DATE DUE			
Dec 15 73			
Dec 18 '74			
Dec 18 7			
Mar 10 '75			
Dec 1 '76			
Dec 15 77			
Mar 7 79			
Apr 26 7			
Nov 5 '81			
Aug 10 '82			

190 —

A Short History of
INDIA

A Short History of
INDIA

Ian W. Mabbett

PRAEGER PUBLISHERS
New York • Washington

BOOKS THAT MATTER
Published in the United States of America in 1970
by Praeger Publishers, Inc.
111 Fourth Avenue, New York, N.Y. 10003

© Cassell Australia, Ltd. 1968

Library of Congress Catalog Card Number: 70–121006

Printed in the United States of America

Contents

List of Illustrations

MAPS

Acknowledgments

I am grateful to the following for permission to reproduce quotations: The Oxford University Press, London, for quotation from P. Spear's *The Nabobs*, and from C. H. Philips' *The Evolution of India and Pakistan*; The Bodley Head, for quotation from Jawaharlal Nehru's *An Autobiography*; the Navajivan Trust, Ahmedabad, for quotation from D. J. Tendulkar's *Mahatma* (vol. 3); and Thames and Hudson Ltd., for quotation from M. Edwardes' *A History of India*.

I am also glad to acknowledge the help given from various quarters in providing photographs and permission to reproduce them: The India Office Library, Commonwealth Relations Office; the Victoria and Albert Museum; the Information Service of India in Sydney and Canberra; the Patna Museum, Patna; the Archaeological Survey of India; and in particular I am indebted to Professor B. L. C. Johnson of the Department of Geography, Monash University, for supplying a number of other illustrations in the book.

I have benefited from the advice of a number of colleagues, not all named here, who have looked at parts of the manuscript, and am grateful to all. Special mention must be made of Professor A. L. Basham and Dr A. A. Rizvi, of the Department of Asian Civilization, Australian National University, who have looked at the chapters on ancient history and Muslim dynasties respectively and made detailed comments and recommendations, and of Mr B. Kennedy, of the Department of History, Monash University, who has similarly checked chapters on the early stages of the British Empire.

I have particularly appreciated the guidance given me by the publishers and by the General Editor, Professor J. D. Legge, throughout the preparation of this book.

I. W. Mabbett
Monash University

Foreword

China, Japan, India and Indonesia are, in their several ways, of tremendous importance to their neighbours and to the world at large. The progress of Communist revolution in China's vast agrarian society, the success story of Japan's industrial revolution, the efforts of India to combine the pursuit of economic development with the preservation of democratic institutions, and the problems of political stability and of population pressure in modern Indonesia, are issues of general and crucial significance. It is therefore surprising that the study of these countries in Australian schools should have been delayed until the 1960s. The present series of volumes is designed to aid that study. While directed specifically to a particular syllabus it hopes, at the same time, to offer a treatment which can interest the general reader.

The authors of the four individual studies which go to make up the series have been left considerable freedom in handling their subjects as they see them, but they have accepted one common principle. They share the view that the study of any Asian country cannot be seen solely in terms of its recent history and its present situation. They recognize the persistence of tradition into the present and the way in which contemporary behaviour may reflect the long established patterns of ancient societies. They share also the view that, quite apart from its importance in interpreting the present, the study of traditional societies is worthwhile for its own sake.

Each of these volumes therefore is concerned to place 'modern' history in the context of the longer history of the country concerned, whether it is the shape of early Asian trade and the rivalry of maritime and land-based kingdoms in the Indonesian archipelago, the artistic triumphs of the Gupta period in India, the character of Confucian thought in China or the contribution of a feudal order in Japan. If history must have a utilitarian purpose it is hoped that, in this way, not only will students be led to a more subtle understanding of the character of the modern countries of Asia, but that they will acquire a measure of respect and sympathy for systems of thought and ways of behaviour which are far removed from their own.

J. D. Legge,
Monash University

(ix)

CHAPTER ONE

India and Indians

(a) THE LAND

The words 'India' and 'Indian' are not entirely straightforward in
meaning. When Columbus crossed the Atlantic and found land in
1492, it was the lands of Asia, rich in spices, that he was seeking, and
he thought that it was Asia he had reached. For this reason, the
native people of America came to be called Indians, though there is
no particular racial connection between them and the Indians of
India. To an American of today, 'Indian' means first and foremost
an American Indian, and an Indian from India has to be called an
Indian Indian to distinguish him.

European interest in Asia at the end of the Middle Ages was
centred on the trade in spices. This was a valuable trade, and it was
the hope of profit as much as anything else that prompted the early
voyages of exploration—westwards across the Atlantic and eastwards
round the south of Africa. In a certain sense it was through this
European interest and activity in Asia, originally commercial, that
there came to be a country called India, the country whose story this
book tells. There was, however, no single country in the beginning.

When the Portuguese and Dutch and British set up their trading
stations, India consisted of a multitude of countries, each with its own
government. In the course of time, the British became dominant and
established themselves as the paramount power. In the nineteenth
century, it became possible to speak of India as a single country,
under a British government. But even then, and even up to the time
of independence in 1947 when the British handed over power to the
Indians themselves, there were still in the country many native
states, with their own kings, that were largely independent.

After independence, these native states were rapidly absorbed
into the new India. But this new India was itself not the same as
that which the British had ruled. The Indian empire of Britain
was divided into two, and each part became a separate, newly
independent, country. The larger part kept the name of India, and
keeps it still. The other part—which, to add to the complication,

1

consists of two separate sections itself—became the Muslim state
of Pakistan.

Thus there has never been a single country called India occupying
the whole of the land that we are concerned with in this book,
although in the nineteenth century the whole of it was under strong
British influence.

It is therefore worth asking what it is that justifies us in treating
India as a unity—in writing a book about India which includes the
India and Pakistan of today instead of, say, India without Pakistans
or alternatively, India, Ceylon and Burma, which in some way,
share a common tradition. What is it that the Indians have in
common in their history?

It is not any single government, nor is it a language. True,
English will get you by in most parts of the region, but this means
only that the educated minority speaks it: most people don't. There
are over two hundred languages in India, and many more if we
count every dialect spoken by remote hill tribesmen. Many of these
languages are spoken by very few people, and are dying out. The
Indian government is taking steps to record and study the rarer ones
before they disappear.

Perhaps it is a culture that the Indian peoples have had in common
through their history. But it is difficult to identify a culture and say
what people have it and what people don't. There are differences
of language and religion for example between the Indians and
Pakistanis of today. Can we say that they share the same culture?

For the purpose of identifying the unity of India, it is best to take
the simple and obvious facts of geography, and this is our starting-
point. A glance at the map is enough to show that the India of this
book is a geographical unity. It is an enormous peninsula jutting
out from the Eurasian land mass, divided from other lands by sea
to the south and by the mighty Himalayan mountain range to the
north. There is to the north-east a narrow and difficult corridor into
Burma, which has not for most of its history been the route of any
very important traffic between peoples. There are to the north-west a
number of mountain passes which link India with Afghanistan and
Central Asia. The most important of these passes, and the scene of
many colourful and dramatic movements critical to India's history,
is the Khyber Pass.

These geographical facts are fundamental to the pattern of history.
They are significant chiefly for an understanding of the movement of
peoples in India and of contacts between them. What needs to be
stressed is the fact that for most of its history India has been relatively
isolated. There has been plenty of commercial traffic by sea, and
indeed the ports of southern India have participated in world-wide

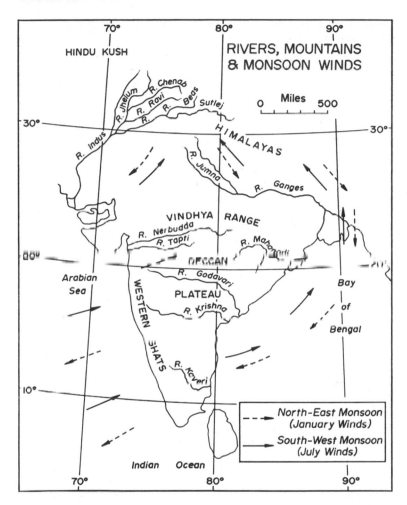

patterns of trade for two thousand years. But trade is one thing: migration of peoples is another. Ships have brought silks, porcelain, jewels, gold, ironware, woollens, weapons, hats and most things under the sun, but until the British came, ships did not bring people in sufficient numbers to govern the course of India's history in any obvious way. The races of India came by land. And because the Himalayas have made impracticable most land routes other than the north-western passes, India has never been completely overrun or lost its identity through the free movement of hordes of people across its boundaries. There have been frequent invasions through the passes of Afghanistan—by Aryans, Greeks, Scyths, Mongols, and Turks to name but a few—but these invaders have usually melted into Indian society and become part of the Indian scene. Thus Indian culture has been largely free to develop along its own lines and assume a distinctive character.

North and South

From this chapter onwards, until the last section where it will be necessary to distinguish between India and Pakistan, 'India' will mean the whole of this land south of the Himalayas. There are of course important differences between the various parts of India, and throughout this book, a distinction will frequently be made between 'the North' and 'the South'. The reason for this is partly geographical.

The northern part of India, between the Himalayan foothills and the Vindhya range, has great, low-lying areas watered by the Indus and Ganges rivers and their tributaries. The Aryans (the earliest recorded invaders), and others after them, spread out across the North. The area is conducive to settled cultivation, because the rivers are fed by the melting mountain snows and therefore have water all the year round. The Vindhyas divide the North from the South. This has meant that, in the course of history, the peoples who entered from the north-west have had less impact on the South. The Aryans slowly spread throughout India; but even today the languages of the South are distinctly non-Aryan, and in many ways the South has preserved distinctive characteristics of its own.

Climate

We tend to think of India as a particularly hot place, and so much of it is; but it is large enough to have a wide variation of climatic conditions. In winter, if you undertake a train journey from Calcutta to, say, the frontier town of Raxaul by the Nepalese border, you will go from a very pleasant climate—warm to hot days, mild nights—to a distinctly chilly one, where overcoats and blankets are welcome on the train. Delhi is chilly for a short while in winter, but its summer is among the hottest in the world. The South, of course, being nearer the equator, is hot all the year round, and does not experience the same extremes of heat and cold.

Winds blow in different directions at different seasons. From about May onwards, the rain-bearing south-west monsoon winds blow across the southern part of the subcontinent; in the North these winds blow from the south-east up the Ganges valley. In the cold season, at the end of the year, the monsoon winds blow in the opposite directions.

It is difficult to exaggerate the importance of the rain-bearing monsoons that herald the wet season. All India depends on them. In the South, where there are no snow-fed rivers, much hangs on the availability of water from the village tanks—large artificial ponds in which water is stored through the year. The North also, with its dense agriculture, cannot rely entirely on melting Himalayan snow for the irrigation of its crops. If the rains fail, the harvest fails, and people are likely to starve. It is almost as simple as that, but not quite.

There are two things to remember: firstly, the rain is scarcely likely to fail all over the country; and, secondly, modern transport and unified administration make it possible to send rice or other crops from areas that have a surplus to areas that have a shortage. It doesn't always work very well, but, especially since the coming of railways, it has been possible to redistribute food and overcome the worst of a famine.

(h) LIVELIHOOD

The Importance of Agriculture

Nowadays, in western countries, most people live in towns. In the countryside, with modern equipment, farms can be run without large numbers of farm hands. But for most people, at most periods of the world's history, agriculture has been the source of livelihood. Even today, though towns are attracting more people in India, the majority of the people still live in the countryside.

Indian farming methods have not been in the past, and are not now, very advanced. It is impossible to have advanced farming methods without equipment, and equipment costs money. Before he can afford to buy equipment (pumps, tractors, whatever it may be) the farmer needs to make profits and save money. Before he can make profits, he needs to have improved farming methods. It is a vicious circle. Those who are well off, and have some money saved, can afford to experiment and risk losing something in the hope of finding better. But those who have nothing saved depend for their life on getting some sort of harvest every time—there is no room for experiment, because if an experiment fails they will starve. For this reason, and others which have to do with habits of thought, Indian farmers have usually been poor, and because they *are* poor, they have remained so.

Rice

The commonly held idea of a typical Indian meal is probably a bowl of white steaming rice and a hot, rich, meaty curry. It is not really typical. Across the north of India, people tend to eat wheat at least as much as rice, in the form of various sorts of bread or pancake.

Rice is associated more with the South. As for the curry, a typical villager probably cannot afford to buy, and rarely sees, meat. Or, if he can afford it, he is quite likely to be a vegetarian anyway. He lives on rice or wheat and vegetables.

Wet rice cultivation is, however, the life-blood of the Asian village economy, and it deserves a word or two here.

The most primitive form of cultivation (of rice or anything else) is 'slash-and-burn' cultivation, and the earliest inhabitants of India farmed in this way. It consists of cutting down the trees on a hillside, burning off the trees and undergrowth, and growing dry crops, not requiring large quantities of water, on the cleared ground. After this has been done for two or three seasons, the soil fertility is depleted and may take twenty years or so to recover. It is therefore necessary to move on.

More than 1,000 years B.C. in some parts, settled agriculture developed. For this, plenty of water is required. Wet rice, grown over much of India, has to be grown in water for most of its life, and therefore needs concentrated irrigation for the period of its growth. The monsoon winds that bring heavy rainfall for a limited period of the year make tropical countries suitable for the cultivation of wet rice. There are parts of India beneath the Himalayan range that get over sixty inches of rain a year. The Ganges plain gets about forty; the inland area of the South rather less.

Nowadays in India, most farmers expect to get only one crop a year; but in early times, when the soil was more fertile, and when there was a less dense population competing for the available water, conditions were more favourable. In such conditions, when the water supply can be controlled, it is possible to get two or more crops a year.

In technically advanced countries it is possible to cultivate rice by highly mechanized methods, but Indian farmers necessarily lack these advantages. Their soil has been depleted of its fertility over many centuries. Their fields are small and scattered, too small to deploy a tractor efficiently. They are too poor to risk experiments with different types of grain. Too few of them can afford insecticide or pumps to keep their fields irrigated, let alone tractors, and there is no question of sowing from an airplane in a region of small landholdings and dense population with villages scattered every-where. Machinery is expensive, but labour is cheap, and everything is done by hand. When the rice is grown, it is cut by hand, threshed by hand, winnowed by hand. In most villages in rural India a visitor may still see groups of women standing under the hot sun, rhythmically beating the piles of rice with long poles to separate the grain. It is as tedious and laborious as it looks.

Trade

Not all those who live in the countryside are directly engaged in agriculture. The village community also needs the services of craftsmen and traders. From early times, there have been people making a living from various skills—metal workers, goldsmiths, leatherworkers, potters, weavers, and many others. India has always been famous for textiles especially, and in villages up and down the country even today, craftsmen work at handlooms to make cotton and silks that are sought after and highly valued. Many centuries ago, there was developed the use of various dyestuffs—such as turmeric for yellow, indigo for blue, madder for red—with which, using many combinations, bright patterns could be made.

Several centuries before Christ, India was trading with the world. Gold has always been especially prized by Indians, and could be obtained over the long and hazardous trade routes by sea to the Mediterranean and the Roman empire and by land to Siberia. The Indians themselves did not always make the entire journey, foreign traders handled much of the traffic. In the last two centuries B.C. references in Sanskrit literature suggest that India became interested in some of the lands of South-East Asia as a source of gold.

By such links, Indian traders built the subcontinent into a world-wide pattern of connection by which India became known as a source of various luxuries and as a possible object of conquest for ambitious rulers in western Asia. Trade was extensive in early times, though there was nothing like the complex banking system that western countries have today to oil the wheels of commerce. Banking did not develop in India until Muslim times—the times of the Middle Ages in Europe. But it is worth noticing that, while our ancestors were roaming the forests of Europe, Indian craftsmen were working wonders with metals and textiles, and enjoying a trade that spanned continents.

CHAPTER TWO

Early Civilization

(a) THE PEOPLING OF INDIA

Diversity

Not only has India had many different states within itself for most of its history; it has always had many different races. When we talk about 'the Indians', we are talking about the people who live in one area, an area that is relatively cut off from the rest of the Eurasian land mass and has some cultural characteristics of its own; but we are not talking about one race of people.

In some parts, particularly inland and in the hills, there are small backward tribal groups that have no racial connection with the bulk of the population. In the north-east, in Assam, there are people with a strong East Asiatic element in their make-up, a link with the peoples of South-East Asia and, more distantly, China. Over the north and north-west there are mingled together the descendants of Turks, Afghans, Persians and others. In the west there are some communities with an African origin. The peoples of the south in general are descended from the dark-skinned non-Aryans. But the remarkable thing is that, one way or another, nearly all these peoples have been absorbed into India, fit into the caste system, and share cultural traditions with each other.

The Aboriginal Tribes

The coming of the earliest inhabitants of India is lost in the mists of prehistory, and there is not a great deal that we know about them. The more backward tribes of India are what remain today from them; efforts are being made to improve their conditions and to introduce them to the ways of the agriculturalists around them. Study of their languages, and of their physical characteristics, shows a number of racial connections between these tribes and others which exist today in Africa, in Ceylon, in South-East Asia and in the South Seas. The Negritoes were the earliest, followed by the Australoids, Mongoloids and others. These racial groups have been named by modern scholars after the tribes of today that seem to be descended from them, or after the areas from which they seem to have come originally. The Australian aborigine of today belongs to the same racial group as the Australoids whose bones have been found in India.

Three Layers of Immigration

History consists of what is recorded in writing, and these early inhabitants certainly had no writing that we know of. The story of India that we are mainly concerned with begins with the coming of the races usually known as the Aryans, who were the first to have any substantial literature that is known to us (though at first it was spoken, not written down). When they arrived in India by the much-trodden north-western passes, they found certain peoples who seem to have had a highly developed culture of their own, with a form of writing that has not yet been deciphered. Several different terms have been used to name these peoples; here we shall simply call them 'non-Aryans'.

By distinguishing peoples from each other by the standards of language and race, it is possible, at the risk of slight distortion, to divide the peopling of India into three general layers.

The first layer consists of the aboriginal tribes, which retreated into the south or into the hills, and which still exist today, some of them, with their own language and culture entirely different from those of the people around them.

The second layer consists of the valley peoples, the non-Aryans, who were responsible for the chief culture of India at the time the Aryans arrived. They have sometimes been called 'Dravidians', after the sort of languages they speak, and they are descended from different racial groups such as the Mediterranean and the Veddoid. Although they had no written history of their own as far as we know, they had, in the Indus valley (now largely in West Pakistan), a fascinating and advanced civilization that we know of through the work of archaeologists who have dug up their bones, their pottery and other utensils, and—most impressive of all—their cities, which are unlike anything anywhere else in India.

The third layer, the Aryans, the light-skinned nomads who came as conquerors to begin the story that later chapters will tell, arrived only when the Indus civilization collapsed; and it is possible that they were the cause of its collapse.

(b) The Indus Civilization

The pre-Aryan people of the Indus valley had a civilization similar to that of Mesopotamia, and likely to have owed something to Mesopotamia in its origin, but it developed along different lines. It lasted from about 2,300 B.C. to about the middle of the second millennium B.C. The chief cities that have been excavated are those of Mohenjo Daro and Harappa. There may be others that have not yet been discovered. There are plenty of towns and villages belonging to the same culture that have also been excavated, all so far in the north-west, chiefly the Indus area and Gujarat. The cities had well-planned streets and buildings of burnt-brick. Some seals have been found with inscriptions on them, but nobody has yet been able to decipher the script in which their language is written. The cities may have been overrun by invaders, and if so it is likely that these invaders were the Aryans about whom we know from their own literature. However, the way in which this civilization met its end is rather obscure.

The Cities

The bare facts of the remarkable Indus people barely hint at the fascination of this ancient culture that is so unlike anything before or after it. We have their bricks, their bones and their pots, but we have very little of their history, their language or their customs. It is rather like a good film without the sound-track: we can see interesting people, splendid scenes, intriguing doings, but we do not know what the characters are saying and there is a tantalizing mystery about the whole thing.

The cities of Mohenjo Daro and Harappa are remarkable chiefly for the planning and the well-developed technology that they show. In a land of peasants, mud-brick dwellings, backward tribes, nomads, and primitive agriculture, these cities stood out as monuments to civilization, with streets, brick houses in orderly rows, good drainage, baths, public buildings of all sorts, and strong fortifications.

The systematic planning is an important feature to notice. Streets are straight and laid out in a grid pattern, at right angles to each other. This suggests that the cities were planned as a whole right from the start, like some Australian and American cities: they did not grow up gradually like London, or like the Mesopotamian cities.

Another feature is the citadel to the west of each city: a group of public buildings raised up above the level of the rest and surrounded by fortifications.

There is a remarkable similarity between the cities: Mohenjo Daro and Harappa have exactly the same sort of plan. This suggests that the Indus valley had a uniform culture if not a uniform government that was shared by the whole area.

Outside Links

The culture of the valley does not appear to have existed in a vacuum. As we have noticed, Mesopotamia may have helped give it

birth, but the differences between the Indus culture and the Mesopotamian are at least as striking as the similarities, and it is clear
that the Indian cities belonged to a separate tradition with its own
vitality.

Many of the artifacts dug up on the sites—or from the Indus
civilization dug up on sites elsewhere—show what trading contacts
there were and where the Indus culture got the raw materials for its
crafts. There were trading connections with the Persian Gulf and
Mesopotamia, and the gold, tin, copper, jade and other things used
must have come from places such as Persia, Afghanistan, and parts
of India to the south of the Indus, notably Rajasthan.

The People and their Life

Skeletons have been found, buried with some of their possessions,
which tell us something about the people. We know that various
races were represented in the cities—Australoid, Mongoloid and
others besides Mediterranean. We have many of their carvings and
terra cotta figurines, some of which show a high standard of artistry
(though it is not quite certain whether some of the things found on
the site really belong to the Indus culture). We know from toy
models and carvings as well as from bones that they had, or knew,
camels and asses as well as other animals, and that they had two
wheeled ox-carts. Examination of their buildings shows that they
had units of measurement—feet and cubits—that were very exact,
and similar in length to units known in Egypt. And we know from
seals that have writing on them what their script looked like,
although nobody has been able to decipher it.

The End of the Indus Culture

In a way, the end of this culture was as sudden and mysterious as
its beginning. It seems that there was a gradual decline—the standard
of building, for example, deteriorated as time went on. But there
may have been a particular time when the cities were violently
overrun. Unburied skeletons have been found, lying about in the
streets and buildings and showing the marks of assaults which were
probably the cause of death. So one theory is that there were
invaders who devastated the cities and left them to go to ruin.
And this happened somewhere around the middle of the second
millennium B.C.

It is like a jigsaw puzzle. Some pieces consist of these facts that
we know from digging at the city sites. Others consist of a different
sort of information: the Sanskrit literature of the Indians of later
times, which includes the ancient hymns chanted by the Aryans at
the time of their immigration into India. These hymns are likely

to have been composed over several centuries before and after 1,000 B.C., and they contain mentions of the dark-skinned enemy non-Aryans, called *dasas* or *dasyus* (slaves), who retreated to their fortified towns.

It is only guesswork, but it is possible to fit these pieces together and form the conclusion that it was in fact the *Aryans*, the ancestors of the northern Indians of today and the founders of the Indian culture (who kept written records, and whom much of this book is about) who blotted their copy-books by laying waste the ancient and cultured Indus cities. However, it should be added that this is simply one possibility, and there is much room for speculation.

(c) THE ARYANS

The third general layer of peopling that we are concerned with in this chapter consists of the tribes known as Aryans. This is the name of a language group rather than a racial group. The Aryan tribes, whose language shows them to be related to the races of Europe, entered the Indus valley and moved across the northern plains round about 1,300–800 B.C., conquering, driving out or mingling with the previous inhabitants. They may well have been responsible for the overthrow of the Indus valley cities. Gradually, the Aryans spread all over India, and, as a result of their mingling with the non-Aryans, a new culture emerged. By this culture, India came to have in common the Sanskrit language—an Aryan language used in ceremonies and, as it developed, for sacred literature—a set of gods, a religion, and a folklore.

The Aryans when they entered India did not have a particularly advanced culture. The advancement came when they settled down to a village life, based on agriculture. Originally they were nomads, small groups moving about the countryside with their herds and often displaying a warlike nature.

Races of men are like families. A family may split up, and spread out across the country; sons may leave home, and set up households somewhere else. In their new setting, they may change, and certainly their children will be different from themselves and their fathers, but there will be a family resemblance. The people who spoke the original Aryan languages split up into different tribes; some tribes became the population of Europe, some went eastwards. In their new settings, their languages became different from each other, and their customs and beliefs also; but the family resemblance was there, and anybody who studies the languages of Europe and the ancient and modern languages of northern India can see the resemblances clearly.

But when a son moves away from home and establishes a household somewhere else, he will not be able to start a new branch of his family unless he marries; and the new branch will show resemblances to his wife's family just as much as to his own. The Indian history that we are going to examine is not just the history of the Aryans after they had arrived and had overcome the inhabitants; it is more like the history of a marriage between the newcomers and those who were already there. In languages, and in the earliest religious beliefs, we can see family resemblances to the Aryans and thus to the people of Europe. In many other things we see what must be resemblances to the culture of the previous inhabitants.

Indian History: Whose Child?

These, the Aryans and the non-Aryans, were the parents of the culture that grew in India during the first thousand years B.C. and gave the world Buddhism, Hinduism, Sanskrit literature, and a highly refined tradition of temple art and sculpture, and stands in direct line of descent to the India of today. Politicians even now use as slogans ideas that appeared in India thousands of years ago— cow protection, the doctrine that cows should not be slaughtered for religious reasons, was a live issue well before Christ, and it is a demand painted on the walls of Delhi at election time today. The Hindu name for India, *Bharat*, that appears on Indian postage stamps, reminds us of the name of one of the ancient Aryan tribes that burst upon the Indus and Ganges valleys three thousand years ago.

The Aryans were the conquerors, and they gave to the new culture its government, its chief languages, something of its religion—for Hinduism is something that grew gradually from the original Aryans' worship of their own gods. What did the non-Aryans contribute?

They did not contribute their cities, because these were abandoned and left to nature. Their languages, of course, survived, especially in the south where the Aryans were slow to penetrate, and the Aryan speech itself was partly affected by theirs. But there is no doubt that Sanskrit, an Aryan language, was the chief form of expression of the developing culture.

The answer, all the same, is probably that they contributed more than we realize. The Aryans did not have the caste system; and their religion at the time they entered India was very different from the Hinduism of later times. It is likely that the caste system and Indian religions alike owe a great deal to the ideas and customs of the pre-Aryan inhabitants, and Indian history as we shall now study it should be thought of as the development of both peoples.

CHAPTER THREE

Indian Society and Culture

(a) CASTE

Two men are walking towards each other along a path. There is plenty of room for them to pass, but one of them jumps nervously aside, off the path, and into a muddy field.

Many soldiers in the Indian army in the 19th century were not supposed to travel overseas, and it was possible to recruit them only on the condition that they would not be sent outside their own country.

One ruler visits another and takes a meal with him in his palace. After the meal, the host has water brought to him and washes in a public ritual, to show that he thinks he has been polluted by sharing a meal with his guest, who is not of the right caste. It is a deliberate insult.

These are examples of the operation of caste, which is a set of principles governing the way people behave. Caste has existed in India for two thousand years or more. It exists today, and some would say it is as strong as ever, though the present Indian government is trying to do away with much of its influence. It is part of the whole Indian outlook and way of life, and it is important that we should have some understanding of it.

Caste, Law and Religion

It is necessary to be clear what caste is *not* in order to understand what it is.

In the first place, it is not exactly religion. But in a way it is certainly part of the Hindu faith, and the Hindu faith is a part of the caste system.

Hindu religion contains ideas about salvation, and it contains a number of ceremonies. According to the religion, whether you can hope for salvation, or whether indeed you are allowed to receive instruction in the religion, depends partly on where you are in the caste system. Again, where you are in the caste system will partly decide whether you can perform a particular ceremony or not.

So the system is bound up with the religion.

But caste is more than a doctrine that is set out in religious texts, and that people follow because they happen to believe in the religion. Caste is a set of rules that people would follow whatever attitude they had to the religion, because these rules are part of Indian society, and of the customs that everybody learns. So caste is a matter of custom as much as of religion.

Law and caste are obviously not the same thing, because nowadays caste is partly against the law. It is possible to describe caste as a set of rules, but these are customs that grew up in the distant past and have evolved and adapted themselves to changing situations. They are not like Acts of Parliament formally drawn up and made official.

India's law, which was religious law, and mixed up with religious ceremonies in the sacred texts, had almost always accepted caste up to a point, as religion had done. After British rule, however—and beginning during it—governments have tried more and more to do away with some of the injustices of caste.

According to caste, people may not take just any kind of job: the sort of work they can do is laid down for them. According to the law, however, anybody can apply for any sort of job. An applicant can be refused if he does not seem to be the right man for the job, of course; but not simply because he belongs to the wrong caste group. This is one way in which modern law comes into collision with caste.

The government is now trying to ensure that at least some low-caste or outcaste men get high-level jobs by reserving certain positions especially for them.

Caste Rules and Caste Groups

A caste is a group of people following certain customs: but what kinds of customs?

Generally speaking, the members of a particular caste are supposed to follow the occupations of that caste. If it is a caste of washermen, for example, they should become washermen. They are born into the caste which their parents belong to, and should not marry outside it. Nor should they take food in company with members of other castes.

In theory, each caste belongs to one of four general grades or classes—the *brahmans* (from which priests are recruited), the *ksatriyas* (warriors or aristocrats), the *vaisyas* (engaged in agriculture or trade) and the *sudras* (servants or labourers). Thus, a caste can be described as a vaisya caste, or a sudra caste, for example, according to its grade. There are many rules about relations between people belonging to different classes. People of lower caste are expected to show deference in various ways to people of higher caste, as in the first example at the beginning of this chapter.

There are many people, called outcastes, *harijans*, or members oi 'depressed classes', who are considered not to belong to any caste at all. They have their own forms of livelihood, and customs governing their behaviour, so that in some ways they are like another caste. But they are expected to show the utmost respect to high-caste Hindus. There are places, for example, where brahmans are not even supposed to see outcastes. Low-caste Hindus and out- castes suffer from all sorts of unfavourable discrimination from their caste superiors. They are not free to live the sort of life they might want to, or might have been able to, otherwise.

Caste rules are not rigid: they can change themselves, or be adapted. If need be, a man who cannot follow the profession of his caste can take some other calling. Because of this flexibility, the system is able to survive even where things are clearly not being done in practice as the theory says they should be.

It would be a mistake to think that people always, or nearly always, marry within their castes, take no food with other castes, follow the professions laid down for them, and so forth: there are many exceptions to the rules. Vast numbers of brahmans became soldiers in the army under the British, for example. And caste groups sometimes change their class, though this is impossible in theory. A group of people in an area may start off by being, say, vaisyas, and in the course of time, adopting new customs and rituals, start calling themselves brahmans, and have other people accept the change.

How did caste groups come into being? The four classes (brahmans and so forth) existed early in the first thousand years B.C. That does not mean that the marriage rules and caste groups within the four classes existed too, however; and nobody really knows the whole story. Some people regard caste as a set of rules that came to be formulated by the Aryan priests in order to maintain society in a hierarchy with the Aryans on top. Other people think that caste customs as we would recognize them existed among the pre-Aryan Dravidians, and that as Aryans mingled with non-Aryans the customs came to be embodied in the religion and ritual of the whole society. However that may be, the castes started as groups of people who married among themselves, did the same sort of work, and lived in the same place. In the course of time, as people moved away from their parents' villages, castes spread out and mixed, so that in one village there might be groups from several different castes, and one caste might be spread over a large part of the country.

Caste in the Modern World

There are reasons why we should expect the caste system to break down in the modern world.

One reason is that educated people, and particularly the government, want to do away with the injustices that it entails. They want all the people to be eligible for the same education, the same jobs, and the same social services.

A second reason is the spread of education. People are no longer so ready to live the same sort of life as their parents and to follow the same old ways. In particular, they are not so happy to accept wives (or husbands) chosen for them from the same caste as themselves.

Again, the circumstances of modern life are against the system, especially in a city. It is difficult to avoid touching an untouchable on a crowded bus. Again it is difficult to avoid taking food from somebody of the wrong caste in a restaurant.

It is generally believed therefore that caste is on the way out. It takes time to change people's attitudes, however, and old-established customs are slow to die. Moreover, caste has a way of perpetuating itself by bending a little here, changing the rules there. If the person who hands you water in a train is a brahman, he is bound to be of at least as high caste as yourself, and you will not break a caste rule by accepting it. Therefore the people employed to carry round drinking water on trains are brahmans, in practice if not by law. Caste may still be a long time dying: although its death seems inevitable.

In the villages a man will have a strong feeling of affinity with his fellow-caste-men. They may be related to him indirectly. They are doing the same sort of work together. Their children and his will marry each other, and they have the same customs and rituals. Thus the caste is a sort of club that will stick together and protect its members against afflictions from outside.

The whole system has this kind of value for the individual, and as a result he does not want to see it destroyed. Even though he suffers from the prejudice, suspicion and discrimination of other castes, he has the compensating security of his own.

(b) CULTURE

Literature

For us, a book consists of a number of printed pages fastened together down one side and bound into a cover which has a spine. For an ancient Indian, however, a book consisted of a number of handwritten strips of palm-leaf, either stitched together top and bottom and folded concertina-fashion, or joined by cords running through holes, and held between two long narrow boards, highly decorated. At the beginning, however, nothing was written down at all; and much of the religious teaching has always been passed on without the use of writing. Instead of ink, there was the spoken word; and instead of palm leaves, there were the minds of men.

Much of the education of brahmans traditionally consists of memorizing the sacred literature.

Much of the ancient Sanskrit literature, of which a great deal exists, is religious. Beside Chaucer and Shakespeare and the whole treasury of English literature, ancient India can range a good deal more than a few hymns and other minor writings. In sheer quantity, Indian literature compares favourably with English: and there is an impressive breadth and variety, with great depth of thought, and with poetry of ingenuity and elegance.

The ancient language of India, and the language of its traditional literature, is Sanskrit. Because the language did not stay the same all the time, but evolved, we can distinguish two types of Sanskrit, representing two stages in its development. Vedic Sanskrit is the language of the *Vedas*, which were the hymns and chants of the invading Aryans around 1,000 B.C. Classical Sanskrit was the standard literary language in later times, and is a more simple form with fewer grammatical complications. The golden age of Classical Sanskrit was in the first four centuries A.D.

Other languages are worth a mention too. Prakrit was the name given to actual, everyday speech. It was not the same all over India, but took different forms in different regions—dialects. The famous inscriptions of the emperor Asoka were in Prakrit, each betraying the influence of the dialect of the place where it was set up. Pali was a particular form of Prakrit, probably a western dialect, and it became one of the sacred languages of Buddhism. These Prakrits were like much simplified forms of Sanskrit. They themselves changed and evolved, and by stages gave birth to the modern Indian languages of the North, such as Hindi and Bengali.

Sanskrit and these other northern Indian languages have non-Aryan elements in them; but basically they are derived from the speech of the original Indian Aryans, and are therefore related to European languages.

After the ten large books of Vedic hymns, most of which are odes to gods, there were various classes of religious works: on the conduct of rituals, and on metaphysics—the inner nature of the universe, and the deepest religious truths.

The sutras were one form of composition. 'Sutra' means literally 'thread', and the sutras were like strings of sayings, in prose, with an explanation of each saying perhaps added afterwards by somebody else. These sutras were on law and ritual and the like.

Sastras were the basic texts on law, duties, ceremonies, the sciences, politics and philosophy. Much of the historian's knowledge of ancient Indian thought and society comes from these sastras.

Among the epic poems, the Ramayana is the story of the mythical hero Rama and his fantastic experiences. It tells of his virtues, his adventures, his battles, his encounters with demons and supernatural beings. Its hero is the great folk hero of Indian myth and religion, and Indians understand allusions to the Ramayana just as we understand (some) allusions to the Bible stories: it is part of their life. The other great epic, the Mahabharata, is of considerable length and more like an encyclopaedia than a story. There is a central tale, about a possibly real conflict between two tribes back in the Vedic past; but interspersed with this are numerous passages containing religious teachings, instruction in politics, and the like.

There were plays, highly stylised but with real character and fine poetry in them, and something of the grandeur of Greek tragedy. There was pure poetry; and no poet of ancient India is more famous than Kalidasa, who lived during the Gupta dynasty, and is called the Shakespeare of India. Poetry was a highly developed art, with complicated rules and a great range of techniques, in which Kalidasa excelled.

There were, finally, the puranas, a set of miscellaneous texts put together in the course of time, mingling religion, history (largely imaginary history), astrology and teachings on various subjects.

One thing to notice about Sanskrit literature is the way in which works borrow from each other. There was nothing like copyright law in India. Whatever was written or passed down was regarded as common property. There was no question of stealing somebody's words. It was a literary tradition that people shared, to do what they liked with: they could forget parts of it, put parts together in different ways, or create new parts with some of the old parts in them.

Art

Imagine that you are standing in a dark and gloomy cave temple hewn out of solid rock. In a recess at the far side is a man with a torch, and in the inconstant light you see eerily illumined the great figure of a stone statue. It is a Buddha, more than life-size, mysterious and awesome in the dim light.

Then a very strange thing happens. The statue seems to be alive. At first the light on the statue is from one side, and the Buddha seems to be intent and frowning. Then the torch is moved, so that the light falls on the statue's face from below—and the expression

on the face changes before your eyes, takes on a look of calm
serenity. A further marvel: the torch is moved again, to the other
side, and once more the expression uncannily changes—quite clearly
and unmistakably, you see the Buddha smile.

This ingeniously carved statue, designed to bear different
expressions according to the direction of the light, is one example
of the ancient artist's skill from the famous cliff-face cave temples
of Ajanta, in modern Maharashtra. In other temples at the same
site, you may see marvellous paintings on the walls and ceilings,
and statues and relief carvings of all kinds: an eye that seems to be
looking straight at you wherever you stand, a pattern on the wall
that glows mysteriously in the dark when the light is taken off it,
a carving of four deer that share a single head.

Painting, sculpture and architecture were not in those days in
India distinguished as separate crafts followed by different people.
A single craftsman—a silpin—combined the various roles, design-
ing a temple, making the sculptures that adorned it, and, often,
painting the walls.

Little of the painting has come down to us, and the temples of
Ajanta are therefore all the more valuable, because several of them
are richly decorated with colourful paintings that illustrate mythical
stories. They date from varying times through the first six
centuries A.D.

Sculpture adorns many temples. As time went on, designs became
more complex; and the later Hindu stone temples, of the ninth to the
fourteenth centuries, are covered in relief carvings and sculptured
patterns. Statues stand in niches on either side of a door, and
wherever there is any excuse to put a niche. There is a preference
for carving human figures, though these usually represent gods or
mythical beings of one sort or another, sometimes hybrid creatures,
half human and half animal. The limbs and bodies are very smooth
and curving—no rippling muscles—and each part of the body was
thought of as representing something from the non-human world:
the shoulder, for example, was carved with the temple of an elephant
in mind.

Some of the common subjects of statuary should be mentioned.
The gods Vishnu and Siva are very often represented; as with other
gods, there is a wealth of symbolism in the way that they are shown.
Strict Buddhism in its early stages was against images of any sort,
but Mahayana Buddhism—a tolerant variety of the religion, which
accepted various practices frowned on by the orthodox—has many
statues of the Buddha. Another sort of Buddhist being is a
bodhisattva—a future Buddha—and we often see these beings

gazing serenely out across the precincts of Mahayana temples. Among other Hindu gods, there are many of statues of Ganesh, with the head of an elephant. Often the epic stories are illustrated, and we see Hanuman, the monkey king in the Ramayana. Female figures are common; goddesses and nymphs stand in graceful poses and represent the Indian idea of beauty.

Architecture

It was not until quite late times that there were erected stone buildings—other than temples—that have survived for us to see. Ordinary mortals, even kings, usually lived in wooden buildings which have perished. Thus, nearly all the monuments to ancient architecture are religious structures such as temples, shrines, a few Buddhist monasteries, and solid monuments.

These solid monuments are among the earliest. They are Buddhist stupas, a stupa being a dome-shaped mound surrounded by stone railings with a monument—shaped like an umbrella—in top of it. It is likely to have originated from the burial mound; but many stupas are large, with the domes raised on elaborate platforms.

Buddhist monasteries are other early architectural remains. One of the most impressive, though not from the earliest times, is at Nalanda in Bihar. It is built of bricks, rises several stories, and consists of square buildings containing rows of monks' cells. The walls are incredibly thick, which is why a number of the buildings survived later attempts by Muslim invaders to destroy them: the marks of fire still remain on the ruins.

The earliest temples that we have are from the fourth and fifth centuries, the time of the Guptas and of the classical period of architecture. The chief feature of the classical period is simplicity. Stone is treated as if it were wood, for architects were not entirely used to dealing with stone, and many features of these temples really belong to carpentry. This is true to a lesser extent of later architecture. The roofs of temples often consist of barrel-shaped vaults, like the thatching on curved bamboo poles that houses had. Imitation beams stick out beneath eaves. There are brackets in the angles of pillars and lintels. But these are incidentals: what is important about the style is the way that a sense of balance and proportion gradually develops.

In the sixth and seventh centuries, the mannerist period of architecture, temples had more elaborate ground plans—no longer plain squares, but with many angles—and there was more and more ornament on the walls and pillars. Pillared verandahs surrounded the temples. Spires began to grow on the roofs. Roofs themselves became more elaborate, rising one above the other in more pyramidal or pagoda-like shapes.

But it was in the next few centuries that the extremely elaborate baroque style really caught hold in India, and indeed ran riot. Everything one could multiply was multiplied—there are multiple slender pillars, multiple terraces, multiple roofs, multiple umbrella shapes on the spires, which grew loftier and more complex in design. There are so many corners and re-entrants in the ground plan that what started as a square turns into more of a star shape. There is carving and there is statuary everywhere; every square inch of surface is covered. Though often overloaded with detail the best examples of this style, like the Rajarani temple at Bhubaneshwar, are real marvels of delicacy with some of the world's most exquisite carving on their surfaces.

The chief feature of the Hindu temples of the South is the gopuram or gate tower. The temple building itself is comparatively insignificant; the focus of attention is outside rather than inside the temple, and all around it are priests' houses, tanks, and other buildings. The gopuram is much more of a tower than a gateway, serving a chiefly decorative purpose. It has a rectangular ground plan and rises many stories high. On top of it is a barrel-vaulted roof, reminding us once again of the thatched roof of a village dwelling.

If these temples and their sculptures were all that remained of India's pre-Muslim past, they would be quite enough to impress us hugely with the richness and sophistication of ancient culture. When we add to this the enormous literature, the art, the music, and the philosophy, it is clear that the cultural heritage of India is as fine as that of any part of the world.

(c) Contacts with the Rest of the World

Nowadays we have all sorts of contacts with other parts of the world. Modern transport, telephone communications, films and books enable ideas, goods and people to move freely between countries; and our whole way of life is affected, more than ever before, by all sorts of influences from overseas. What we may not realize, unless we stop to think about it, is the isolation of all pre-industrial societies. And India was, perhaps, particularly isolated, the wonder being that what cultural contact there was between East and West ever took place at all.

The Importance of Trade

This contact, as we have seen, came largely through the arrival of successive waves of invaders, so that India was like a field constantly being fertilized with fresh life.

But what brought the invaders in? Two sorts of forces can be distinguished: one pushing them, one pulling them.

Often, invaders were pushed from behind, displaced from their homelands by other races who invaded them. Much of the history of Central Asia and the adjacent regions looks like a game of musical chairs.

But often they were attracted by India, and their knowledge of its wealth, of its arts and crafts, its great and prosperous kingdoms waiting to be conquered, its temples with their gold ornaments waiting to be plundered. India, like China, was often looted by the nomads of the steppes, their knowledge of the place coming from the most important sort of contact of all. This was trade: and trade, despite all the natural hazards, throve through thousands of years, and made links with all parts of the known world.

We know about this trade both from the written accounts of it that have come down to us—from Arab merchants, Chinese administrators, pilgrims, and so on—and from the evidence of archaeology. Especially for the earliest times, it is the pottery, the glass, the seals, the figurines and the like that show us what trade went on. An Indian pot dug up in Malaya is evidence of trade between those two places: we need no written account to spell it out.

Commodities

Goods from China which were exported to many parts of the world included earthenware, porcelain, silk yarn, satin, damask, brocades, gold, iron, beads, and coins. The graceful designs of Chinese pottery are one of the most impressive features of its culture.

From South-East Asia, through much of the Christian era, came the spices that were sought after by all the world—spices to make unrefrigerated meat edible, spices that in later times brought Portuguese, Dutch and others all the way from Europe in search of profit. Mace and nutmeg from the Banda islands, cloves from the Moluccas, and many luxury goods from the Malay peninsula and the islands that are now Indonesia: gold from Sumatra (and—much later—pepper); sandalwood from Timor; camphor from Borneo; pepper and slaves from Java; tin and gold from the Malay peninsula.

From the Arab countries to the west, and, from the Mediterranean beyond them, came cotton, perfumes, opium (from the Arab countries), dyed woollens, copper, steel, mirrors, beads and glassware among other things, all mostly in the Middle Ages. During the life of the Roman Empire, gold was one of the exports most prized by Indians.

From India itself, textiles of various kinds were, and until quite

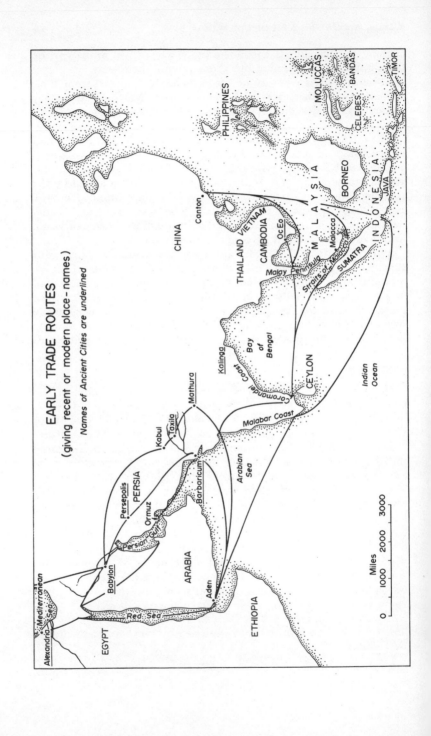

EARLY TRADE ROUTES
(giving recent or modern place-names)
Names of Ancient Cities are underlined

modern times always have been, the chief export: cottons, silks, dyed cloth intricately patterned, and brocade.

The Course of Relations with the World

This was a flourishing trade; but it was not until the early centuries of the Christian era that it really developed. India's earliest connections with countries elsewhere were not so numerous.

Babylonian ships in the sixth century B.C. reached India, but we do not know of Indian ships participating in the traffic. During the Buddhist period, however, it is clear that Indians carried on at least a coastal trade in their ships, and reached Ceylon: and Indians in the fifth century fought alongside Persian soldiers. After about the third century, Indian goods reached Egypt by the Red Sea route, being transhipped at entrepôts like Aden; and in the first century there was a luxury trade with Rome (though it appears that the export of gold from Rome came to be prohibited, because too much was disappearing).

At about the beginning of the Christian era, Egyptian sailors found that instead of hugging the coasts in their voyaging, they could use the monsoon wind that blew in certain directions in certain seasons, and sail straight across the Arabian sea to India. In the next few centuries there was flourishing trade with south-east Asia, and goods were carried across the Malay Peninsula overland to be re-shipped for trade further east (later the Straits of Malacca, between the peninsula and Sumatra, became the chief avenue of trade in south-east Asia). There were connections between India and east Africa. After the fifth century A.D., Arabians as well as Egyptians were active in the trade from the Middle East.

The South of India took a considerable part in this traffic. From the fifth to the eighth century, the Pallava kingdom was prominent in trade; from the ninth to the eleventh, the Cholas with their empire were dominant. Ports on the east and the west of the peninsula throve, serving as entrepôts for the long-distance overseas trade, terminals for Indian trade overseas, and collecting centres for Indian goods of their regions.

(d) INDIAN LIFE

Society

An important feature of Indian social life is the extended family, which has existed from time immemorial. Children did not leave home when they married and set up new households; the sons brought their wives into their parents' homes. When they died, however soon this was, their wives were not expected to marry again, and were thus condemned to live out their lives virtually as servants in the houses of their in-laws, with no hope of marriage thereafter.

There was a custom, not in fact observed very much in the lower levels of society, by which a widow was supposed to commit suicide on the death of her husband. There were plenty of families where the custom was maintained; and eventually the British put an end to it.

The caste system meant that, at least in theory, everything was highly organized. Everybody knew, because there were rules about it, what he was to do with his life, whom he should marry (a girl chosen for him by his parents), what people he should work with and eat with, where he should live, and so on. With wives being brought into the family house, cousins once or twice (or more) removed were living together under the same roof, with their common grandfather or great grandfather exercising authority over them. Generations were short—parents wanted to have as many children as possible in order to be sure of continuing their lines of descent and having others to look after them in their old age—so children were married off as soon as possible. They were even betrothed to each other long before they were old enough to have children.

This meant that families were much larger than those of western society today; and that, since authority in a family was exercised by a patriarch, most people did not experience much responsibility until they were quite old. The decisions were made for them by their fathers or grandfathers.

Looked at from the outside, the family system does not seem very attractive; but we have to recognize that it shared with the caste system one great advantage for the Indians seeing it from the inside: it offered security. Life was hard and the rather rigid-seeming organization of society meant that each man was not alone: he was part of a group, and was surrounded by supporters.

There were, of course, enormous inequalities; and the caste system maintained them. Everybody was conscious of his position in the caste scale, and would be unwilling to do anything for those beneath him. But at least the system meant that there were clearly defined rights that everybody had. Even the low castes had their own occupations, which nobody else was supposed to follow. Thus, in any village or group of villages, a caste group of sweepers had a monopoly of sweeping; nobody else did the job, and they were a tight brotherhood—they could dictate their terms to anybody who wanted to employ them. Nobody belonged completely to anybody else. True, slaves existed—chiefly in the cities, where the wealthy could afford to support them—but even this was a form of security for the slaves (who had often become slaves as a way of working off debt) since their masters were under obligation to support them.

Much of this is a description of a state of affairs in modern or recent times. The pattern of society is likely to be an old one, however, since it is a state of affairs characteristic of a rural society which for two thousand years has had little reason to change radically.

The Economy

We have seen that most people worked on the land, and that some were engaged in trade—a trade by which India was linked directly or indirectly with all parts of the known world.

It was a luxury trade rather than anything else, however; and, far from reaching every villager, its products came to precious few. Ample coins remain to prove the existence of money; but this does not mean that everybody had money, and bought whatever he could afford. Most people had few possessions—furniture, farming and household utensils, and clothing. Some of these they made themselves; the rest were obtained by barter, their crops or the products of their labour being exchanged for their needs.

Rich curries (with plenty of pepper from the South), and fruits to follow them, were the daily fare for very few. For most, rice—or wheatcakes, where wheat was the staple—constituted the standard meal, cooked with maybe a few vegetables. Cattle were used in the fields, and not regarded as a source of meat or milk. Religious beliefs prevented most people from slaughtering cattle; and meat was a comparative rarity.

Though poverty set a limit to what could be bought or obtained by barter, there were plenty of crafts catering to the wants of society. There were workers in all manner of precious and semi-precious stones; ivory workers; goldsmiths; and especially—from about the sixth or seventh century onward—carvers of stone, who furnished the temples with their reliefs and statues. There were weavers producing muslin, calico, silks and other fabrics. 'Chintz' is an Indian word in origin, as are several other words for types of textiles.

But two things above all limited a villager's ability to obtain more than the bare necessities of life. These were the weather and the political situation. If the rains failed, there would be no harvest. Even if the weather was good and there was a fine harvest, a king in dire straits or a callous tax collector might take most of it. Standard official rates varied from the traditional one-sixth to a half of the crop. Even if the government didn't take more than was fair, an army might be quartered nearby, and would demand food from the villages. Or if law and order had broken down, robbers might come plundering and looting. There were many doubts and uncertainties to life.

Administration

The government was a rather remote thing, and something to be feared. Government officials who came round from time to time were likely to be interested at least as much in profiting from the powers given them by their position as in the welfare of the subjects. The king himself might be regarded as a great man, as a superior sort of being; but the individuals who represented him in practice were seldom loved.

However, long periods might go by without sight or sound of a government official. The local officer might put in an appearance only at tax-collection time. So although the government could constitute a burden, it could also be very lightly felt. Villages very largely ran their own affairs. Headmen, who were probably largely hereditary, arranged the apportionment of tax contributions, and were in some of their functions rather like magistrates. People in a community would club together to do such things as making wells or rest-houses, providing salaries for local priests, arranging defence against armed bands, and the like. In the South there came to be regular village councils, called panchayats, on which elders would deliberate about matters of concern to their communities.

Conclusion

Life for the Indian was, then, a strange combination of dependence and freedom. He was dependent on the weather, on family heads, on the political situation and the government; yet he had independence from the government for most of the time, freedom to do things on his own, and to evolve his own customs—local customs being recognized as authoritative in law.

It was a hard life, and it is understandable that people should turn to religion as an important part of their lives. The austere doctrines of the orthodox Hindu schools were softened in village usage to something warmer and more easily understood by ordinary people— mixed with all sorts of local cults, the worship of spirits, with elaborate ceremonial to give people a feeling of participating in something important. In the course of time, and contrary to the original spirit of Hinduism and Buddhism, there grew up in Indian religious tradition a belief in a God of love.

CHAPTER FOUR

Hinduism and Buddhism

(a) INDIAN RELIGIONS

When we think of Indian religions, perhaps we think of a turbaned man lying on a bed of nails, or perhaps squatting cross-legged, wearing only a loincloth, as he meditates. Such images are so strange and so remote from our own experience that some of us may not try to understand why he does these things, but may regard him as an oddity, a mystery, perhaps even a joke. On the contrary, it is worth some effort to learn about Indian religions.

There is a large body of holy scriptures first of all. Hinduism is like a cluster of religions, each with its own sacred texts; and these texts have been studied in ancient times by learned men who have composed other texts about them. Buddhism has as the sacred literature of its orthodox school the Pali Canon—Pali being the language in which the texts are written. No longer used today, it was a North Indian language, though the books were first actually written down in Ceylon. The Canon is the set of books that are regarded by Buddhists as their authorities on religion. This set is called the three baskets, because when books were written on palm leaves, they were kept in woven baskets.

India has always had enormous respect for men of religion, and the doctrines that they have propounded are worth the most serious consideration. They are not easy to understand. You cannot do justice to Hinduism or Buddhism simply by reading a few books, let alone the few words that are all there is room for here. Indian religions are part of Indian life, and like life they have to be lived. We would not expect somebody from a non-Christian country to find out what Christianity is really like from a glance at the Bible, because Christianity has been going on for two thousand years and has developed many varied characteristics in different places that cannot very well be understood without living in those places. In the same way, we should not expect that a superficial survey will be enough to remove the mystery from Indian religions and make them seem natural and straightforward.

Rebirth and Fatalism

We probably don't expect, when we die, to be reborn in the world
in some other form, such as a cat, a worm, or a flea. The Indian
outlook, however, embraces this idea; and behind it lies a perfectly
logical doctrine that helps to make life intelligible for those who
accept it. It is taken for granted that we go from life to life in
different bodies, much as those who can afford it go from car to car,
buying a new one every so often. In each life, we get the rewards and
punishments for what we have done in the past. This, to many
people, makes just as good sense as does our belief, for instance,
that the earth is round.

There are quite frequent references to the 'fatalism' of the East.
The people of India, and indeed the rest of Asia, are said to be
resigned to whatever fate does to them, unwilling to try and change
their position in life. They are said to be pessimistic people, not
expecting to be able to make life happy for themselves.

There is probably a fair amount of truth in this idea, though it
is difficult to make generalizations that are true about all or even
many Indians, especially nowadays. There may indeed be a lot of
pessimism about the outlook on life of many villagers, if only because
life is fairly hard for most of them and they know very well that they
cannot expect any dramatic improvements in their lot. Whether
their religions are pessimistic, however, is another question—as we
shall see.

If we want to understand what Hinduism, for example, can mean
for a believer, we have to see what positive thing it offers. And we
find that it offers him the hope of salvation, the hope that by his own
efforts he can obtain for himself deliverance from suffering—not in
this world or in this life, but in the future.

Christianity makes much the same kind of promise to its followers.
But it is a different sort of salvation, a different sort of deliverance
from suffering; and there are important differences between the
general characters of religion in the East and in the West.

In the first place, religions in India are more tolerant of one
another than Western religions are. This is not true of the relations
between the later religions of Hinduism and Islam; but as far as the
ancient Indian religions are concerned, all kinds of different beliefs
have lived together without any notable conflict: nothing, at any
rate, like the fearful clashes between rival Christian sects that
turned into some of the bloodiest full-scale wars in European history.

It has been said that the religions of India are like a net—all the
things in it are joined together, as the knots in a net are; and if you
take up one, you pull up others as well. This is to say that, although
there is a great deal of diversity, all the sects—orthodox and un-

orthodox—share certain underlying assumptions and purposes;
they are all parts of the same way of life, and the historical and
cultural connections between them bind them into a single pattern
of thought and action. Much of what we can say about Hinduism is
true about Buddhism, which started life as one of the unorthodox
sects of Hinduism but developed into an important religion in its own
right.

(b) HINDUISM

Hinduism and Buddhism

Indian religion, then, consists of a large number of sects with
partly overlapping sets of beliefs. Hinduism is not so much one of
these sects as a central cluster, a group of beliefs and practices which
have been regarded in India as orthodox and which go hand in hand
with law, caste, science and other features in Indian life. For you
cannot easily distinguish these things from religion as separate
activities: everything in Indian tradition has a religious colour to it,
and the laws, the caste rules, the scientific knowledge, and so forth,
are written down in the same class of books that contain purely
religious principles, regulations for holding sacrifices, and the like.
Orthodox Hinduism, then, is the repository of ancient Indian
wisdom studied and practised by the orthodox priests, the brahmans

Buddhism is not quite the same sort of thing. Hinduism is a group
of religious traditions based on certain central ideas; Buddhism is
one particular unorthodox tradition that detached itself from the
teaching of the brahmans and established its own school. It shares
many of the basic ideas of Hinduism, but does not have the same
rituals and is not tied up with the caste system, as Hinduism is.

There are several distinctions that can be made between the two
religions. In the first place, we must remember that, whereas
Hinduism could scarcely help being strong in India because it has
been the orthodox Indian religion, Buddhism is something that split
off and has since become very weak in India. Although there were
times in Indian history when Buddhist monks were everywhere, and
rulers in all parts of the country supported their activities, Buddhism
in India eventually retreated again before the orthodox religion of
the priestly class—the brahmans. But in spite of losing ground in the
country of its origin, Buddhism has become the official religion of a
number of other Asian countries to which it was exported.

Again, as we have seen, Hinduism is diffuse, containing within
itself so many different elements that have grown into it in the course
of Indian history that it is difficult to define it. Buddhism, on the
other hand, is a more precise set of teachings based on a set of sacred

texts. Especially in Buddhist countries other than India, however, many beliefs and practices were also developed. For example, there are three divisions of Buddhism: the 'Great Vehicle', the 'Small Vehicle', and the 'Vehicle of the Thunderbolt'. It is not easy to talk about 'Buddhism' then, without saying what type of Buddhism is being referred to.

Another important distinction between Buddhism and Hinduism, which has been too seldom recognized by students of the two religions, is that Hinduism is orthodox in India. It consists not only of doctrines but also of rituals—just as Christianity consists not only of what is said in the Bible but also of services in church, some regular and some for special occasions. It is often the rituals that mean more, practically speaking, in the lives of average villagers—they leave the doctrines to more educated people. And these rituals—sacrifices and so forth—require the services of a priest, or brahman. There have always been large numbers of village priests making their living by performing ceremonies for the villagers.

This has meant that Hinduism is something built into the caste system, in which the brahmans are the most important. Buddhism is not part and parcel of the caste system, and is not tied up so much with rituals and ceremonies. It concentrates more on the teachings, which used to be preached by monks who wandered about the country, spreading the doctrines of the Buddha to the people by word of mouth. This sort of activity was not really the job of the brahmans, since Buddhists who wanted to preach were expected to give up their settled family lives and devote their lives to the search for enlightenment, wandering about and living off forest products, or begging their food.

Hinduism and Society

Hinduism has its own thinkers and profound philosophy, however—just as Buddhism does—and Hindu ascetics, too, are dedicated to a simple life of meditation. Four stages are to be included in the life of a pious Hindu, indeed; and of these four, the last two entail devotion to the private search for religious truth. In the first stage, the pious Hindu is a student, living in the household of a religious teacher, and learning from him. In the second, as a young man, he has left his teacher and gone out into society to be a householder—an ordinary citizen, raising a family and working for a living. In the third, he is a forest recluse, and in the fourth, a wandering religious beggar.

At no time in India's history, of course, were all the people following this pattern of life. On the other hand, it was generally thought good to do so; and religious beggars were by no means regarded as nuisances who ought to be working for a living. There were always quite a number leaving their villages to lead simple, austere lives, and the Buddha himself followed this well-established tradition in abandoning his life of luxury at the palace for hardship and seclusion in the forests.

Most people had, and still have, their positions laid down for them in or out of the caste system, although probably only a minority went through all the stages of life laid down by the Hindu religion. The most important feature of the social order for the purposes of religion was the set of four classes we saw before—brahmans, ksatriyas, vaisyas, and sudras. These four classes comprehended all the people who were 'in caste'; outcastes did not, and do not, belong to any of the classes.

In the religious books, a great deal is written about these classes (varnas). The first three, the higher ones, are said to be twice-born. That is, they have two births: one is the actual physical birth into the world and the second is symbolic—they are said to be born again when they are initiated into the faith of the Aryan Hindus by being invested with the sacred thread which is placed around them in the course of a ceremony. It is as if, in Christianity, we said that baptism was a 'second birth'. But the ceremony of the sacred thread occurs later in the life of the Hindu than baptism does in the life of most Christians.

There are constant references all through the sacred literature to the different rights and duties of the respective classes. There are many ceremonies which are different for different classes. And the sudras—the servants and labourers—are given very little opportunity for involvement. The sudras are admitted to be in the caste system—thought, that is, to be descended from the original Aryan immigrants. But they are not to be initiated into the religion. They are not to be taught the sacred books, or even to overhear readings from them. They are treated in every way as inferior creatures.

This is a point where it is difficult to disentangle religion from other things, because in the texts of Hindu thought religious things are mixed up with secular things like law and politics. The discrimination between class and class is not just a discrimination in matters of religious initiation and ceremonies therefore, it is also a discrimination in matters of law and justice. Whenever crimes and the penalties are described, we find that different treatment is set out for the four classes. Usually (though not always) a crime against somebody of higher class, especially a brahman, is more severely punished than a crime against somebody of low class; and crimes by sudras are more severely punished than crimes by higher classes.

The Evolution of Hinduism

So far we have been talking about Hinduism as if it never changed. Although much of the theory of the religion has in fact remained virtually unaltered, there have also been many changes. The religion evolved into new forms as the Aryan tribes entered India and spread across the North, mingling to some extent with the earlier inhabitants, their small communities becoming settled kingdoms with government organizations, and the Indian culture growing and flourishing, establishing rich traditions in literature and the arts.

There are three very general phases that we can notice in the formative years of Hinduism: the worship of the original Vedic gods by the Aryans entering the subcontinent about three thousand years ago; the development of mysticism and the basic doctrines associated with Hinduism today; and the development of the main sects that are associated with Hinduism today.

The Vedic gods—the gods of the Vedas—are those worshipped by the nomadic Aryan tribes with whom the written record of Indian history starts. The Rig Veda contains the hymns that were chanted by their priests. The hymns were originally memorized and handed down by word of mouth; they were divided into ten parts and were eventually committed to writing. (The last of these ten books is thought to have been composed later than the others.) An enormous variety of gods are celebrated in the hymns, most of which consist of praises to them—descriptions of their might and glory and requests for their help. They were sung on the occasions of sacrifices, at which it was thought that the god in whose honour a sacrifice was being held would come down and feast with the worshippers.

This type of worship is characteristic of fairly undeveloped peoples living in small communities, and it shows links with the religions of the other Aryan peoples—some of the names of gods show similarities to those of Aryan tribes who founded the civilizations of Greece and other parts of Europe. The immigrants to India brought with them similar gods and sacrifices to those which their cousins in Europe had, and which in a way, we ourselves have inherited. Some of our weekdays are named after old Norse gods—Wednesday after Woden, Thursday after Thor. And Woden and Thor lived in the same Nordic landscape as Zeus, the father of the gods. Now Zeus is really the same person as the Roman god Jupiter, under a different name—the first syllable, *Ju*, is the Latin version of Zeus. And far from the Mediterranean, even further from the cold mountains of Viking lands, on the sweltering plains of India, the cousins of these European tribesmen worshipped the same god under the name of *Dyaus*.

These then were Aryan gods rather than Indian gods, and this

type of religion differed from later developments in Hindu belief
with the domestication of the Aryans and the fusion of their culture
with that of the original inhabitants. These gods are perhaps a bit
like the Aryan tribesmen themselves—they have strong characters,
they are individualistic, they are fierce and powerful, they are
warriors. Their worshippers bow down to them in fear at least as
much as in reverence, being afraid of the consequences of the gods'
displeasure. In the hymns addressed to them, it is clear that the
motive of the worshipper was often to avoid the gods' wrath as well
as to obtain benefits by flattery.

In a later age, from about 800 or 700 B.C. onward, we find the
character of religion changing. The books no longer consist of hymns
to gods. Instead there are increasingly complicated rules for the
conduct of sacrifices and obscure texts in which mystic doctrines are
propounded. There is a preoccupation with the magic power of
words, the chanting of the right syllables at sacrifices, the distillation
of the truth and the key to the infinite in the utterance of sacred
formulae. One class of books worth mentioning is the upanishads.
Literally the word means 'sitting down beside', and the meaning is
that the books contain secret doctrines about the universe which
were to be whispered privately from one person to another.

Among the doctrines of Hinduism, the personal element is now
less. We no longer find gods whom we can recognize as personalities.
Instead we find an attempt to describe the inner truths of life.
Sometimes indeed a god is named, but he is then more of a symbol
for some abstract idea than a person. The meanings of the word
'brahman' need to be mentioned. One form of the word means a
more or less personal being who created the world. Another form
means a sort of spirit that is spread through the universe. And from
these meanings develop the ideas of 'divine', 'sacred', 'priestly', and
so we have a word 'brahmana', meaning a certain sort of sacred text,
and of course the familiar word 'brahman' meaning priest.

This tradition of Hinduism—the mystic tradition—is the one
most familiar to the West: the idea of meditation leading to some
direct awareness of an inner truth or of God.

The mystic vision and the inner awareness were naturally not
things that every Indian could hope for or was interested in. For the
villager, religion meant ceremonies for all the occasions of life that
needed to be marked by a sense of moment and religious significance,
and the worship of known, familiar beings who would listen to
prayer, share in the sacrifice, and give rewards or perhaps punishments. No longer, indeed, did people feel the need of the hearty
bustling Vedic gods; but they needed some person to focus their
reverence upon. This person was not to be, like the Vedic gods, a

human being writ large—especially mighty, but subject to misfortunes and acts of fate outside his control. He was to be more than
this—an almighty, majestic being far above the scale of mankind,
a king reigning supreme and separated from men by an extensive
hierarchy of supernatural beings. But still, the god was to be a person,
not an abstract principle.

Gods came and gods went. Even in Vedic times, the Aryan
Dyaus was past his heyday, and a more awesome god named
Varuna took pride of place. As time went on, the celestial palaces
came to be inhabited by a few majestic and awesome gods, rather
than a large number of highly personalized ones.

The gods and goddesses worshipped in post-Vedic times, in the
early centuries B.C. and onwards, are Indian rather than Aryan:
that is, they represent a tradition in which the Aryan character has
been softened and turned inwards by a new style of life, or by
contact with the pre-Aryan peoples of India, or both; and love, awe,
mystery, reverence take the place of cheerfulness and bawdiness.
Vishnu and Shiva are the chief deities of this phase, and come in the
course of time to preside over the two main branches of the Hindu
religion. Eventually, practising Hindus could be divided into those
who adopted the worship of Vishnu (Vaishnavism) and those who
adopted the worship of Shiva (Shaivism).

Vishnu was the god of creation, and was always shown in statuary
holding symbols of creation. Shiva was the protector, the god of
procreation, the preserver. And such gods are made the subject, not
of hymns that praise their virtues and celebrate their powers, but of a
great treasure-house of myths that tell hundreds of stories about
them, and thus weave them into lore and literature. There are for
example stories of the various incarnations of the god Vishnu, who
was said to have been born numbers of times in different forms,
sometimes as an animal, sometimes as a man or as a supernatural
being, and the whole complex tradition of divine activities was part
and parcel of Indian life; everybody knew about the gods and their
doings, how to pray to them, what were their symbols, and in the
temples every statue was full of symbolism.

Transmigration

For a few people, Hinduism meant the search for enlightenment
through mystic experience. For most people, it meant familiar gods,
often-repeated sacrifices, a wealth of literary and artistic traditions,
and the sense of security and community that goes with participating
in a shared tradition or activity. But there was something in between
the mysticism of the yogis and the gods of the villagers something
that built a bridge between the sophisticated and the commonplace

and made of Hinduism a thing that everybody shared. This was the set of basic ideas at the root of Hinduism and of the other religions of India as well.

Transmigration was (and is) a central idea. This is the belief that the souls of all beings pass from life to life from one body to another. The world is like a stream that rushes onwards, carrying everything with it, and each creature in it is carried along willy-nilly—death does not put an end to anything, because presently the same creature is reborn in another form. This then is the doctrine of rebirth that is taken for granted by so many people as a natural and reasonable idea.

For us, this notion seems to have a cheerful aspect. It means that death is not a final end to everything. But for the Hindu it is not as simple as that. For him, being born into the world is a matter for despondency. In Buddhism especially, life is regarded as suffering, and the doctrine of rebirth is in a way like a prison sentence—it means that when we die, instead of escaping from the miseries of existence in the world, we are condemned to another life, and after that to another, and so on in an infinite series unless we should chance somehow to escape from the need to be reborn. The world itself, according to many Indian religious doctrines, is an illusion, and therefore to be born into it is to be ensnared into illusion; all suffering is born of illusion, and if, by being born, we are trapped in illusion, we are trapped in suffering also.

This is a rather difficult idea to digest, but it is an important one in Hinduism and other beliefs. We must distinguish between everything that we mean by 'the world'—space, time, life as we know it—and, on the other hand, the spaceless, timeless eternity in which there are no separate beings with their own selves, no separate existences, but all things are merged into one. This state, this eternity, cannot be described by the use of words, because all the words we have are able to cope only with the world of space and time, the world of illusion; so when we talk about the world of reality we have to keep saying 'it is not like this' or 'not like that', but it is impossible to say what it really is like.

Karma

Indian religions say that it is possible to escape from the world of illusion and return to the world of reality, where one's self disappears and there is no more rebirth. It is possible to escape by cultivating virtue and by doing away with passions and attachments to things in the world. We are then able to avoid the need to be reborn by the operation of Karma.

This is a Sanskrit word which has several shades of meaning, but in the context of religious doctrine it means the law of good causing good and bad causing bad.

If we are good, then there are good results for us—not necessarily in this life, but in a future one. Similarly, if we are not virtuous, or if we hanker after things of the world, things which are after all illusions, then in the future we suffer for it. What we sow, we also reap.

In a way, this means that what happens to us is out of our hands, there is nothing we can do to avoid it, because it has been determined by what we have done in the past. But in a way also, it means that we can control our destinies—what we do now affects our future.

Thus, life may be suffering, but we are able to do something about it; we can lift ourselves up by our shoestrings, as it were, and put an end to the cycle of rebirth. Because, if we accumulate sufficient merit in the course of our migration from life to life, and if we free our minds from attachment to worldly things, then at the end, there will be no rebirth for us, and we shall be merged into the world of reality—not the world as we know it, of space and time, but the world that cannot be described. As we go from life to life, we might rise or fall in the scale—now a man, now a god, now a ghost, now a monkey—but there is hope for all of us that one day we shall be able to move up the scale and out at the top.

Salvation

One thing to notice here is that it is not the ultimate aim of the Hindu to go to a heaven. There are several heavens, but they are all part of the world of illusion. This is another rather difficult idea to digest, but it too is quite important. Any state in which there are separate existences is part of the world of space and time and therefore illusion. In the heavens, there are separate gods who have separate lives, so they also are in the world of illusion and suffering. Theirs is a higher state than ours, true, and there is less suffering; but still they are re-born they have not yet obtained final salvation.

The Hindu idea of salvation, then, is not like that of the Christian. For the average villager, it may indeed be that rebirth in a happier state seems to be the chief benefit that his religion can give him. But for those who make a serious study of their religion, for educated brahmans, and for ascetics, 'going to heaven' is not the end and object of existence; and indeed the wish to go to heaven is itself an example of attachment to illusory things, of hankering after the pleasures of the world. It is therefore likely to cause bad karma— to have a bad effect in a future life.

Hinduism is not an easy religion to enter into—it seems very austere, because it demands a total rejection of everything that we

The Great Bath at Mohenjo Daro, one of the sites of the Indus Valley
civilization

Bodhgaya monument: the stone pillars have mortises to hold railings, being carved as if they were of wood

Stupa at Sanchi, an early Buddhist monument

Buddhist monumen
at Bodhgaya, said t
be the scene of th
Buddha's enlighter
ment

normally value. It demands the deliberate cultivation of passionlessness, of indifference to the world, even, in a sense, to other people. But, for the Hindu, this is not to be thought of as coldness, as frigidity. It is poise, serenity and inner peace. It is the road to mystic experience, the condition in which a living being still in this world can have a taste of what it is like to lose one's self and escape from the world and shake off all illusions. This state is called (in Sanskrit) samadhi. In Buddhism, much the same thing is meant by 'nirvana'. Literally, the word 'nirvana' means 'extinction'. It is like the snuffing out of a candle. But what is being snuffed out is the illusion. Our separate selves happen to be part of the illusion, but that does not mean that, when the selves are gone, there is nothing left. The Hindu would say that the world of reality is left.

(c) Buddhism

There was once a Buddhist monk who had a very saintly character. Everybody thought that when he died he would be reborn in a much higher condition than the life of men. He was extremely virtuous; he followed all the precepts of Buddhism; and he had purged his mind of worldly attachments.

But there was just one little thing that was not as it should be; there was just one form of attachment to worldly pleasures that he had not got rid of. He was very fond of his yellow monk's robe. He wore it with pride. But pride is illusion.

This was of course only a small thing, no great crime; but it just happened that, when the time finally came for him to die, he had in his mind a trace of his attachment to his robe. Now, the thoughts in the mind at the moment of death are very important in determining the next life. This monk's interest in the robe caused him to be reborn as a louse crawling about on it.

This may seem rather a cruel stroke of fate. He was, after all, a saintly monk. But his rebirth as a louse did not mean that all his good karma was wasted. A few days later, the louse died, and he was reborn in the highest heaven.

This story comes from the Buddhist literature. It illustrates several things. In the first place, it is a good example of the way in which Buddhism was presented to people. They were taught the doctrines, not by theological explanations, but by stories like this that were readily understood.

It shows also how the doctrines of rebirth and of karma—good causing good, bad causing bad—were thought to work. It points to the importance of what is in the mind rather than what one actually does. And it shows how, in the end, everything works out so that justice is done.

Finally, the story shows what a lot there is in common between Buddhism and Hinduism. The ideas here are exactly those we have just been discussing in connection with Hinduism. We are not dealing so much with two distinct religions as with a world of thought—the Indian world of thought, to which the Buddha belonged. What he preached shared the basic ideas of the other sects in the India of his day; but some of his teachings put his followers outside the mainstream of orthodox belief. In particular, Buddhism was not tied to the caste system. The Buddhist belief was that anybody had a chance of obtaining salvation, even directly after this present life, whether he was of low caste or high; whereas for the Hindu, a low-caste man could not hope for better in the next life than to move up a notch in the caste scale.

The Life of the Buddha

This appeal to men of all castes, without discrimination between them, helps to account for the considerable popularity that Buddhism came to enjoy for centuries after the Buddha's death. He lived in an age when new sects were active and new ideas were afoot. The importance Buddhism came to have later is the reason for our giving so much more attention to it than to other non-orthodox schools of religion: during the Buddha's lifetime there already existed a variety of doctrines, to which the Buddha's teachings were a further contribution. Another sect—the Jains—were important in his day, and have continued to the present day.

The Buddha himself came from a noble family in the North, among the Himalayan foothills. This was an area where, in the sixth century B.C., there were many small kingless states; they were governed by assemblies of aristocratic families. The Buddha belonged to the Sakya clan, and came of a family that lived in royal style.

Many stories have grown up about his life and become part of the Buddhist tradition. It is often difficult to tell what core of truth they may contain, but many of them are obviously pure inventions— full of magic and fantasy, part of the myths of the religion. It is scarcely likely, for example, that the infant Buddha, at the moment of being born, took seven symbolic steps and announced that he had been born into the world for the last time. Such behaviour in a new-born baby today would be distinctly alarming for everybody; but for the Buddhists it was a way of representing the supernormal quality of the Buddha, and the importance of his birth.

Similarly there is no certainty that, before he was born, his mother had a dream in which an elephant entered her side. That story is told, however; and it is said that the wise men were asked to

interpret the dream. They said that she was going to give birth to a
son who would become either a great teacher or a great emperor.

We are told that the Buddha's parents went to a great deal of
trouble to prevent him from becoming a teacher: they wanted him
to carry on the royal traditions of the family, to take over his father's
inheritance and raise the family from the level of a noble lineage
in a small state to that of an imperial dynasty. If he became a teacher,
that would mean that he would leave them and go away into
solitude—become a beggar or a hermit—because that was the sort
of life that all religious teachers were expected to follow.

The story runs that the child Buddha (or Gautama, for Buddha,
meaning 'Enlightened', is a name that he was given later) was
made to lead a very sheltered life and given every sort of luxury,
so that he would be content with the style of living of the palace
and not turn his mind to speculations and doctrines. Eventually a
beautiful wife was found for him, and he was constantly surrounded
by attendants with food, music, entertainments of all kinds,

He was a virtual prisoner in the palace grounds, however; and
when he finally did go out, by stealth, into the world, the things he
saw made a deep impression on him. It is said that he saw an old
man, ancient and decrepit and ugly, and this was something new to
him. Then he saw a sick man, diseased and suffering Thirdly, he
saw a corpse, all puffed up. Now all these things were deeply disturb-
ing to him, because they showed him that there are sorrow and
suffering in the world, and that death comes to all of us.

Fourthly, he saw a religious beggar, an ascetic who devoted himself
to religion and relied upon others to put rice in his bowl. This man
seemed to be so poised and serene that Gautama thought that this
sort of life must be the right way to understand the sorrows of
earthly existence and rise above them.

Accordingly, Gautama stole out of the palace one night, after
much heartsearching, and dedicated himself to the life of an ascetic.

At first he tried the method of self-inflicted suffering which many
ascetics followed—going almost entirely without food in the effort
to make themselves independent of worldly concerns. But he found
that this did not help him to obtain the enlightenment that he was
looking for, so he broke his fast and ate. This seemed to others with
him a poor thing to do.

But Gautama was not abandoning the quest for enlightenment;
he was looking for a new way. He sat down under a peepul tree at
Bodhgaya and resolved not to leave the spot until he saw the truth,
the inner meaning of life.

At Bodhgaya today, a large monument stands at the place, and
is much visited by tourists. For many centuries the place has been a

magnet for Buddhist pilgrims. To one side of the monument there grows a tree, spreading its bright green foliage wide; it is said to have grown from a cutting that has descended, cutting by cutting, from the very tree under which the Buddha sat. There can be few sites so permeated with history.

The story goes that, after a long meditation, and after grappling with powerful temptations offered by demons, the Buddha finally rose—for now he really was Buddha, the enlightened—and went to preach the new teachings that under the peepul tree, had come to be understood by him. He preached the doctrine of the Middle Way—that truth is to be found, and enlightenment is to be gained, neither by austerities, self-torture, whipping oneself, fasting, and the like, nor by a soft life of ease, ignoring the suffering all around, but by a middle course between these two extremes. He rejected as useless for the purposes of enlightenment both the worldly life and the methods practised by so many of the ascetics of his day, people who would subject themselves to all manner of torture, maiming them-selves, or holding arms up above their heads until the arms were withered and useless.

What the Buddha preached was a life of simplicity and tran-quillity. Sufferings would only hinder the search for truth. But poise and serenity would come from following the Middle Way.

The rest of his life is a story of his teaching as he moved about gathering disciples and spreading his doctrines. Kings patronized him. People came from far and wide to hear him speak. At the time of his death, he had founded a new movement, an order of monks, called the *sangha*. It was his wish that after his death there should be no single leader to run the sangha, but that his teachings themselves should act as the leader.

There is a great deal about the Buddha's life and teachings in the Buddhist literature, as we have said; and it is often impossible to know what to believe. We have to remember that the Buddhist traditions were not written down until about five centuries after the Buddha's death: until that time they were handed on by word of mouth. Perhaps we can say that the doctrine of the Middle Way and the appeal to Indians of all castes originated with what the Buddha himself said; perhaps he preached the eightfold path and the four noble truths. But there is little that we can be sure of.

The Eightfold Path and the Four Noble Truths

The Buddha was not a theologian. He was not concerned to propound new metaphysical doctrines, though his followers did that for him later, and in abundance. We have to realize that the Buddha regarded himself as a guide whom people could follow in pursuit of objectives that were familiar in India, and already well understood by many. He regarded his teaching, not as a body of doctrines to be learned by rote, but as a technique for rising above sorrow and attachment to worldly things, and heading towards enlightenment. It was a skill, like learning to ride a bicycle, not a piece of memorization, like learning multiplication tables. What mattered was that it should work. The Buddha compared his teaching to a raft on which one crossed a river. It is needed for a limited purpose only. When you have crossed the river, you abandon the raft, because you don't need it any more.

It is in this light that we should look at doctrines like the eightfold path and the four noble truths. They are intended as tools for the use of people who are seeking the peace and serenity that right understanding can bring; and who are ultimately seeking, like disciples of the other Indian religious schools, release from rebirth.

The eightfold path consists of the means by which a disciple should discipline his mind and get rid of attachment to worldly things. The eight things to be cultivated are: right views, right resolve, right speech, right conduct, right livelihood, right effort, right recollection and right meditation.

Something else that his hearers very probably took for granted was the Buddha's view that life is full of sorrow, and the object of a devout man should be to get rid of sorrow by forsaking his entanglement in the affections and pleasures of worldly life. Birth, said the Buddha, is sorrow. Age is sorrow. Disease and death are sorrow. There is sorrow in experiencing what is unpleasant, in leaving what is pleasant, and in having wishes unfulfilled. These facts constitute the first of the four noble truths, the truth of sorrow, which is the main bar to progress for a man who wishes to gain enlightenment.

The second is the noble truth of the arising of sorrow—it arises because of our attachment to worldly pleasures, to possessions, to friends and family and so forth, which causes us to be reborn again and again. The third is the truth of stopping of sorrow, which is to be achieved by stopping our thirst for worldly experiences and relationships and for all that is pleasant. The fourth is the truth of the way to stop sorrow, which is to follow the eightfold path.

The Development of Buddhism

Buddhism, like Hinduism, was not a static unchanging religion. In later centuries much was added to it—and in particular a great deal of abstract philosophy—so that there came to be different brands of Buddhism in different places.

As we noticed before, although the religion eventually became very weak in India itself, it became very strong in many other places. Ceylon, in the first place, was according to tradition the place where the Pali canon, the sacred texts of Buddhism, was written down, and Ceylon became the home of orthodoxy—where the monks studied the scriptures closely and transmitted a tradition of Buddhism that was firmly rooted in the scriptures themselves, and was therefore not likely to change very much in the course of time. From Ceylon, Buddhism was exported to other countries, where it took root and flourished. The kingdoms in the area of modern Burma, Thailand and Cambodia received this orthodox brand of Buddhism from Ceylon.

In India, especially during the period of invasions from the north-west in the centuries before and after Christ, there was a ferment of ideas, as different peoples with different religions came into contact with each other. Modifications were made to people's Buddhist beliefs, making the accent on sorrow and the need to escape from the world seem less austere and pessimistic. A different, non-orthodox style of Buddhism developed, and found its way to China—where it became one of the chief schools of thought, along with Confucianism and Taoism. In Japan it became dominant.

There are, then, two general divisions of Buddhism. Although we have been calling them the orthodox and the non-orthodox, these are not very good terms; what is unorthodox in one country, for example, might be orthodox in another. It is possible to call 'orthodox' the Ceylonese type because it insists more on the actual words in the scriptures than does the other 'unorthodox' division, which is more tolerant of various practices and beliefs that are not strictly part of Buddhism, and which has a less chilly doctrine of salvation. It would now be a good idea to examine these two divisions further using their correct names.

Mahayana and Hinayana

The two main schools of Buddhism are known by Sanskrit names, which are rather cumbrous; but they really need to be learned, because they are so often used.

'Hinayana' means literally 'lesser vehicle'. It refers to the orthodox tradition that existed in India for some centuries after the lifetime of the Buddha, and which found its chief home later in Ceylon. It was called the lesser vehicle because it seemed to the unorthodox Buddhists to be rather strict and narrow, less accommodating than their own brand. The Hinayana Buddhists themselves use the term Theravada, 'the doctrine of the elders', to describe their doctrine; so Theravada and Hinayana overlap, although there were once Hinayana sects which were not Theravada.

Hinayana Buddhism is opposed to sullying the religion with the mingling of foreign elements, especially elements that smack of idolatry. Images of the Buddha had been forbidden; and indeed it was not until some centuries after his death that any statues of the Buddha were made. Hinayana is therefore not so much associated with art, sculpture, temples and so forth, although Hinayana art and sculpture are found in many Buddhist sites in India and Ceylon.

Mahayana Buddhism is more tolerant and therefore in Mahayana Buddhist countries the religion has been more mixed with other things. The word 'Mahayana' means 'great vehicle'; it is a broad, capacious wagon on to which all sorts of strange ideas and practices will fit. The spirit of the Mahayana doctrines is quite different from Hinayana Buddhism—there is the idea that some beings, who have accumulated enough merit to escape rebirth, choose to stay in the world of sorrow and pass on some of their merit to other people and in this way to help them. This brings an element of compassion into the doctrine. There are many Buddhas, for a Buddha is an enlightened one, one therefore who will not be reborn again; there has been a whole series of these, and more are to come. A man who is a potential Buddha, but stays in the world to help others, is called a bodhisattva. It is possible that we all may become bodhisattvas and Buddhas in the course of time, if only we accumulate enough merit in the course of our rebirths.

These then are the two schools of thought that gradually appeared and drew apart from each other in the centuries that followed the Buddha's death. At a council of Buddhists held by the emperor Asoka (third century B.C.) Hinayana was established as the orthodox school. There were not at that time any Mahayana sects as such, but in the course of time unorthodox schools developed until there came to be two distinct traditions, Theravada and Mahayana. They have not fought each other with swords; and today Buddhism, despite the vicissitudes of its history, is the religion of as many people as ever before.

CHAPTER FIVE

The Ancient Indian Kingdoms

(a) VEDIC INDIA

From about 1,300 B.C. to about the seventh century B.C., the first period of history that we can take for examination, the Aryans were spreading across the North of India and settling first the Indus and then the Ganges valleys, and establishing kingdoms. In the process they turned from warlike nomadic tribes into a race of settled farmers.

In this early period, the Aryans were still distinct from the rest of the population as a conquering class, with their own language and religion and customs that they had brought with them from beyond the Hindu Kush. As time went on, the races merged. In modern times, the races that make up the Indian people are very much mixed. The southerners are generally darker-skinned than the northerners; and the high-caste Hindus may have in them rather more blood from the original Aryan invaders than have low-caste Hindus or outcastes: but no clear dividing lines can be drawn between the races. Only some of the backward tribes in the interior have kept separate from the rest of the population and have thus kept their racial and cultural characteristics fairly distinct.

The Vedic Tribes

The Vedic period of Indian history is so named because practically all of what we know about the Indians of the time comes from the Vedas.

There are, of course, other sources also. Archaeology can give us several glimpses of their culture. We know, among other things, about the grey painted pottery that they had in the North, their iron ware, their horses, their polished black ware that was later traded with the Deccan—the central belt of India where the non-Aryans were still strong. But our knowledge is still very scanty, and we have to puzzle out what we can about the early Aryan tribes from what the Vedas tell us. This is rather unsatisfactory, because of course the Vedas are not intended as history books. They are intended as religious documents, as praises for the gods and instructions for sacrifices and so on. There are only incidental mentions that give us, for example, the names of the Aryan tribes. These were often at war with one another, and some of the legends of later times are based on conflicts that took place back in those days.

Though they were often fighting amongst themselves, they were all hostile to the native peoples, whom they called the dasas or dasyus—presumably the non-Aryans.

Social Organization

During the period of the Vedic literature, it is evident that the Aryans changed their style of life and gradually became agriculturalists, using the well-watered lands of the river basins for the cultivation of rice, wheat, barley and pulses (peas, beans, lentils). The roving clans settled into village life and kingdoms or states, ruled by large-scale gatherings of elders, came into being.

Throughout the Vedic period, families and clans were very important in people's minds. Many words are used to refer to the larger and smaller groups of relatives. These groups were contained within each other, like nesting tables: each person would belong to a family, let us say, the family would be part of a clan, and the clan would be part of a tribe. Each group would command its own loyalty from its members, who would fight together in battle. But we do not know much about the system in detail, and the words for these groups are not always used with the same precise meaning.

The Vedic Indians did not have the caste system as we know it from later times. The caste system is something that grew up from the practices of the non-Aryan communities, or from the relations between the non-Aryans and the Aryans.

But, late in the Vedic period, the Indians did use the idea of society as something divided into four classes—priests, nobles or warriors, agriculturalists, and labourers, in descending order of importance but all necessary to each other's existence. This is not the same thing as the caste system. It does not mean that there were many groups with elaborate rules of marriage, dining, occupation and so forth. But the fourfold division was nevertheless the scheme into which the caste system came to be fitted: each caste reckoned itself as belonging to one of these four classes.

Political Organization

The Vedic tribes were under the leadership of nobles, members of the leading families. The word 'raja', meaning 'king', is well known, because the colourful rajas of India in more recent times played so big a part in the country's history. The Vedas have the word too, but it need not have meant anything so precise in those days. Literally it means 'shining one', and may originally have referred to leading tribesmen taking part in religious sacrifices. It doesn't matter very much: either way it is clear that there was a noble class in society. And as tribes turned into settled villages and larger communities, this noble class provided the kings.

The kings, or leaders, did not govern the tribes despotically, wielding complete power over them. Even if a tribe had a single chief, who was responsible for the decisions, the noble class as a whole made its views felt. There were important ceremonial occasions on which, amid pomp and pageantry, all the great men would assemble and all manner of business would be discussed.

Vedic Culture

So tribes were becoming settled communities, and political leadership was developing. The Vedic period was the cradle of the Hindu tradition and of Indian society as we know it from later times. Wild tribesmen, who had (perhaps) been the despoilers of Harappa and Mohenjo Daro, were learning the arts of civilization and developing their trade and culture. They began to merge with the indigenous population, and probably to adopt some of its ways.

The literature of the Aryans reflects the development. The earliest texts are the *Rig Vedas*, ten great books of hymns. These show us the original Aryans with their fierce gods. But the later texts consist increasingly of more technical things: elaborate instructions for rituals, spells and chants, and eventually subtle philosophy, highly abstract and metaphysical, of a sort the original tribesmen would not perhaps have understood.

(b) BUDDHIST INDIA, c. 600–321 B.C.

Religions

It is easy to use religions as labels for different periods of Indian history. The Vedas, representing a variant of Aryan religion from which Hinduism was to grow, gave their name to the 'Vedic age' as we have seen. 'Buddhist India', the subject of this section, is the India of the Buddha's time and several centuries after it. 'Hindu India' is a term often used to describe the later classical age, and 'Muslim India' seems an appropriate way of describing the time when most of India was ruled by Muslim invaders. Such labels are convenient, but may be misleading. It is misleading if we think that at a particular moment, for example, the whole of India suddenly became Buddhist, and at some later time it stopped being Buddhist and became Hindu. We have to remember that, right through history, there was one main religion, Hinduism, which developed from the religion of the Aryans and perhaps took much or most of its special character from the religion of the Dravidians. But this religion was not a precise, single thing; it was a variety of different schools of thought with different gods but with some ideas in common.

Buddhism was very strong for much of the six centuries before Christ, but there were other schools as well, such as the Ajivakas and Jains, and the regular priests—brahmans—and their Hinduism still existed. Similarly, in Muslim India, only the ruling classes and a minority of the population that was converted were Muslim.

Kingdoms

Like the Vedas, the Buddhist literature is not designed to tell us history: it serves a religious purpose, and we have to put together our jigsaw picture of the land from random mentions here and there. But one thing is very clear—there was in this period a very distinct political development. India was entering the era of the settled kingdom, too large to be governed by an assembly of elders or aristocrats. It was ruled by kings who wanted power for themselves and their families, who would marry the daughters of other kings in order to extend their influence, and go to war against their neighbours to build up an empire.

This is the striking feature of the North of the time (there is still little information about the South), but it is not the only one. There was a twofold pattern.

Through much of northern India, especially the upper Ganges, where agriculture was developing and settled communities were growing fastest, there were many kingdoms of the sort just described. Northward, towards the Himalayas, and to the north-west, in the Punjab, there were kingless communities run by assemblies.

Of the kingdoms, we know the names of several, into which the area of Aryan settlement was divided. They include Anga, Kasi (the ancient name for the sacred city of Benares on the Ganges), Kamboja, Gandhara (away to the north-west, and subject for much of its history to influences from outside India), Kosala (the largest) and, most important for our immediate purposes, Magadha.

Magadha was the first significant empire in India. We know about its king, Bimbisara, reigning during the sixth century B.C.,

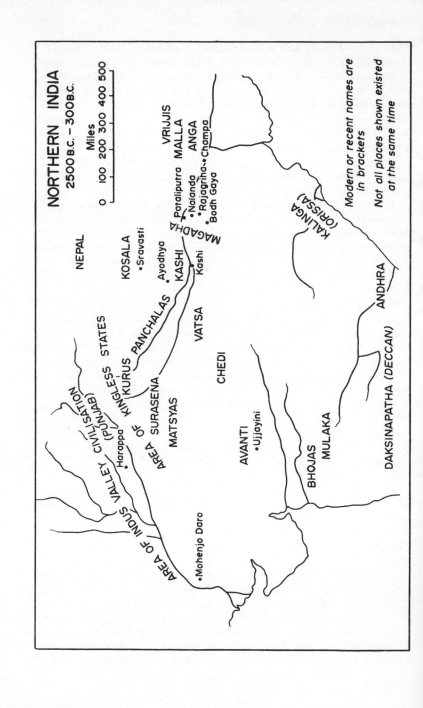

NORTHERN INDIA
2500 B.C. – 300 B.C.

Miles
0   100 200 300 400 500

Modern or recent names are
in brackets

Not all places shown existed
at the same time

NEPAL

KOSALA
•Sravasti

KASHI
Ayodhya

VRIJJIS
MALLA
ANGA
Pataliputra •Champa
•Nalanda
Rajagriha
Bodh Gaya

MAGADHA

KASHI
•Kashi

KALINGA
(ORISSA)

ANDHRA

KURUS
PANCHALAS

AREA OF
KINGLESS STATES
(PUNJAB)

SURASENA

VATSA

CHEDI

MATSYAS

AVANTI
•Ujjayini

BHOJAS
MULAKA

DAKSINAPATHA (DECCAN)

•Harappa

AREA OF INDUS VALLEY CIVILISATION

•Mohenjo Daro

who married the sister of a neighbouring king and also the daughter of a chief of a kingless community, thus extending his influence by dynastic marriages. He also extended it by war, as most Indian kings through much of their history seem to have done. Bimbisara was no exception. He was also a great patron of Buddhism and welcomed the Buddha himself to the court to preach. This interest in religion did not contradict an interest in war. Most kings were interested both in religion and in war—war was their way of life, just as performing sacrifices was the way of life of the brahmans.

The kingdom of Magadha had its capital at Pataliputra, near the modern Patna on the sacred river Ganges in Bihar. Pataliputra was for many centuries the focal point of North Indian political power; later emperors had their capitals there, and philosophers, artists and preachers came to their courts. In the sixth century B.C., the Buddha spent much of his life wandering in this area and spreading his teachings; consequently some of the chief shrines of Buddhism, monuments and places of worship to which Buddhists made pilgrimages, are located in Bihar. Bihar was a stronghold of Buddhism even when most of the rest of India had turned away to Hinduism.

The rise of Magadha and the other kingdoms, and the beginnings of empire, were the chief political development in the period, and, at its height, Buddhism was the dominant feature in culture. But not everybody lived in a centralized kingdom like Magadha, with its large class of government officials and its king constantly going on tour to show himself to his subjects and hear their grievances. Many people lived in communities that didn't have a king at all, and it is worth remembering that the Buddha himself came from one of these, the Sakyas.

The Kingless Communities

'Kingless communities' is a rather clumsy phrase to use in describing them, but it seems to be the safest: because different people who have studied them have different ideas about how they should be described. Sometimes 'republics' is the word used, sometimes 'oligarchies'. Either way, the chief point about them is that they were not monarchies in the same way that Magadha was a monarchy.

As we have seen, they skirted the area of the kingdoms to the north and north-west; the monarchies developed largely in the Ganges area, where rice came to be grown and where society became more organized; the kingless communities were among the foothills of the Himalayas, partly in modern Nepal, and in the forested parts of the Punjab. In general, they were smaller than the kingdoms, although a few of the kingdoms were very small. We know their names—there were among them, for example, the Licchavis, the Sakyas, and the Moriyas. These are the names of the people, the tribes, rather than of the territories they inhabited. It is possible, therefore, to see these communities as survivals of the old Vedic type of tribal organization. The Licchavis, for example, would all consider themselves to be related to each other, one large clan or tribe, and within this group there would be leading sub-clans or families which constituted a sort of aristocracy.

This is one way of looking at the kingless communities, regarding them as a continuation, with modifications, of the sort of tribal pattern that had been known before. The Vedic tribes had kings; but the important thing about them was that they were tribes, with strong family consciousness and some families claiming leadership, and the Licchavis and others were perhaps rather similar.

But there is another way of looking at them, which has sometimes been adopted by historians, and that is to regard them as reactions against the kingdoms. The people objected to the authoritarian control exercised by kings, and set up their own communities that were run by assemblies of the people, who thus had more to say in affairs. Thus they were little republics.

Whichever way we look at them, it is possible to describe them as republics, because they did not have single kings. But the word is likely to be misleading, because it makes us think of modern republics, such as the United States of America, which are large and democratic. These Indian ones were small and quite likely un-democratic. They were run, not by the entire population electing representatives, but by assemblies of noblemen, who were competing among themselves for influence and jealous of each other's families.

Buddhist Literature

There are many matters (such as the nature of the kingless communities) over which historians have disagreed, and it would not be right to set things out as facts, when they are not really known for certain and when scholars dispute them. The reason for much of the uncertainty, as we have noticed, is that we have to piece together our knowledge from occasional references in a literature that was not designed to tell us history. For what we are calling 'the Buddhist period', the Buddhist texts in Pali are the main sources for our knowledge. It is worth mentioning therefore what they consist of. We have already seen that they are composed of three 'baskets'. The one containing 'thread'—strings of sayings, or stories—includes many things that give us a picture of the times. The Jatakas especially, stories of the Buddha's various (imaginary) former lives, show us something of the nature of village life. We see the villagers running their affairs, doing for themselves many of the things that are nowadays done for them by the government, such as roadmaking and the building of assembly halls. We see a great deal about the quality of life, but we do not get history in the sense of an accurate narrative—an account of things that actually happened.

This problem applies to much of ancient Indian history. It didn't seem important to people to make accurate chronicles. The literature does not contain anything that can really be called a history for a thousand years after Christ, and even then the facts given are very uncertain and mixed up with legends.

(c) Alexander and the Rise of the Mauryas

From late in the fourth century B.C. onwards we have more varied and abundant material from which to learn what was happening in northern India. The South, yet to experience the full impact of the Aryans with their Sanskrit literature, is still largely a closed book to us at this stage. But the Sanskrit texts of law and morals, the epics, the inscriptions of the emperor Asoka, these and other things—though they were not all composed as history and may not all have been composed in the last three centuries before Christ—certainly tell us more about India in the pre-Christian era.

There is a long period before us now, from late in the fourth century B.C. to early in the fourth century A.D., in which the North of India witnessed many invasions and the rise and fall of many kingdoms and empires. Among the empires, the most illustrious was that of the dynasty of the Mauryas, based on Pataliputra. Among the Maurya emperors, the most important, or at least the most famous, is the great Asoka, whose name is one of the best known in Indian history. We shall therefore concentrate especially on him. But much went on before and after his reign—wars, cultural achievements, upheavals—and we must also see what were the chief features of the period.

Alexander the Great

Late in the fourth century B.C., based on a territory in the north of Greece, Alexander, son of Philip of Macedon, carved out a mighty empire for himself—probably larger than the world had ever seen. Wherever he went, he conquered: it was said that he seemed to exhaust the scope of possible conquests, and sighed for fresh lands to conquer. His reign is part of Greece's history. But it is also part of India's.

In 326 B.C. he crossed the Indus and entered the area of Indian settlement. He found an India divided among all manner of petty kingdoms and tribes. In the North-West, there were numerous comparatively small communities quarrelling amongst themselves and unable to combine to meet the invader. In the North-East, Magadha was not its former self. It is said that there was a series of nine kings, the Nanda dynasty, who by one account were all brothers who started off their career as a robber band. There is also a story that the first Nanda king was a barber of *sudra* class. It is difficult to know how much truth there is in such stories. But at all events the Nanda kings seem to have been oppressive and unpopular in their kingdom.

If Alexander with his army had penetrated to the region of the Ganges, he might have found the opposition stronger, because Magadha was at least a more powerful kingdom than any of the patchwork of communities in the Punjab; or he might have succeeded in displacing an unpopular ruler and made himself master of the North. We cannot know, because after overcoming one by one the North-Western communities Alexander stopped and turned back. The reason for his retreat was that he was far from home, he had been years away, and his army was unwilling to push the campaign further. He left behind him generals to look after his new-won empire, which after his death split up. But the last general, Eudamus, left India in 317 B.C., and nothing remained of the mighty conqueror's Indian empire.

The significance of Alexander's invasion is chiefly in the contribution it made to cultural contacts between India and the lands to the west. Traders and ambassadors had been passing to and fro for some time, but one particular thing that followed from Alexander's invasion, and a thing that had not happened before, was that a Greek ambassador, Megasthenes, went to an Indian court, at Pataliputra, and wrote a description of India as he saw it. Unreliable though the surviving versions of his description are, it is a valuable aid to us in learning what things in India were like.

Chandragupta Maurya

The court which Megasthenes visited, some time after the invasion, was that of Chandragupta Maurya at Pataliputra, the first king in the Maurya dynasty. Chandragupta took advantage of the turmoil caused by the invasion to overthrow the last of the Nandas and establish himself as ruler of Magadha and eventually of a great empire.

This empire appears to have been nearly as large as that of Asoka, the most powerful of the Mauryan rulers. Chandragupta Maurya was able to secure possession of the lands conquered by the Greeks in the North-West when the empire of Alexander eventually broke up, and thus extended his influence beyond India into modern

Ajanta cave 1. Painting showing initiation of a prince

Terracotta female figurine with elaborate head-dress, from region of Pataliputra, Mauryan period

Statuette of four-armed
Vishnu, eleventh century
Bihar

South India: rock carvings
Mamallapuram, near Madra

Afghanistan. Northern and much of central India were in his empire. The administration of it kept him very busy, and if Megasthenes' account is reliable he was preoccupied all the time with hearing cases in court and running a highly organized administration. However, we cannot know exactly how effective government control really was in all parts of the empire, and it is to be expected that outer provinces were semi-independent under governors or ex-kings who passed on tax or tribute to the emperor.

We are told that he had an enormous standing army (but it is difficult to believe some of the figures we get from these ancient sources), that the administration of the capital city was under six committees dealing with different affairs, that there was no slavery (but in this Megasthenes was probably wrong), and it appears that much was done for irrigation—a large dam was constructed in one place, for example, from which an extensive lake was formed. From Megasthenes and from references to Chandragupta Maurya in later inscriptions we get a picture of him as an energetic, empire-building monarch.

Bindusara

Chandragupta's son, Bindusara, reigned from 297 B.C. to 272 B.C. We do not know a great deal about him except that he had relations with Antiochus I, ruler of part of Alexander's former empire. And such details as we have about him come largely from the records of contacts like this. But Bindusara's son, Asoka, left plenty of sources of his own.

(d) ASOKA, c. 269-232 B.C.

Every day millions of Indians hold in their hands one memento of the most impressive, the most glorious, and in a way the most puzzling chapter in their country's ancient history. That memento is the group of four proud lions which appears on the face of many of their coins. The same lions have been adopted as a national emblem, because they are the sculptured group that stands on top of one of the pillars that were constructed by the emperor Asoka.

Asoka the man and Asoka the emperor are splendid and mysterious. For a great part of history, he has been little more than a name in a list of kings. But in the last century or so, more and more information has come to light about his reign: enough to show something of the enormous extent of his empire, something of his government, of his concern with religion, of his administration of justice, of his conquests, of his character and the way he wanted to be seen by his subjects. Yet, despite all that has been written about him, he is still a shadowy figure. We do not know anything of the

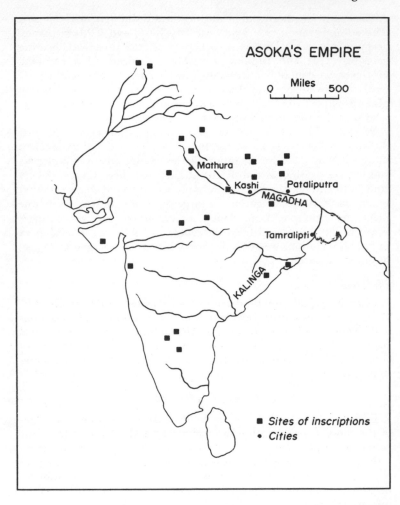

ASOKA'S EMPIRE

Miles
0   500

Mathura

Kashi

Pataliputra

MAGADHA

Tamralipti

KALINGA

■ *Sites of inscriptions*
• *Cities*

personalities who surrounded him or his dealings with them. We do not know what his subjects thought about him, or what his wife thought. It would seem that he set himself up as a father to everybody: kindly, tolerant, preoccupied with the virtue and behaviour of his subjects. But was he really like that? And how did he seem to them? How did he get on with his ministers? How exactly was an emperor expected to behave, and how did Asoka actually behave?

The information we have about him comes partly from the rock and pillar inscriptions that he had erected throughout his dominions, and what is particularly significant about these inscriptions is the positioning of them—they have been found in most of the extremities of India, north, east, and west. Only the far south is without them. This shows that his influence, if not his sphere of control, extended over an enormous area.

Also, we have information about his reign from Buddhist tradition —stories and beliefs that have been handed down from generation to generation among the monks of the Buddhist order. These stories and beliefs, however, are not altogether reliable, because the purpose of them was to teach morality rather than history. They were intended to show the actions of those who do not follow Buddhism in a bad light, and it is possible that the truth is distorted.

However, the information that we are able to get reliably allows us to identify a number of the features of his reign. There are several things that can be noticed here: the policy of conquest by righteousness, the administration of government under the supervision of moral commissioners, the various public works that were undertaken for the purpose of public welfare, the fostering of religion, and the fatherly idea of a king's authority.

Conquest by Righteousness

Certainly, unless Asoka was an arrant hypocrite, he forswore the use of military force to enlarge his empire. After the conquest of Kullugu, he adopted the policy of conquest by righteousness. He did not renounce the use of force altogether. The Mauryan emperors had large standing armies, and there is no reason to believe that Asoka dismantled his, or found no use for it in the suppression of disorders. But his professed aim was to increase his influence and prestige by means of righteousness (*dhamma*), not elephants.

Dhamma is a word that occurs again and again in the inscriptions of Asoka, and for that matter it is an important idea throughout the whole of Indian literature. It can be translated as righteousness, but it had a special meaning for the Indians that is difficult to convey exactly in English. It carried with it certain tones that we today do not hear in the word 'righteousness': it suggested duty, and obedience, and submission to authority and to what fate decreed. Right behaviour, then, consisted of doing what was required by one's position in life, and what Asoka wanted was that all men should be pious and dutiful, and not try to disturb the settled order of things.

Administration

With this in mind, he undertook certain administrative experiments. One of these was the institution of the dhamma-mahamattas. Now these dhamma-mahamattas—ministers of righteousness—

were high officials who were given posts of great responsibility by Asoka. His inscriptions record the establishment of this office, and proclaim to the subjects that these men are to be sent round the empire teaching the subjects how they should carry out the duties given them by their various stations in life. Sons were to obey their fathers, wives were to obey their husbands, and so forth.

It should be clear that these officers, who went round Asoka's empire representing him, settling local disputes, and exhorting people to peaceful and pious conduct, were not doing the same sort of job that civil servants do nowadays. They were doing partly the sort of job that we expect the church to set itself. Several of the inscriptions are about his subjects' religious life, and exhort them to be tolerant of other religious groups besides their own. Men are to be generous, restrained, obedient and considerate. Colleagues, acquaintances and priests are to be honoured.

Public works

The emperor's welfare undertakings were another expression of his concern for his subjects: he showed himself very anxious that his power and wealth should be used for their benefit. 'All men are my children', he said. He regarded his ministers as nurses looking after his children. They were to see that the subjects behaved well and that they came to no harm. Among the provisions for them, rest-houses were built and shade trees were planted along the roads, medicinal herbs were grown, various relief measures and support programmes were instituted. All his wealth, the emperor said, was for his subjects' good and not for his own. Many Indian kings showed a keen interest in welfare, at least in what they said, but few seem as zealous as Asoka, who built up this interest into a philosophy of action. It was a part of his programme of Dhamma, intended to turn the whole empire into one great family acknowledging the overlordship and fatherly responsibility of Asoka himself.

Religion

The idea of dhamma as a programme of government tells us at once that Asoka was anxious to foster religion, because government itself seemed to be a religious activity. This does not mean that one particular religion was turned into a state religion, and that everybody was compelled to belong to it. No such thing. There was no idea, at least in Asoka's mind, that one religion is right, so that others are wrong, and the right one must be propagated at the expense of the others. Certainly, Asoka showed himself very interested in Buddhism, but he displayed interest in other sects as well.

Asoka was not tolerant of everything that went under the name of religious practice, however. In one inscription he condemns the observance of trivial and superstitious rites. These rites, which he condemned as useless, consisted of all manner of little sacrifices and offerings to various gods for the purposes of petty benefits. From the condemnation of these as superstitious, we may suppose that Asoka was opposed to the large class of priests whose living was gained simply by the performance of such small-scale rites, and not by preaching, or by wisdom in the deeper truths to which religion claimed access.

An effort must be made to realize the importance in Indian religious life of this theme: the constant potential opposition between the priests, who were performers of sacrifices and professional mediators of divine favours; and the ascetics and monks, who devoted their lives, or the latter part of them, to searching out the meaning of life. These two kinds of people were doing two different kinds of job. The ascetics were not supposed to perform sacrifices, and the priests were not supposed to preach dhamma. We can easily imagine that there might be tension between them; but we do not really know that there was. There is much in the life of the times which is still wreathed in mists of obscurity.

Moral authority

To sum up Asoka's reign, then, the most striking thing about it is the moral ideal of authority. Other ancient kings had the same general quality of ideal, but it gets its best and fullest expression in Asoka's declarations, and that is why it is worth while to pay so much attention to the implications of these declarations. The emperor saw himself as responsible for the goodness of his children. This we have called the idea of moral authority.

It is an idea that can be looked at in various ways: we may like it, or we may not. We may think that it represents a high moral standard that was aimed at by ancient Indian governments and a sense of security and responsibility in public life that is lacking today. Or we might see Asoka's government as a rather old-womanish concern, poking its nose into people's private lives and setting itself up as an arbiter of matters that were the concern of the monks and priests rather than of the government.

No matter how we see it, we have to remember that what we are discussing all the time is the ideal that Asoka set up. He seems to have been a very selfless man, to judge by the ideal—but the point is that it is an ideal, and we have little detailed knowledge of how far he succeeded in putting it into practice.

(e) THE LATER MAURYAS AND THE INVADERS

The decline of the Mauryas

When we talk about the age of the Mauryas, we do not imply something that began and ended at particular points in time. Under Asoka, the Mauryan empire dominated most of India. It did not go on dominating most of India until it died, and then give way to another dominant empire. It gradually faded away, shrinking by degrees into just one among a whole lot of competing kingdoms. The moment when it finally disappeared was not the end of one era and the beginning of another.

So it is with most of the kingdoms and little empires There are periods of history when our attention is turned on just one that holds the centre of the stage; but it existed before the time when it came there—it may even have been quite important—and there are plenty of other kingdoms, parts of an empire but with their own hereditary rulers biding their time and waiting for a chance to reassert their independence and carve out their own empires.

The reasons why the Mauryan empire faded away are then the same as the reasons why all the other empires faded away—there is nothing special about the Mauryas except that, under their first three rulers, they were more successful than most.

But the sheer size of any great empire was against it. There were no telegraphs then, no trains, no paved roads, and it was difficult to keep such a ramshackle structure together for long.

Again, an empire was a rather arbitrary thing. Its boundaries were not the boundaries between one country and another, between two sets of people who felt themselves to be different from each other. Its boundaries came wherever a king happened to be able to get with his army. An empire was whatever shape and size its rulers could make it. There was nothing about it to make its inhabitants feel that they really belonged, and they were quite ready to give their loyalty to some other ruler. So any empire was like a jack-in-the-box, or (worse, from the ruler's point of view) a whole lot of them combined, any one ready to spring out when the lid was opened.

Further, vassals and state officials were not reliable servants who could be trusted to do whatever the emperor wanted; they came of high birth, they were important people in their own districts, and were usually ready to take any chance that offered to become petty kings themselves. Plotting, scheming and treachery abounded on every hand.

The wonder is that dynasties could last as long as they did, and that under the impulsion of strong personalities and good generals,

empires could be held together at all. The Mauryan dynasty, like
the rest of them, eventually became a line of kings jostling with
others, a principality in the north-east. In 183 B.C., the brahman
general Pushyamitra Sunga ousted his master from the throne and
set up a new dynasty of his own.

The Invaders

From the second century B.C. to the third A.D. there were many
successive waves of invaders of various races who entered India
from the north-west, overcame the medley of small kingdoms they
found in the same way that Alexander had done, and set up empires
large and small in the north.

First there were the Yavanas. This is the Sanskrit name for Greeks,
but it is used very loosely to refer to a number of races from the West.
The first Yavana ruler in India was Euthydemus; his son Demetrius
was master of a large territory in the area of the Punjab in the earlier
part of the second century B.C. In the later part, another ruler,
Menander, was lord of areas in Afghanistan as well as the Punjab.
This king was a patron of religious teachers, and is famous for the
discussions he had about Buddhism.

Then there were the Sakas—the Sanskrit name for Scyths—and
the Pahlavas, who were from Persia, in the first century B.C. The
Kushanas, who appear to have been Turkish, were notable for the
emperor Kanishka, who was responsible for a strong dynasty and an
empire that covered much of north and north-west India.

In the first three centuries A.D., in the west of India, there ruled
the Western Satraps. The most important of the rulers for us is
Rudradaman, for whom was composed a long inscription com-
memorating his fame. Like other such inscriptions, it is concerned
to praise the king rather than to record facts accurately. But we
learn several things from it—in particular, that Rudradaman
ordered the repair of an old dam dating from Mauryan times
(against the advice of his ministers to whom it presumably seemed
too big an undertaking).

What became of them all?

These were some of the invaders and some of the kingdoms they
established. There are many more. One or two things need to be
said about them all.

After so many foreign conquerors had come in, it might be thought
that there would be nothing left of the India that existed before;
that the Indians would turn into slaves, groaning under the weight
of several layers of foreign nobles. But it was not like this at all.
India stayed the same, and the foreigners changed. In the first place,

there were many millions of Indians, and at every stage the new-comers would have to spread out very thinly or else remain small compact groups within a larger society. In most cases the alien races merged into Indian society, adopting Indian languages and religions, and each fitting into the caste system as simply one more group. The same applies to other conquerors later in the Christian era—the White Huns, for example. It is often difficult to tell just what became of any particular one. Sometimes the names and the geographical distribution of more modern castes suggest that they were descended from immigrant races. It was only with the time of the Muslim invasions that India began to find it difficult to digest so many foreigners, and the process became less smooth.

Links with the world

All these incursions illustrate a fact about Indian history that was mentioned at the beginning of this book—that the subcontinent was open at the North-West to a whole series of contacts, peaceful and warlike, by which the major epochs in its development were shaped. The Greeks and Scyths and others were following a path that had been followed by the Mediterranean races in prehistoric times, by the Aryans, and others, and which further waves of conquerors were to follow later.

Nor was the movement entirely one-way. Apart from India's trade in goods, one export in particular, going out by the landward route, played a big part in the history of Asia. This most important export was an idea in the mind—Buddhism—finding its way to China by a roundabout route; out by the passes of Afghanistan and then, turning east, across the troubled regions to the north of Tibet, to the centres of Chinese culture. Though Buddhism waned in India, it became one of the vital forces in Chinese life.

In India itself, the early centuries after Christ were a time of resurgent Hinduism. Vishnu and Shiva held sway, and with them came an opulent classical age in India's culture.

(f) THE GUPTA PERIOD

The Guptas were based on Pataliputra, the old capital of Magadha, and fashioned for themselves an empire which in the fourth and fifth centuries A.D. was the dominant power in the north of India, and much of the south. The first Gupta king known to us is Chandragupta I (not to be confused with Chandragupta Maurya of six centuries earlier) who was reigning in about A.D. 320. His son Samudragupta, whose succession seems to have been contested, reigned from about 335 to about 375, a long and eventful reign in which many conquests were made. Most of northern India,

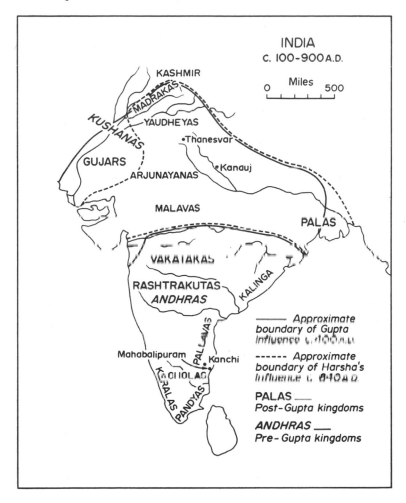

INDIA
C. 100-900 A.D.

Miles
0   500

KASHMIR
MADRAKAS
KUSHANAS
YAUDHEYAS
•Thanesvar
GUJARS
•Kanauj
ARJUNAYANAS
MALAVAS
PALAS
VAKATAKAS
RASHTRAKUTAS
ANDHRAS
KALINGA
PALLAVAS
Mahabalipuram
Kanchi
KERALAS
CHOLAS
PANDYAS

——— Approximate
boundary of Gupta
Influence c. 400 A.D.

------ Approximate
boundary of Harsha's
Influence c. 640 A.D.

PALAS ___
Post-Gupta kingdoms

ANDHRAS ___
Pre-Gupta kingdoms

including Bengal in the east and the Punjab in the west (to use modern names not then current) were brought into the empire. Chandragupta II reigned from 375 to about 413–415, and added a bit more to the empire in its south-west corner—the territory of the Western Satraps. Chandragupta II had a notable reign, marked by flourishing art and culture generally and by the visit of a Chinese pilgrim, Fa Hsien, who has left us an account of his travels. Kumaragupta (about 415–455) had an uneventful reign, as far as we can tell, except that towards the end of it his empire was troubled by raids from the Huna peoples, who in later times overran much of northern India and reduced Gupta power to a shadow of its former self. The next king, Skandagupta, is likely to have been the last under whom the Gupta empire remained really strong.

Why name a 'period' after the Guptas?

These few bare facts go a little way to show why we talk about the Gupta 'period' of Indian history generally, even though these kings were only one dynasty in a subcontinent where dozens flourished, and themselves fell to insignificance after less than two centuries of glory. As far as political importance goes, their heyday was longer than that of most dynasties, and their empire was certainly greater.

But there is more to it than this. The phrase 'the Gupta period' conjures up more than a few dry facts about kings and empires. It conjures up the atmosphere of an epoch. It is a label for the era when a whole multitude of ancient India's most fascinating artistic creations were produced—sculptures fashioned, temples built, plays and poems written—a great array of cultural achievement that calls to us now as if from another world. The statues were not then strange stone shapes, and the plays and poems were not worm-eaten mouldering manuscripts; the temples were not strange ruins used by nobody and visited only by tourists. They were all part of the everyday life at least of the cultured classes, and had meanings bound up with the whole complex of myths and beliefs that were shared by all and familiar to all.

It needs a big effort of the imagination to build up from stones and manuscripts, taken out of their proper contexts, a sense of the flourishing cultural life of ancient India. But it was under the Guptas that art and literature reached a pinnacle.

Gupta empire

The Gupta monarchs were patrons of the arts. Samudragupta, the conqueror, was said to be no mean player on the lute himself. But whatever the Gupta kings may have been—cultured men, great men, wealthy men—they were not masters of India, and their empire did not give them despotic control of the lives of their subjects. We should not be blinded to the fact that there were many other monarchs in India, who did not lose all their power even if they were under the Gupta empire.

We are able to learn something about Samudragupta's empire from an inscription carved on an Asokan pillar at Allahabad. The inscription was intended to celebrate his reign, and it is likely to exaggerate his might and glory. But, be that as it may, the inscription lists an impressive number of conquests and records the extent of the dominions which Samudragupta had brought into his empire.

He had two classes of influence. He had influence in some places through having entered into friendly relations with local rulers and receiving tribute from them as an acknowledgment of his overlordship. This was obviously not the same thing as taking over the administration of them. For example he is said to have received tribute from Ceylon, but it is most unlikely that he could have assimilated any part of Ceylon into his empire in any real sense. The other form of influence was through having conquered a territory. Such a territory might indeed be taken over by his own officers and administered as part of his own kingdom. An inscription certainly states that certain kingdoms were violently uprooted. But it could happen that a conqueror would put somebody else on the throne of a conquered king, perhaps a relative either of the conqueror or of the victim, and then go away. The new king would then run the kingdom as his own and give help and tribute to his overlord. Sometimes it happened that a conquered king was actually restored to the throne that he had lost. What the conqueror wanted was acknowledgment as emperor; tribute; and an ally.

Perhaps it would be better therefore to think of the peoples or kingdoms listed in the Allahabad inscription as Samudragupta's allies and vassals rather than as parts of a tightly controlled empire.

Kingless Communities

One thing worth noticing about Samudragupta's pillar inscription is the mention of a number of probably kingless communities among his vassals—the people who acknowledged his overlordship.

We met these kingless communities before. They were an ancient feature of northern Indian political life, and they seem to have been particularly strong about the time of the Buddha. They were fairly small units, small enough to run their affairs through meetings of elders or nobles assembling in one place to discuss their affairs, and they were thought of as communities of people rather than as countries or places. The Samudragupta inscription refers to them as 'the Yaudheyas', 'the Madrakas', 'the Arjunayanas', 'the Malavas' and so forth—naming the people, not the lands they inhabited. In a way, they are something like tribes, but we should not think of them on that account as being any more primitive than the kingdoms and empires around them.

By the time of the Guptas, kingdoms and empires were well developed institutions, and the kingless communities were now, apparently, much fewer, less organized and less powerful than their neighbours. Yet they still existed, for nine of them are listed as parts of Samudragupta's empire, chiefly in the north-west, in Rajasthan. What sort of communities were they, that could be absorbed into successive empires and still keep their identity?

There are two things that can be said about them. The very fact that they continued to exist for so long suggests that they had some degree of independence even when they were parts of empires: when the empires faded away, they re-appeared on the scene. Another fact about them is something stated in several ancient Indian texts: because they did not have the central authority of a king, their government was not firm and stable. Their government was carried on by debate between a lot of people, all claiming noble descent and a voice in the control of affairs. As a result, they were given to dissension, and constantly torn between rival groups with no controlling hand.

In fact, there is little that can be said of them with real certainty; even the few remarks offered here are rather speculative. We know that in various kingless communities there were large numbers of nobles who called themselves rajas, and when the government was in their hands, the communities would be oligarchies. But sometimes one of these rajas would have overriding authority, subject to the support of a large group of nobles, and there would then be little difference between this situation and kingship.

Administration

It is clear that, in the Gupta empire, there were different sorts of vassal communities—with or without their own kings—with different relationships with the emperor. This does not mean that the emperor did not have power over his vassals. If he was wealthy, and maintained a strong army, and was successful in diplomacy, he could have a great deal of power over the parts of his empire. But if he did not have those things, there was nothing to stop the empire from reverting to a lot of independent countries.

The structure was a sort of pyramid, then, with the emperor at the top, a number of chief vassals below him owing him allegiance—tribute, and support in war—these vassals having their own sub-vassals, and so on down the line. This pyramid is probably what Indians themselves had in their minds when they thought about political authority, though it by no means always corresponded to the reality.

Another pyramid existed within each kingdom, matching the pyramid in which the kingdoms themselves were arranged. This was the pyramid of administration.

We know from inscriptions that each unit in the empire had, in theory, quite an elaborate system of administration. At the top was the king, or vassal, or governor appointed by an overlord. Under him were governors for the various provinces, and each province was divided into districts, the districts into groups of villages, the groups into sub-groups, and so on. Each unit in this hierarchy had its own official in charge, who was subordinate to the men in charge of the group to which his unit belonged, and in command of officials running the smaller units within his own.

These officials were responsible for the collection of taxes—especially in the form of a share of crops grown—for organization of forced labour (a sort of national service, which took the form of working on public undertakings—cultivating the king's own crown lands for instance, or maintaining roads), for giving effect to the king's orders in their own districts, and so forth. And each official in the administrative hierarchy of a kingdom had a certain degree of independence. In particular, officials often took their salaries out of the revenues of their districts, instead of being dependent on the central treasury for payment.

Fa Hsien

Inscriptions of kings are not the only source from which we learn about the administration and other details of the Gupta empire. There is quite a lot that can be derived from Sanskrit literature written at the time. And there is one particularly interesting account left by a foreign traveller, who described what he saw in India. This foreign traveller is the Chinese pilgrim Fa Hsien.

Fa Hsien was in India during the earliest years of the fifth century, and tells several things about what he saw in the empire of Chandragupta II. According to him, bureaucratic control over the citizens was not oppressive—people were not much troubled by red tape concerned with household registration and the like—and the justice of the courts was lenient by the standards of the time. It was possible to rebel against the monarch, and be caught, without losing more than a hand as punishment. The Indians, as Fa Hsien saw them, had strict and abstemious habits amongst themselves, and the rules of the caste system were strictly kept.

Conclusion

The north of India in the fourth and fifth centuries did not see the blossoming of a bureaucratic and centralized empire with control over most of the subcontinent, but it did see an age of cultural splendour. The art, architecture, music, and literature of this period have lent it the name of India's 'classical age', an age to which Indians of later centuries looked back for inspiration. These early centuries also saw the beginnings of new invasions that were to erode the older order, break up the patterns that were becoming familiar, and introduce new elements into India's ever-changing scene.

(g) From the Guptas to the Muslims

Like the Mauryas, the Guptas withered away. Long after they were really important, we find their name perpetuated by small kingdoms which could make no great claims to empire. And their passing reminds us that the story of India's rulers is not a story of successive great empires. It is rather a story of numerous invasions and numerous small kingdoms struggling against each other. The great empires exist, but they are just episodes.

We have seen that the Gupta empire was not a close-knit organization with a centralized government. No Indian empire was. And so, in the course of time, pressures from outside and inside made it disintegrate. The next major stage in the political life of the subcontinent was the coming of the Muslim hordes several centuries later.

We come then to another long stretch of time in which there was a bewildering variety of small kingdoms—small, that is, beside Asoka's empire—and it is impossible to do more than notice a few of the more important features in the landscape. In the fifth and sixth centuries there were invasions by a new race, the savage Huns. In the seventh, the empire of Harsha with his court of opulence and culture revived something of past glories. In the eighth, ninth and tenth, up to half a dozen of the more powerful kingdoms in the North and the Deccan vied amongst themselves for hegemony.

The White Huns

The Huns of Central Asia, roaming and invading, got a reputation for fierceness that the Indian branch of them seems to have lived up to during the short period when there were Hun kingdoms in India.

The Huns came, like the other conquerors, from the lands beyond the Hindu Kush which had from time immemorial been a melting-pot of races—Turks, Afghans, and Iranians, with a constant warlike traffic of Scyths, Greeks, Mongols and others surging to and fro across the indeterminate region between China, India, and the Arab countries further west.

The later Guptas had been troubled by their incursions. After about A.D. 465 the Hun Toramana had a kingdom in the Punjab. His son, Mihirakula, had a kingdom based on Sialkot.

In the sixth century, the Huns fade out of the picture, and there is some uncertainty about their fate. Claims are made for a rather mysterious king Yasodharman as a conqueror of the Huns around

A.D. 530. Losing their political dominance, the Huns were absorbed into Indian society, and the descendants of them and of other foreign intruders may be represented by later castes such as the Gujars.

Harsha

The most notable name from seventh century history is that of the emperor Harsha, of the Vardhana line, who ruled from A.D. 606 to about 646–47. A son of the ruler of Thanesvar, he moved his capital to Kanauj as his dominions expanded, and for long after his time Kanauj, on the upper reaches of the Ganges, was a centre of power fiercely contended for among the aspirant emperors of the North. If we are to believe the traditional story of his reign, the kernel of his empire was constituted by three kingdoms: his father's, Thanesvar; that of the ruler whom his sister married, Kanauj; and that of the king who attacked Kanauj and overthrew his sister's husband, Malava. But he added many kingdoms to his domain, and his empire extended as far as the Himalayas and the river Narbada to north and south, and to the Indus tributaries and the Bay of Bengal to west and east.

Such a large empire yielded ample tribute, and his court could well afford to be a centre of culture. Harsha himself was no mean writer, and created several Sanskrit plays. His reign is particularly notable for the visit of a Chinese Buddhist pilgrim, Hiuen Tsang, who has left for us an account of what he found in India. As a pilgrim, he was chiefly interested in Buddhist shrines and monasteries, and his account illustrates that, though Buddhists were not particularly strong in numbers elsewhere, Bengal and Bihar, with so many historic Buddhist sites, were the home of a small active faith. Being Chinese, Hiuen Tsang himself subscribed to Mahayana Buddhism, and it appears that he was able to influence Harsha in the same direction—though Harsha was originally a member of the Theravada school.

The later centuries

The Islamic faith, later to be exported with fierce crusading zeal to so many parts of the world, was born about the beginning of the seventh century; and early in the next century there were Muslim Arabs in India with a kingdom of their own, in Sind. However, it was not they but the Turks who were destined in later times to be the bringers of the faith to the greater part of the subcontinent, and Islam was not carried beyond the boundaries of their state, though there were certainly some Muslims in other parts—chiefly the Deccan coastal districts.

It was the Hindu kingdoms that still held the stage, vying for power: and Kanauj, with its central position and its imperial tradition, changed hands more than once as empires rose and fell.

In the eighth century, Kashmir from its mountain fastness in the far north, made short-lived a bid for power in the plains.

In the east, in Bengal, the Pala dynasty started a regime that lasted for four centuries and gave to Bengal a period of imperial splendour. Under this dynasty, the arts throve, universities were established, and Buddhism took new forms.

In the ninth century, almost the whole of northern India came under the sway of the Gurjaras, who built an empire on their base in the west. In the following century, it waned, and a new challenge came from the south, from the Rashtrakutas of the Deccan, in alliance with the Arabs of Sind.

There is no need to add to the confusion of detail: what matters is the overall picture. Lingering memories of the Maurya and Gupta glory, and the need for each king to establish his claim to be a legitimate ruler by success in competition with other kings and with rivals around his own throne, spurred on ruler after ruler to try his luck in the arena of imperial aspirations.

Visualize the map of northern India at the time, and it is as if the contestants took it in turns to reach into the centre of the arena, trying to extend their influence across the whole of it. It was the *mandala* theory in operation, the theory known to the Sanskrit literature of politics that each king should aim at empire, treating his neighbours as enemies and looking for friends on the other side of them. This was the world of Indian politics that the Muslims entered when in 1018 Mahmud of Ghazni sacked Kanauj, and the eleventh century saw a contest involving the new Islamic powers.

(h) The Kingdoms of the South

If you visit Madras, in the south-east, for more than a day or two, you will probably want to visit Mahabalipuram (or more strictly, Mamallapuram). Here, in a quiet little town, there are reminders of a past empire, a vanished culture, a forgotten splendour. For a few pennies you can hire a bicycle which will take you round to the rock carvings, to the 'rathas'—stone shrines and sculptures carved out of living rock, each a single piece, not built up of different blocks—and to the shore temple. For Mahabalipuram is a coastal town, a 'seaside resort' as the tourist brochure calls it (though it is quite unlike the commercialized resorts familiar in Western countries). From the shore temple you can stand under the hot south Indian sun looking out across the Bay of Bengal towards the distant lands of south-east Asia, to which, from this place, ships plied with varied cargoes more than a thousand years ago.

Little remains in Mahabalipuram from that time. The wooden buildings have perished. But the stone structures still stand—carvings, shrines, temple—and they make a link with a different world, a world where this quiet spot was an outpost of Aryan civilization, a thriving mart carrying on trade with the fabled spice islands of the eastern seas, an arena of fierce competition between kings. Today the waves lap at the temple, and if you stand on an eastern wall to take a photograph you are liable to be drenched with sudden spray. But these crumbling ruins, this peaceful scene disturbed only by the sound of waves and the chattering of tourists from time to time, were nevertheless once at the heart of a southern culture which is all too easily left out of the Indian story in our preoccupation with the northern empires.

The importance of the South

There are several reasons why the North often gets more than its fair share of attention. In a sense, history began there earlier—the early literature and the early inscriptions from which we build up our picture of ancient Indian history come chiefly from northern centres. Again the most notable comings and goings were there: when new races came to conquer and set up kingdoms and empires, they came overland, from the north-west. The conflicts and contrasts, the rise and fall of empires, attract our gaze northwards. Further, in British times, the chief territorial gains, the centres of administration, and the scenes of the most momentous changes, were again in the North.

But most Indians will tell you that you should not leave the South out of any tour, for from there have come many of India's most gifted writers, artists, politicians, and philosophers; from there come some of the richest traditions of Indian culture—dancing, singing, music.

The North was an area that suffered invasions, and where newcomers to the subcontinent were constantly being assimilated. But the nature of the South's dealings with foreigners was different. Across the Arabian Sea to Arab lands and, beyond them, the Mediterranean, and across the Bay of Bengal to south-east Asia, the South conducted a flourishing trade.

The North was the homeland of Aryan culture in India. In the South, though Aryan culture had spread, though Sanskrit was the literary language of the courts, though the same religious sacrifices were performed as in the North, this culture was more of an imported thing.

The languages of the South are also different. Sanskrit is a dead language now, but it shows a strong influence in various of the

Northern languages. It has far less influence on the non-Aryan
languages of the South, of which Tamil, Kannada, Telugu and
Malayalam are the chief modern representatives. These are quite
different in structure and vocabulary from, say, Hindi or Bengali
speech.

The Andhras

A lot of what we can say about the earliest historical Southern
kingdoms is rather speculative. We have to piece it together from
incidental mentions in some of the inscriptions and the early
Sanskrit literature.

From such sources we know something about the Andhras, a
people in the South whose kingdoms flourished between about the
third century B.C. and the third century A.D. They were not down
in the peninsula but in the Deccan.

The most important dynasty of the Andhras was that of King
Satakarni, who pursued a career of conquest in the western Deccan
and north of the Narmada river, and challenged Kharavela in
Kalinga. Other Andhra kings also challenged the might of some of
the ancient Northern powers, taking advantage of their possibly
weak and unsettled condition during and after the disintegration of
the Mauryan empire.

There are two interpretations of the pattern of Andhra development: one is that, originating in the eastern Deccan, they built an
empire westwards; the other is that they originated in the west and
extended eastwards. The latter is much more probable. Such
uncertainties illustrate the fact that much of our knowledge of the
earliest times is speculative.

The Deccan kingdoms

From about the fourth century onwards, we find a flourishing
culture among the Pallavas, who were on the eastern side of the
Deccan and extending southwards into the area of modern Madras.
Their capital was at Kanchi (south-west of Madras). This was a
great centre of Hindu culture, with a centre of Sanskrit studies
operating as early as the fourth century.

The Vakatakas were another Deccan people, who had their
centre near modern Nagpur.

Not all the peoples and kingdoms need to be noted here, but the
Chalukyas are particularly important. They are important by
virtue of the extent of the Chalukya empire that was carved out in
the seventh century by the famous king Pulakesin II (who acceded
in the year 608). This empire spread right across India, forming a

belt of Deccan power that Harsha was unable to break. There came to be two Chalukya kingdoms, the one in the East lasting until the eleventh century and the Western empire, larger in extent, being worsted in the eighth century by the powerful Rashtrakutas.

The Tamil kingdoms

In the extreme south, in the peninsula, were several Tamil kingdoms with a long history. The three main ones need to be mentioned by name: the Pandyas, the Keralas, and the Cholas.

Some of the most important contacts between India and other parts of the world were made by these kingdoms, which, as their geographical position alone might suggest, were interested in overseas trade. An embassy from the Pandyas, of the very tip of the peninsula, appears to have reached Rome as early as the first century B.C. As late as the ninth century, we find the Pandyas engaged in wars and diplomatic manoeuvrings with their neighbours and also with Ceylon.

North of the Pandyas were situated the Keralas, on the west coast, and the Cholas on the east coast. King Kharavela of Kalinga mentioned the Keralas as one of the three Tamil kingdoms of a confederacy. In the tenth century, we find the Keralas in conflict with the Cholas. The modern Indian state of Kerala has inherited their history and the site of their kingdoms.

Perhaps the most important of these peninsular powers was the kingdom of the Cholas, which in its long life had periods of dominance in the south of India and maintained links with many of the remoter parts of the known world. Chola trade with south-east Asia and with Egypt and the countries of western Asia and the Mediterranean flourished. Cotton, pepper, silks, and precious stones passed through the Chola ports. In the late tenth century, under the famous king Rajaraja, victories were claimed by the Cholas over the other Tamils, the eastern Chalukyas and other powers besides. By the end of the tenth century the Cholas were dominant in southern India, and indeed under Rajaraja and Rajendra achieved maritime expansion to Ceylon and south-east Asia, where the Sumatran ports among others were important trading partners.

Conclusion

This is no more than a brief glance at the histories of a few of India's kingdoms. The general impression is of a kaleidoscope. The myriad kingdoms with colourful histories, far-flung trade, aspirations to empire, hectic conflicts with their neighbours or opulent cultural achievements clamour for our attention on every hand, and the effect is bewildering to the eye. This was not a stagnant or a monotonous India—it was an India teeming with life and variety; and when the Muslim invaders came, they added simply one more element to one of the most heterogeneous and cosmopolitan civilizations in the world.

CHAPTER SIX

Islamic Faith and Culture

(a) THE ISLAMIC FAITH

The Muslim invaders who troubled India from the tenth century onwards and came to make themselves masters of most of the country, differed in at least one vital respect from previous waves of conquerors, who had settled down and merged into the Indian scene: their religion set them more apart from their subjects, and was an obstacle to their assimilation. For centuries they were invaders, carrying on the government of their empires from camps, or from camp-like fortresses. In the eyes of an orthodox Muslim, all non-Muslims were infidels. War must be waged on them, and they must be either converted to Islam or killed. Christians and Jews were exceptions to this, for particular reasons. But outside the homeland of Islam, wherever the Muslims went, they went as warriors.

Now, this is not to say that they went as warriors simply because their religion was one of war against unbelievers. We could just as well put it the other way round and say that they had a warlike religion because they had a warlike nature. If we are to understand properly the reasons why with increasing frequency they surged into India and made themselves masters, we must look not only at their religion but also at their social organization and the quest for gain which drew them into India in the first place.

But in this chapter we are concerned with Islamic religion and culture, not with economic or other motives of the Muslim invaders; and we see, firstly, that their religion was one that preached war. Secondly, Islam very uncompromisingly declared a faith in one God.

'There is no God but Allah'—that is the central belief of Islam, the starting-point from which all the other beliefs proceed. It is sheer blasphemy to invent any more gods than one, to have images of different gods with different characteristics, because there is only one, who made the world and everything in it. Here, obviously, Islam is like Christianity (although there are important differences as well), whereas Hinduism was full of different gods. Vishnu and Shiva were only the most important; there was a whole treasure-house of myths and legends telling of gods for all occasions, and every Hindu temple was for the Muslim like a portrait gallery of his enemies, for all the statues in and on them were in his eyes blasphemous images of false divinities.

For these reasons the two cultures and the people who created them did not mix easily. It was, at least in theory, the mission of Islam to convert or destroy those of all other religions. Islam and Hinduism were opposite in character. The wonder therefore is that there was any mingling at all. In fact, there was quite a lot. Hindus, in the event, were not all either destroyed or converted, though some of them were; most managed to co-exist readily enough with the conquerors. Art, architecture, political organization, military techniques, language—everything came to blend in itself elements from both traditions. The question is not so much: why was more blending not possible? It is rather: how could there be so much?

Mohammed

Islam, unlike Hinduism, started from the words of one man, the prophet Mohammed.

He lived from about A.D. 570 to 632. The early part of his life was spent at Mecca, in Arabia, later the centre of pilgrimage for devout Muslims. He was quite successful in a worldly sense, marrying a rich widow, but the things of this world did not satisfy him and he took to meditating in mountain caves not far from Mecca. Eventually, he claimed that he had received revelations from God, and with the support of his wife and a few relations he started a new religious group in Mecca.

His views were not popular, and indeed he raised so much opposition against himself that he had to flee from Mecca. He denounced idol-worship in strong terms, insisting on the oneness of God. This offended the Meccans, who had innumerable divinities in their temples. So, in 622, Mohammed made his way to the rival city of Yathrib, afterwards called Medina. To be unpopular at Mecca was a recommendation here, and Mohammed was able to establish a dominating influence in the community and build up a following for his teachings. Much of his followers' time was taken up during his lifetime with waging war on the hostile Mecca and also on the local Jewish and Christian groups who did not accept him as their prophet. His teachings included doctrines about the organization of the Muslim brotherhood—laws and regulations— as well as religious ideas, possibly reflecting his experience of the practical problems of organization. We should not, however, divide his teachings sharply into doctrinal and political: he saw the affairs of his faith and his followers as a whole.

Reforms of Mohammed

In order to understand the teachings of Islam properly, it is necessary to understand something of the particular situation in which the religion was born.

There were various things wrong with the Arabia of Mohammed's day, in his eyes, and it was part of the concern of his teaching to put these right. Both in religious doctrine and in law, his purposes were concerned with the Arabia of his day. In the sphere of religious doctrine, what seemed to need correction was the corrupt and polytheistic form of belief and practice which he saw current among the Arabs. At Mecca, literally scores of different gods were worshipped. He wanted to cleanse religion and give it a pure clear programme, insisting that there was but one god, the creator of the world. Oddly enough, in this detail Mohammed found himself ranged against the beliefs of his fellow Arabs, and on the same side as the foreign religions that were practised by minority groups in Arabia—the Jewish religion and Christianity. Jews and Christians alike believed in one God, whereas the Arabs generally did not, so that the Jews and Christians were his allies, up to a point. They were known by Muslims as keepers of the book, and their own scriptures, the Torah and the Gospel, were recognized as revelations by God, though they were considered to have falsified the teachings given to them. And it became Muslim policy, instead of trying to destroy them or convert them, to tolerate them under Muslim rule and merely impose a special tax on them. Later, the same principle came to be applied in India, where the Hindus were taxed.

In the sphere of law, Mohammed set himself to oppose injustice and to establish firm principles. The subordination of women was one sphere in which he felt reform to be necessary. They had few rights, and men were able to take as many wives as they pleased. Mohammed laid down the rule, which became law in Muslim countries afterwards, that no man was to have more than four wives (though a number of concubines was allowed as well). To us, this may seem rather extravagant, because we are used to the idea of having only one wife at a time. But it was not really extravagant at all: it was an attempt to introduce a bit of responsibility and restraint into the scene. Similarly, Mohammed set out rights for women, who, theoretically, should be treated fairly and have entitlements to property and so on. In fact the position of Muslim women was, and is, stronger in theory than in practice, because in practice the custom of giving women an inferior place was so strong that their rights didn't count for very much. Actual attitudes to the position of women were similar in India.

By looking at the background of Islam in its original setting then, we can understand something about its introduction into India. The tax levied on the Hindus by their Muslim rulers was, in the rulers' eyes, not so much an imposition on them as a privilege, making co-existence possible. And, whatever Mohammed may actually have said, the customs of his countrymen and the ideas of those who later edited and re-edited his sayings were not so very different from those of India.

Religious teaching

The actual sayings of Mohammed were, within a short period after his death, collected from the many sources where they had been copied down, and from the memories of his hearers, and assembled to build up the holy book of the Muslims, the Koran. This consists of sayings which were supposed to have been put into the prophet's mind directly by God. It was a revelation, and nobody could question the truth of anything in it. Within about a hundred years, an official version of it was more or less established, with minor variations.

The Koran consists of 6,226 verses arranged in 114 chapters, or Suras. The Suras have been placed in order, with the shortest first and the longest last.

To the Muslim, as to the Christian, God was not a sort of glorified angel. God was unique, the creator of everything, the judge of all men, the rewarder of all virtue and the chastiser of all evil. He was merciful and fair, omnipotent and everywhere. Various descriptions of God became traditional, and a list of ninety-nine 'beauteous names' of God was established.

In spite of the mercifulness of God, there was no escaping damnation for evil lives. At the creation of man, there was an agreement by which man recognized God as his lord, and all those who did evil and thus broke this agreement were liable to damnation.

There were five central points of Islamic belief and practice regarded as essential to the religion and known as the five pillars. The most important of all, the kernel of the revealed truth, was contained in the statement: 'There is no God but Allah, and Mohammed is his prophet'. This contains two assertions. Allah is the name of God, and the saying is a claim that there is only one God. It is also a claim that Mohammed has a special position as the

South India: Srirangam Temple, Trichinopoly

South India: Srirangam Temple carving. The girl is applying an ornamental spot (*tilaka*) to her forehead, just as Indian women do today

Indo-Muslim architecture: the Red Fort at Delhi

Indo-Muslim art: the attempted
assassination of Akbar at Delhi

Taj Mahal,
famous monu-
ment at Agra,
built by the em-
peror Shah Jahan

Indo-Muslim art: Akbar's forces
besieging Ranthambor Fort,
Rajputana

South India: an early nineteenth century portrayal of engineer officers about to survey a Hindu temple

One of a set of views of Calcutta by James Fraser: the Black Pagoda on the Chilpore Road

prophet or messenger or representative of God, the man to whom the divine truth was revealed in the words of the Koran. Other prophets were recognized as having been given by God the same sort of special position in the past—Noah, Abraham, Moses and Jesus. Later, Muslims added the Buddha to the list. But Mohammed was regarded as the 'seal of the prophets': that is, he set the seal on the rest, he was the last of the series, and his revelation was the completely definitive and authoritative one.

Perhaps we can think of Islam, the faith, as a great towering structure like one of its mosques. There is a central pillar: the belief in Allah, one God. There are four flanking pillars, which are also important: the pilgrimage to Mecca, the giving of alms, the month of fasting, and daily prayer. These are parts of the life of a Muslim, who is expected to observe them all.

Every believer is expected to make a pilgrimage to Mecca at least once in his life, and at the shrines in the city there are ceremonies in which thousands of Muslims from all over the Islamic world take part. Nowadays the Islamic world extends from the north of Africa to the archipelago of south-east Asia.

The giving of alms may be either voluntary or compulsory, as a form of tax, but either way all are expected to make contributions which can be used to help the needy.

It is easy to recognize the fast as a custom originating with the Jews. It reminds us too of the Christian Lent. The Muslim fast is for the month known as Ramadan, and it does not of course require that everybody should go without food or drink for the whole period. The rule is that the believer shall allow nothing to pass down his throat between sunrise and sunset throughout the month.

As for daily prayer, the chief feature of Muslim habits as compared with Indian is that prayer is an activity in which people come together. It is not a private thing. At noon on a Friday, the chief time for prayer, impressive numbers of Muslims come into their mosques, all facing towards Mecca, and repeat the words of their prayer-leaders in unison.

These are the chief features of the religion as it developed and as it is practised even today. The differences between Islam and Hinduism are plain to see—different ideas of God, different forms of worship, different attitudes to the outward practice of religion, different places of worship. And yet, in spite of this, there was in India a most interesting fusion of cultures, an accommodation between two religions that allowed each to influence the other, and to be subtly transmuted—even though the enmity between the adherents of the faiths continued scarcely below the surface, if not actually on it. To understand this better, it is worth examining the form of Islam which was most acceptable in India and which had perhaps most real influence on Indian minds—Islamic mysticism.

(b) SUFISM

Part of our conventional idea of India is the picture of the fakir or the yogi with marvellous powers that seem supernatural. We see him throwing a rope into the air: magically, the rope freezes into a vertical position, and he climbs up it. Or we see him walking on glowing coals, even putting them into his mouth without any apparent pain. Perhaps it is all a cunning trick designed to deceive. Or perhaps there is really something in it. Perhaps the East really is mysterious, and the people there are in touch with forces that we with our modern civilization no longer know.

This is one aspect of India and its religions, and one of the best known. Like many conventional ideas, it will be thoroughly misleading if we believe that this is what Indian religion is really like. However, it is not in fact false: such powers certainly have been claimed, and there is some evidence for their existence. Whether they are tricks or not is scarcely a question that can usefully be considered here, fascinating though it may be; and whether the powers themselves are real or not does not matter. The *display* of them is showmanship, and mystics are not just showmen. These powers are a part of the mystic schools, and they really have been claimed as a consequence of the self-discipline that a mystic undergoes. They are not just a tourist spectacle.

Mysticism

So far we have been considering two things together: Muslim mysticism and Hindu mysticism, and the statements made so far apply to both. This fact is significant. It shows that, though the regular practice and belief of the two religions show great differences between them, the mystic schools have some things in common. And this is part of the explanation of the way in which Islam and Hinduism came together in India to the extent that they did.

But let us now turn our attention to Muslim mysticism. In most religions, there grow up numbers of people who are not satisfied with the rules and dogmas of their faith. They find these too restrictive, too cramping. They are less interested in the words, the doctrines, than in the experience, the religious life of the believer, and they devote themselves to seeking direct experience of God (or whatever name they have for the highest level of reality) by meditation. Such people, in Islam, are the Sufis.

Origin of the Sufis

The Sufis were not an organized school or sect within the Islamic community so much as a movement, without precise rules of membership—a movement of asceticism, of austere and simple living, of devotion to the contemplation of Allah. The name 'Sufi' is derived from the Arabic for 'wool', and was applied to many groups of mystics because they customarily wore simple garments of undyed wool. Sufism gradually took institutional form, beginning as a term for mystics generally, especially for a large number of groups in Iraq, and developing into a programme for religious reform and spiritual regeneration of the individual. The Sufis were inspired by a spirit of love and devotion, which perhaps owed something to early Christianity, and was popularized by Persian poetry. There came to be three orders of Sufis in India—the Chisti, the Firdausi and the Suhrawardi orders.

The Sufis were at least as important as the conquering kings in the spread of Islam, though no doubt both were necessary. You can lead a horse to the water, but you can't make it drink. It required a different sort of influence to affect men's minds—a gentle persuasion—and this was supplied by the Sufis, among other teachers, with a form of religion that was more congenial to the Indians, and later to the Sumatrans and Javanese, than the stern one-God dictum of orthodox Islam. Sufism gave to Islam a great momentum, especially in the thirteenth century, when Sufi communities ranged far and wide through Asia, carrying their religion with them.

The life of the Sufis

The Sufis normally lived very simply in small communities, commonly in buildings provided for them by their supporters. They set up these communities wherever the Sufi teaching spread and gained sufficient adherents and supporters, and the teaching spread in the first place, partly through the movement of Muslim religious groups who had their own political leaders and carried on their own overseas trade. Often, it is probable, religious teachers went with regular trading vessels as chaplains, and were thus able to transmit their faith in foreign countries.

The mystic wishing to have direct experience of God had first to be initiated into his order and then to live with his teacher—the shaikh, or leader. In the course of time, after prolonged practice of meditation, he would become a master or leader himself. Five stages in his spiritual progress were recognized. These were: complete submission to God's will, love of God, private meditation, the wisdom that came from the study of God's nature, and finally the supreme experience of ecstasy—direct communication with God, in which his own individual nature disappeared like salt dissolving in water.

Sufism and orthodoxy

If we think a little about these aspects of Sufism, we can see that there might well be friction between the Sufis and the orthodox Muslims. In the first place, the orthodox Muslims were very insistent on the rules that marked out a Muslim from other people—the regular prayer and so forth. The mystic, on the other hand, regarded these things as outward, superficial things of no very great importance. He was more interested in his own inner experience. In the second place, the mystic experiences of Sufis led them to make statements about God that seemed heretical or even blasphemous. The nature of the experience, so far as it could be described at all, was to lose any sense of individuality, to be dissolved in God. Statements of this sort were shocking to many orthodox Muslims, to whom God, being supreme and omnipotent, was on an infinitely higher level than men could ever reach.

But both these features of Sufism, which made the school suspect in the eyes of some of its own co-religionists, served in India to make it a bridge between Islam and Hinduism. Because it did not insist on the exclusive nature of Muslim doctrines, was tolerant of all sorts of practices, it was more easily assimilated by the Hindus with their idea of a world spirit rather than a single God and their numerous sects and divinities. And, because Sufism was a mystic tradition, it struck a chord in India, which had its own rich, varied and highly developed mysticism.

Indeed, the mystic tradition in any religion can serve to link it with other religions—Christian, Muslim, Hindu, or anything else— because the experience sought by mystics is the same: there is one destination, the direct awareness of the supreme reality under whatever name, though there are different approaches to it.

(c) ISLAM IN INDIA

A few words about the way the Muslim faith fared in its new setting will underline the statement that, despite their apparent incompatibility, the two religions of Hinduism and Islam showed a remarkable degree of mutual influence, each borrowing something from the teaching and the associated culture of the other without losing its own character.

Bhakti

Just as, on the Muslim side, Sufism went some way towards Indian ideas, so, on the Indian side, there was a form of religion—

a popular one, not an obscure secret doctrine known only to a few ascetics—that went some way to meet Muslim ideas. This was the movement of Bhakti.

Islam had the element of devotion because it was aiming at the submission of the self to a generous and merciful God. In this it was rather like Christianity. And Bhakti was a movement to put into Hinduism this spirit of love and devotion. In effect, it used the names of the familiar Hindu divinities as names for the single supreme God of a sort similar to the God of a monotheistic religion like Islam or Christianity. It said that this supreme God could be loved and worshipped under any name, whether Shiva, or Allah, or anything else. And the Bhakti movement was characterized by a warm, poetic spirit well represented by Ramananda (fifteenth century), and by Kabir, who lived in the fifteenth and sixteenth centuries and founded a sect in which elements of Hindu Bhakti were mingled with Sufism.

The Sikhs

By contrast with this sort of development, a particular sect with a very different character is worth noticing—the Sikhs. This too was a new sect, that broke away entirely from Hinduism and blended some Hindu and Muslim elements; but, in spite of the liberalism and tolerance implied by some of its teachings, it became a fierce and rigorous sect.

It was founded by Nanak (died 1538), who kept some of the basic ideas of the Indian religions such as rebirth and karma; but he rejected the more superficial features of Hinduism, as he saw it— the caste system, the divine truth of the Vedic scriptures, and so on. His followers formed a new community with its own customs, and he was followed by a series of teachers whose doctrines guided the Sikh community. The last in the series, Govind Singh, is especially revered today by the Sikhs.

The Sikhs became, not just a religion, but a geographical unit— a kingdom of their own—when Sikh rulers became dominant in the Punjab; and though Sikhs have scattered widely, the Punjab is their chief home. This is where the beards and turbans are to be seen in greatest density. They are a part of Sikh custom, for Sikhs are not allowed to cut their hair, which is kept in turbans, and their beards are allowed to grow. They have other distinctive customs: they carry daggers (called kirpans) and wear steel bracelets. They are renowned as warriors, and many have for generations been recruited into the Indian army. They are worth noticing because they are a fairly energetic and prosperous community that has played quite a part in Indian history.

(d) INDO-MUSLIM CULTURE

One of India's best-known express trains is known as the Taj Express. It runs from Delhi to Agra, the old city in Uttar Pradesh where so many monuments are to be seen. The carriages are smart and clean, and even in third class, with wooden seats, there is a proportion of Westerners among the passengers. There seem to be more white people on that one train than in any other place.

The reason is that they are making a tourist excursion to Agra to see some of India's most famous monuments. In the course of a single day it is possible to go to Agra, tour round in a coach, and return to Delhi.

The train is nicknamed the Taj Express for the obvious and very good reason that it is the train by which tourists go to see the Taj Mahal at Agra—the most looked-at tourist spectacle in the whole of India. It is said that the best experience of the Taj Mahal is by moonlight, because then you see the inlaid patterns of semi-precious stones seeming to glow, and the soaring white building looks like a fairy castle. We may well think that this building is one of India's crowning cultural achievements, but there are two things we should not forget. One is that, though architecture was the most spectacular and enduring of the art forms practised in Muslim times, it was only one of many. Painting, music, and literature flourished as well. The other is that the Taj Mahal belongs to the culture of an originally non-Indian race. The interesting thing about Muslim architecture in India is the way in which it borrowed native Indian features, and became eventually blended with the Indian tradition. But it was not the same thing as the Hindu temples described in an earlier chapter. The Taj Mahal has many Indian touches, but it is very different from, say, the Rajarani temple at Bhubaneshwar.

Art, music and literature

Among the Muslim rulers of India, particularly the Moguls (often also spelled Mughals) of the sixteenth and seventeenth centuries, the arts owed much to the example and patronage of the rulers themselves. It was they who provided the money and made it possible for poets to write, musicians to play, and architects to design.

Humayun, the father of Akbar, spent a part of his life in exile in Persia before he could regain part of his Indian empire; and from Persia he brought the artist Mir Sayyid Ali, who was responsible for the development of a school of art in India blending Persian and Indian styles. Muslim artists excelled in the illustration of books with pictures, and many examples of their work remain.

Music, to take a subject that deserves more attention than it can be given in the space available in this book, was a highly developed art in ancient times, and it was abundantly fostered under the Muslim rulers as well. The ancient Indians had a variety of instruments—strings, woodwind and percussion—some of which are in common use today. But one instrument that was invented in Muslim times has become perhaps the best-known in the Indian classical tradition as it is followed today—the sitar. Indian music has been getting more popular in the West in recent years, and concert tours by top performers in western countries have been very successful. It is no coincidence that 'sitar' resembles 'guitar'. It is thought that they both developed from the same source and that the 'zither' is another variant of the same thing.

Some rulers were themselves no mean writers: the first Mogul, Babur, is especially noted. Other rulers, especially the illiterate but intelligent Akbar, patronized writers and poets at their courts. Akbar's court, which accommodated a galaxy of talents in all the arts, supported such people as Abul Fazl (who wrote a history of Akbar's reign) and Abul Faiz.

We must not forget that all this activity was activity within an imported tradition. All the time, Hindus were continuing with their own traditions. And one of the most famous of Indian poets, Tulsi Das, was working at the same time as Akbar's protégé. He wrote in Hindi, not Urdu, and he was unknown to the Muslim nobles, or unmentioned by them. But his poetry about themes of Indian myth such as the life of Rama, deeply religious and devotional, are a source of inspiration to Indian readers today.

Indo-Muslim architecture

In the earlier centuries, the rulers were more conscious of themselves as an invading race, surrounded by potential enemies. When they did not build fortresses, they made buildings that looked like fortresses, and the full flowering of the architecture was not until the sixteenth century.

Their works are different in style and function from the corresponding Hindu traditions. The mosques are different from the Hindu temples because they are large halls where people meet to pray—not dark and secret places where worshippers come individually to the statues or symbols of their gods. The tombs are different: they are enormous buildings, raised at enormous expense, designed to perpetuate forever those who were loved and had departed, and to advertise the devotion to them of those who were left behind. The government buildings are different: the famous Red Forts of Agra and Delhi, battlemented enclosures full of palaces, audience halls and government buildings of every kind; or Akbar's new city of Fatehpur Sikri, full of jewels of architecture.

The materials are different, and to some extent the use of different materials required different styles. The earlier Islamic tombs use a lot of pink sandstone, and, as in the case of Humayun's tomb erected by his widow, the pink is combined with white to accentuate all the features of the design. Of Akbar's successors, Shahjahan especially used marble—above all in the Taj Mahal itself. And the pure white marble that was used was not suitable for the elaborate carving that covered the face of Hindu temples. A different sort of ornamentation was required by the material: trellises and grilles of delicate design— letting all the breezes pass through to cool the interior—and inlay work of semi-precious stones (called pietra dura).

So there were important differences between Islamic and Hindu architecture. But, particularly under Akbar and progressively under his successors, there was a smooth and entirely successful blending of Persian and Hindu features into the Mogul designs. Domes were a typical feature of the Islamic tradition—great domes over the centre of tombs, small domes raised on pillars to make rooftop pavilions. Humayun's tomb and later works have double domes, each with an inner and outer shell. The domes remained as the dominating feature, unlike the tiered pagoda roofs of Hindu temples, but another Hindu feature was increasingly adopted. Square windows, doorways, and so on were introduced, whereby the weight of a wall or terrace above is carried by a lintel laid squarely across two pillars. In the Persian tradition, on the other hand, openings of whatever sort were without square tops, the weight being carried by true arches. Shahjahan made much use of the cusped arch, made up of several intersecting curves. But other buildings, such as the audience chamber at Fatehpur Sikri, used the square Hindu technique.

The Taj Mahal, with its white marble, its pietra dura, its double dome, its false tomb (Shahjahan's queen is actually laid to rest, with himself, in an underground chamber beneath the elaborate tomb room at the centre of the mausoleum), its surrounding parkland, waterways and fountains, represents the apex of Mogul architecture. It is a high point which perhaps later rulers did not achieve, and a worthy monument to a vanished age.

CHAPTER SEVEN

The Muslim Rulers

(a) THE IMPACT OF ISLAM

The dynamism of Islam

Islam was a driving force that swept impatiently across continents. The century in which Mohammed's death occurred saw Muslim rulers already in India: the Arabs who set up a kingdom in Sind, at the mouth of the Indus. The time for the conquest of the subcontinent was not yet, however. The Arabs of Sind did not push their warring, their government, and their religion far afield. Though Islam originated with the Arabs, it was not Arabs but later recipients of the teaching of Mohammed who eventually came to India as conquerors and brought with them a new era in India's history.

These were the Turks of central Asia, the lands around modern Afghanistan and Persia. Spasmodically and intermittently at first, but with increasing frequency and causing upset and disturbance to the local Indian kingdoms, foreign armies burst in through the familiar corridors of mass intrusion, the high passes through the mountains of modern Afghanistan. In the eleventh and thirteenth centuries they came as raiders, desecrating the Indian temples that were to them an abomination.

What brought the Muslims into India?

If this were a history of Muslim peoples, or a history of the Turks, it would be necessary to give a great deal of attention to the forces at work to bring wave after wave of foreigners to the plains of northern India from the eleventh century onwards. Some of these forces we can think of as propelling them from behind, some as attracting them from in front. It is part of the historian's work to seek to understand such forces, however imperfectly, and if we content ourselves with an over-simple or superficial explanation of them then our picture of the Muslims and the age of Indian history that they began is unsatisfactory and lacks perspective.

In this space we can afford to do no more than glance at three types of explanation. There is no suggestion that one is right and the others are wrong. One does not exclude another, and each has been favoured by different historians at different times. Probably each one is right as far as it goes.

This will serve as a reminder to us of an important fact about history: many of the details of it may be established without any room for argument, but there is always room for new interpretations. Historians are constantly making fresh explanations of things, fresh emphases, fresh perspectives; and we should not expect any one style of interpretation to be completely right and to cancel out all the others. Each new interpretation may add depth to our knowledge, but there is no telling whether there can be a point at which the deepening comes to an end, at which knowledge is complete.

So it is with the Muslim invasions. There was a time when a religious explanation of them seemed to be satisfactory, and indeed it is probably valid as far as it goes. Nowadays, however, historians consider that it does not go far enough, and look for other sorts of explanation as well.

This then is the first of the three: the religious interpretation. It is simply put. Islam was a missionary and intolerant religion. In the eyes of a Muslim, the sight of a non-Muslim is an abomination. Any unbeliever, anyone who does not accept the teachings of Mohammed, is an infidel. He must either be converted to Islam or be killed.

So we can say, following this interpretation, that the invading Turks were warlike because they had a warlike religion, a religion that preached holy war (*jehad*) against unbelievers.

But we could just as well say that the Turks had a warlike religion because they were themselves warlike, and for other reasons.

These reasons could be social and political, and this gives us the second type of explanation. They were organized, and because they were organized they were powerful. Instead of being split up into a multitude of competing caste and regional groups, they had a strong sense of corporate identity. They were ready to accept discipline and ready to work together. It would be possible to over-state this degree of organization, but it was certainly something which gave them an edge over neighbours with different forms of society, something therefore which put a weapon in their hands—a weapon of war.

This explanation is quite consistent with the first. Indeed, we could say that they had a religion that taught them submission to discipline. But we could equally say that they accepted that sort of religion because they respected discipline.

The third explanation is economic. Pressure of population on resources, competition with neighbours for available land or wealth, the search for riches and the spoils of easy victory—need and greed—

these are the forces which we can see pushing and pulling the Muslims as they spread around Asia with their religion, if we adopt the economic explanation. In the early days of Islam, pressure on resources and the need for space and livelihood were behind the warlike expansion of the Arabs. Later, with the irruption of the Muslim Turks into India, we can see economic forces also, not least the attraction of loot that India offered in abundance, with its temples full of gold and jewels. We can say that the Muslims desecrated the Indian temples because they were insults to the one true God, or we can say that the Muslims did so for the sake of wealth. Both may be true. But historians nowadays place more weight on the second.

Why no unified defence?

If the Muslims had never been let in at all, if the Indians had united to keep them out, the future course of Indian history would have been entirely different, and there is no telling, because the case is so hypothetical, whether on balance the differences would have been for the better or the worse. Perhaps it was India's misfortune; but it would be foolish to blame its people for their blindness to dangers which we now know were threatening in the centuries before the reckoning came. Moreover, India then was not a single country, but a host of countries, a civilization; and its 'disunity' is to be compared, if at all, to European disunity in the twentieth century. It could be said, for example, that Europe would have done much better to forget the squabbles that brought two world wars and to unite for strength in a new modern world, where there is no room for the segmented European powers from the past beside America, Russia and China, at the summits of power and decision. Such a judgment has as much right, or as little, to be applied to either case.

In India, the old pattern of warring kingdoms continued to the thirteenth century; and was indeed perpetuated beyond, around and beneath the looming Muslim empires. Kanauj, on the upper Ganges, remained a target for the reaching grasp of surrounding kingdoms anxious to make little northern empires of their own. And the raiders from beyond the passes were at first a nuisance, or a possible ally, but little more to most.

(b) THE RAIDERS

There were two stages in Muslim penetration. In the first, Turks from the area of what later became Afghanistan were raiders. Their capitals were outside India, in Afghanistan; they crossed into the Indus valley on raiding excursions for the sake of what they could get out of it, and then returned. In the second stage, which started

in the thirteenth century with the Sultanate of Delhi, there was a
new empire based in India—at Delhi—but run by people who still
felt themselves to be foreigners.

Mahmud of Ghazni

Ghazni was the centre of an uneasy kingdom beyond the passes.
Mahmud, the first of the Turks from (modern) Afghanistan to walk
upon the stage of Indian history in a major role, became king there
in 997. From the following year onwards his raids into India,
usually successful, were a regular occurrence. Harvest was a good
time to lead an army into the Punjab, and this he often did, because
then the army could easily be fed off the countryside, and there was
no need to carry bulky stores.

The chief characteristic of his raids was his amazing mobility;
he was able to move rapidly from part to part of the Punjab and back
across the passes to deal with some other enemy in the twinkling of an
eye. Thus he was not a conqueror; he came for booty, and departed.
With fine Arab horses in his cavalry, mobile tactics, and well-
organized channels of reinforcement, he was more than a match for
what the Indians could put up against him; and what he dealt out
was a taste of things to come. By 1026 he had overrun the Punjab
piecemeal. In 1018 he got as far as Kanauj, but did not trouble to
occupy the cities he took: it was India's fabled wealth, in gold and
jewels, that he was after as much as anything else; and the temples,
as chief repositories of precious things, became his chief target. One
other form of wealth that he could find in India was slaves. Slaves
in vast numbers were carried off into the conqueror's land, especially
after the raids of 1018.

The eleventh and twelfth centuries

The Ghazni Sultanate had a province in the Punjab, but there
was as yet no other dramatic change in the Indian scene. Powers
contended with each other as before. Kingdoms took it in turns to
bid for empire, and enjoyed a spell of glory, and faded again. From
time to time the names of the dynasties changed, and the capitals
changed, but the overall pattern was much the same.

There were the Gahadavalas at Kanauj, the Kalachuris at Tripuri,
the Karnatakas in Bihar, the Senas in Bengal, the Tomaras at Delhi,
and the Chauhans at Ajmere, to name some of the more important.
In the Deccan, the Chalukyas enjoyed a spell of prominence, and
struck north as far as Kanauj. In the South, the old Tamil kingdom
of the Cholas had a phase of dramatic expansion in the eleventh
century. According to an inscription, King Rajendra Chola mounted
in 1025 a far-ranging raid upon all the major ports of south-east

Asia—possibly as reprisals upon overmighty trading rivals. There is, however, little evidence to support the claims made in the inscription, which may be exaggerated. But, on the mainland of India, Rajendra Chola certainly extended his power considerably. The Chola empire of the eleventh century stretched right up the east coast of India as far as the Ganges.

The Rajputs deserve special mention. They were a caste of warriors or princes—members of the ksatriya class in society—who headed many small kingdoms, especially in the area of Rajasthan. Not all of them are likely to have been descended from the same original caste group. It is possible that some of them were descended from earlier invaders who had settled down in the north-west as a sort of aristocracy, and that others came to be admitted to the caste by virtue of having control over territories and thus qualifying as petty princes. Suitable family trees were invented for them, tracing back their ancestry to mythical races identified with the sun or the moon. Many of the native Hindu rulers with whom the Muslims had to contend were these Rajputs, and the name occurs a great deal in mediaeval Indian history. The Tomaras, Chauhans and others were examples of Rajput kingdoms.

Muhammad of Ghur

Muslim probings started again in real earnest towards the end of the twelfth century with Muhammad of Ghur ('the name is spelled several alternative ways). One of the Rajput kings, Prithviraja III of Ajmere, was leader of the Hindu forces arrayed against him. Ghur was another of the centres of power beyond the passes, and from his stronghold there Muhammad essayed his luck in India.

Penetrating, unlike his predecessors, right across the North of India, he reached Benares. By the early part of the thirteenth century he left in the hands of his successors the foundations of a great empire.

(c) THE SLAVE DYNASTY, 1206–1290

The north of India came under the domination of Muslim lords, who were first foreign conquerors, then rulers of an Indian empire with its power confined to India. This was a new style of domination. The people were from outside India, the religion they brought with them came from outside India, the language they brought with them was not Indian.

The Turks and their empire

In a way, there were two worlds in India—the world of the people and the world of the rulers. This is unlike anything we are familiar with in Western countries today. However distinct an aristocracy may be as a class, we expect it to share language, culture, and history with the people it rules. The Turkish rulers of the Delhi Sultanate were not like this.

In the course of time certainly, their partly Persian culture began to merge with the cultures of India. Their religion, architecture, language and dress came to be adopted by many Indians, and Muslims for their part adopted some Indian ways. But for all that, we should not think—though it is tempting, and easy, to think—that Muslims and Hindus came together easily. They did not. They never have. To realize this, we have only to think of the conflicts between Muslims and Hindus in modern times.

The first thing to remember about the Sultanate of Delhi, therefore, is that the Turks were, on the one hand, a part of the Indian scene, with roots in India, but, on the other hand, remained a distinct class. What needs to be emphasized is that there was not a straightforward conflict between Muslims and Hindus.

There were many different communities of Hindus, who had always been jealous of one another in the past and did not unite now. There were many different groups and individuals among the Turks, all anxious for power and self-preservation. The conflicts were between sultans and independent-spirited provincial governors, or between rivals for the sultanate. Succession to the sultanate rarely went uncontested. When a certain queen, Raziyah, was killed, there were various relatives wanting to succeed to the sultanate, and trying to get support among the nobles. Bahram Shah succeeded first, but he didn't last long. He was imprisoned and executed by his army. His brother Ala-ud-din Masud Shah followed, but failed to keep the support of the warlike nobles and was himself executed after four years.

These conflicts were largely conflicts within the ruling class. They were partly between personalities. Military governors, the lords of aqtas—military assignments, areas of greatly varying size—were always trying to assert their independence, and the Hindu chiefs were often rebellious. Balban, for example, had to cope with rebellion and invasion in the Punjab, to the north-west; with Indian chieftains in Rohilkand; and with a rebellion by his own governor in Bengal, to the east. He succeeded; but the cohesion of the empire could never be taken for granted.

The government

This example shows that the Hindu Indians as well as the Muslim Turks were competing in the general turmoil although they did not unite to form a single opposition. The Hindus were not wiped out by the new Muslim aristocracy. The processes of revenue collection and much of the other business of government were in their hands.

There were not enough Muslim lords to go round. The existing apparatus of small Hindu kingdoms had to be relied on. Hindu rulers often became tax farmers. That is, they collected taxes in their kingdoms on behalf of the Muslim overlords centred on Delhi, and passed on a fixed amount, keeping the rest for their expenses. Except when some of them brought on themselves the anger of the sultans, and were slaughtered, they continued to exist as the local rulers.

Besides the part played by the Hindus as agents, there are two other features of government that need to be noticed. One is the role of the nobles. The other is the way in which the line of sultans we are discussing came to be called the Slave Dynasty.

We have noticed how rivals for the sultanate needed to get the support of parties of nobles. These nobles were turbulent warlords living on the proceeds of Muslim rule. Sometimes, a weak sultan might be little more than a figurehead for these people, or for a powerful group of them. A group which originated at the time of Sultan Iltutmish was known as the Forty, and was powerful enough to influence the affairs of government at every turn. It was not a formally established institution so much as a pressure group composed of independent-spirited and ambitious men. It came to be called the Forty, but never consisted of exactly that number, and was not an organized society or a single interest; yet a sultan had to be acceptable to the Forty, or he could not survive. The one queen in the dynasty, Raziyah, a remarkable woman who did her utmost to overcome the disadvantages of being a woman doing what was regarded as a man's job, was always handicapped by the reluctance of the nobles to give her wholehearted support. Possibly hoping to overcome this handicap, she married a leader of the Forty. But the opposition of the others was too great; the Forty did away with her and were able to make or break later sultans.

There remains the question of why the Slave Dynasty, the first in the series that occupied the Delhi Sultanate, was so called. It is quite true that this dynasty originated from the rule of slaves. The first sultan, Qutb-ud-din Aibak, was originally a slave of Muhammad of Ghur, who conquered much of Northern India as far as Delhi, and made possible the creation, after his death, of a new Muslim empire within India. Qutb-ud-din Aibak, then, ascending the throne in 1206, was the first sultan with an Indian empire split off from the Muslim possessions elsewhere. And he was a slave of the conqueror who laid the foundations of his empire.

This was no ordinary slavery, however. The Muslim Turkish lords had a practice of buying slaves and training them up in their royal households for positions of responsibility. It was a recognized ladder to success. The slaves themselves were most often from chieftain families, captured in war. They might become generals, they might become sultans and have slaves of their own.

Summary

The Slave Dynasty, then, was an offshoot of the Turkish Muslim power, of the empire of Muhammad of Ghur, which established itself in Delhi and ruled for almost all of the thirteenth century. It did not claim territory outside the Indian subcontinent. It was preoccupied with extending control eastwards from Delhi and consolidating its power. Qutb-ud-din Aibak, the first ruler of the Delhi Sultanate, was a slave and later a successful general of Muhammad. He and other Turks created an empire extending to Bengal.

Iltutmish (1211–36) was a great conqueror, recovering and consolidating dominion in the Punjab and much of Rajputana. It was during his reign that the mighty Jenghiz Khan was active in Asia, but, although the Mongols came as far as the Indus in pursuit of their enemies, India was saved.

Balban (1266–86), loyal servant of the previous sultan who had been a retiring figure, and rewarded for his loyalty and ability with the sultanate itself, did much to revive and to organize the variable power of his dynasty. He had to deal with rebellions everywhere, but he showed determination and gave no quarter to his enemies.

These are perhaps the chief names to remember from the dynasty. Maybe we could add Raziyah (1236–40), the queen who strove hard to be a king, but could not overcome the resentment of the Forty.

The sultans were perpetually in conflict with relatives and governors and Hindu rulers. The Forty, established by Iltutmish, was a group of nobles who could be a powerful support to a sultan who pleased them, but an insuperable obstacle—indeed an executioner—to a sultan whom they did not find acceptable.

The Turks in India, as a whole, were a class apart from the Hindus, a military caste, but they were not a compact group warring with the Hindus, any more than the Hindus were a compact group warring with the Muslims. The Hindu rulers often rebelled, but they did not unite. Maybe if they had united, from the earliest times, the history of India would have been very different.

(d) India under the Sultanate of Delhi

The political map

From the thirteenth to the seventeenth centuries the chief feature of India's political map was a strong Muslim empire, based usually on Delhi, with one or two changes of capital to Agra or (Akbar's short-lived creation) Fatehpur Sikri. The empire of the Muslims was not fixed for all time; its boundaries were usually fairly hazy, for it exerted a varying degree of control over the chiefs or Hindus who ruled the parts of it, and generally speaking those further from the centre were more independent of their overlord. According to the varying fortunes and abilities of the Sultans or Great Moguls at the head of it, the empire expanded or shrank like a balloon; and when in the eighteenth century it ceased to be an effective major power in the land, it did not fall apart all at once, but gradually lost provinces by a piecemeal process until there was nothing left but a piece of territory around Delhi.

The Sultanate of Delhi was the regime of Turks from the present Afghanistan, an Afghan dynasty; it consisted of a series of dynasties of which the Slave Dynasty was the first. The Slave Dynasty was important as the first Muslim imperial regime based on Indian soil. The Moguls, a fresh wave of Muslims from beyond the passes in the sixteenth century, are important because of their achievements, especially those of the most famous of them all, Akbar. Between the two dynasties came the remainder of the Sultanate of Delhi, a number of dynasties trying, often with success, to consolidate their hold in the North, to extend their power into the South, and to secure their north-western frontiers.

In the South during this period, a new twofold pattern emerged: in the Deccan were Muslim rulers who were independent of the Sultanate; to the south of them were the surviving Hindu kingdoms, of which Vijayanagar was to become the dominant one. Later, the Muslim powers in the Deccan were separated from their Muslim brethren of the northern empires by the rise of a new Hindu power in the West: the Marathas.

The Sultans

The sultans of Delhi seem bigger than life size. They may be villains, but they are villains on a grand scale. Perhaps this impression is affected by the point of view we get, because what we know about them comes very little from the accounts of European visitors; it comes chiefly from what was written by people at the courts of the rulers. And these naturally took for granted a lot of the things that a foreigner would have described, such as inefficiency and lack of organization, and made their masters seem great men.

However that may be, there is a sense of style about these sultans. Their careers are certainly colourful, and their achievements and their failures are alike spectacular.

The Khaljis

Consider the careers of the Khalji rulers around the beginning of the fourteenth century.

There is one name to notice in particular: Ala-ud-din (1296–1316). The reign of Ala-ud-din was remarkable for his distrust of his officials and nobles. It was said that, in his court, the nobles did not even dare speak to each other aloud, for fear of being overheard by spies. They communicated with each other by signs. It would be a sorry thing if the members of a modern Western government felt obliged to conduct their proceedings in the same way.

Ala-ud-din was a very stern ruler, and we can imagine that all those who came within the immediate reach of his arm had good cause to be nervous. He tried to prevent his nobles from meeting each other. He was hostile to the Hindus, and tried to impoverish them by taxes and depredations. He prohibited drinking and gambling. No alcohol was to be brought into the cities, and those who were caught smuggling were flogged and put in holes in the ground.

We might get the impression that the sultans (as well as the Hindu rulers of the same and earlier times) were unmitigated villains without any human feelings at all. The chronicle of dynasties seems to be one long record of usurpations and assassinations, with sons murdering their fathers generation after generation. Unsavoury though it is, it is not entirely pointless and wanton violence. To a great extent it was self-defence. We have to remember that the rule of succession to a throne did not always indicate clearly who was the heir. The fact, especially, that there were numbers of queens who went in and out of favour complicated the issue. So, towards the end of one monarch's reign, his sons were naturally suspicious of each other; and, in an atmosphere of violence and plotting, each prince knew that if he did not strike first, somebody else with a claim on the throne might kill the king and himself and all the other princes as well.

To explain this is not to defend the Khaljis, for it is not a situation where praise or blame is appropriate. However, there are tangible positive achievements to be placed on the credit side of the Khaljis' record. The picture is brightened, for example, by the victories of Ala-ud-din as a prince and as a ruler, by economic measures such as market reform and price control, and by other constructive achievements which deserve more space than they can be given here.

The Tughluqs

The Khalji dynasty tottered to a close. A son of Ala-ud-din had a short and unhappy reign, after which the throne was taken by Ghiyas-ud-din Tughluq, a frontier commander, who established a new dynasty. His own reign was short and successful; his successor's was longer, colourful and eventful; a third reigned still longer, and was quite wise and tolerant; but the reign ended in weakness and confusion to be followed by a series of short violent reigns and the havoc wrought by a Mongol invader.

The first Tughluq, Ghiyas-ud-din (1320–25), was a capable general and ruler, and laid a good foundation for his successor Muhammad bin Tughluq (1325–51). Muhammad seems from the accounts we have of him to have had an odd mixture of qualities, capable of the greatest strictness and the greatest generosity, stern towards others and stern towards himself as well. For him, as for other devout rulers, being a good Muslim meant keeping to all the rules of the faith, such as regular prayer, and he took the utmost pains to see that the rules were kept. But he shows many sympathetic characteristics, especially in his attitudes to Hindus and to people of lower social levels. He was the first Muslim emperor to appoint a Hindu as an amil, the highest level of ruler or governor under the emperor, and he employed in high positions many men, who seemed to him deserving, from the less favoured classes of society.

His reign was notable for a number of events: he moved the capital to Daulatabad, and back again; he had trouble keeping the empire together, losing parts of the east and south of his dominions; he experimented with a token currency made of copper.

The next sultan, Firuz, reigned from 1352 until 1388. He had capable servants, notably a converted brahman with great influence over him, who ran the kingdom for him during a great part of the reign and supervised a well-organized revenue system that did not bear too harshly upon the peasants, and encouraged the development of cultivation. Many slaves were imported and paid by the state. Possibly they represented an attempt to build up a body of men who would be loyal to the sultan.

Matters deteriorated rapidly towards the end of the reign, however, and it was followed by ten years of confusion and disorder in which a number of claimants came to the throne, and left it. In 1398 occurred an event that finally put an end to Tughluq power, and shook India to the roots: the invasion of the Mongol hordes under the savage leader Timur.

Throughout mediaeval and much of modern history, the Mongol tribes of Asia were a constant threat and a bugbear. They roamed widely, and under great leaders like Kublai Khan, Jenghiz Khan and Timur achieved extensive conquests. At the end of the thirteenth century they had overrun China, and established their own dynasty there. They played a part in the histories of all the lands around the Asian continents; their raids took them into China, into India, and

to the borders of Europe, and they were feared by all. In India they
played an important role in many ways from the thirteenth to the
fifteenth centuries, but not as conquerors and masters: the chief
visible mark they left upon India was in the ruins of the places they
had sacked. Delhi was ravaged by Timur's army. A hundred thousand
slaves were taken. The Mongols went as far east as Meerut, but then
turned back; and the next dynasty at Delhi, the Sayyids, sprang from
the family of the viceroy of Timur.

The fifteenth century

This brings us to the fifteenth century, the period that remains
before the Mogul conquest. It is a period that is rather difficult to
deal with. This is because there is no single focus of interest that we
can concentrate on in the course of this rapid survey, and if we
attend to all the kingdoms in India that seem to merit discussion,
the result is confusion. Something must be said about the Sultans at
Delhi, for fresh dynasties rose to claim the authority of past empires.
Something must be said about the South, and particularly about the
Hindu kingdom of Vijayanagar. But we could perfectly well devote
whole sections to other powerful kingdoms with colourful histories.

Gujarat in the west, for example, asserted its independence under
Muzaffar Shah at the end of the fourteenth century and through the
fifteenth enjoyed a turbulent history of its own. Notable are the
exploits of Mahmud Shah (1458–1511), who was frequently at war
and earned himself a prodigious reputation. He it was who had
dealings with the Portuguese when they reached the west of India,
and offered them a site for a trading settlement at Diu.

Neighbouring Malwa deserves equal attention as a powerful and
independent kingdom. Malwa and Gujarat alike were much exercised by the Rajputs—Hindu chiefs enjoying considerable power in
much of western India. In particular the successes of the Rajput
Rana Sanga, of Mewar, are significant for later developments in
Indian history, which must be discussed in their place. In the east,
far from the centre of the Sultanate's power, Bengal with its Muslim
rulers and powerful Hindu chiefs had a chequered history of its own.

Important though these kingdoms are, there are so many of them,
and the frontiers change and the centres of power shift so often, that a
catalogue of names and events would be a long and confusing one.
But this need not be attempted.

In the North, at Delhi, two dynasties arose to claim the powers of
the old sultanate. The Sayyids claimed by their name that they were
descended from the prophet Mohammed himself, but so did a lot
of other people, and the whole Muslim world was full of false claims
of one sort or another. They gained power at Delhi in 1414, and

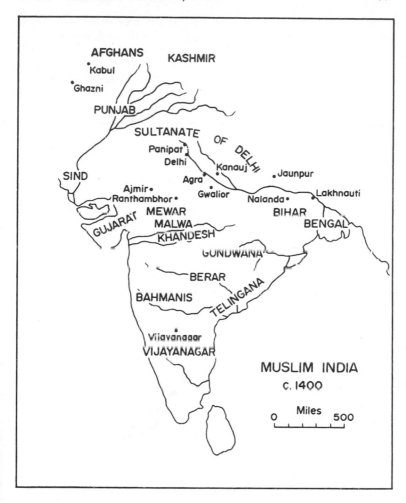

AFGHANS KASHMIR
Kabul
Ghazni
PUNJAB
SULTANATE OF DELHI
Panipat
Delhi
Kanauj
Jaunpur
SIND
Ajmir
Ranthambhor
Agra
Gwalior
Nalanda
Lakhnauti
MEWAR
BIHAR
GUJARAT
MALWA
BENGAL
KHANDESH
GUNDWANA
BERAR
TELINGANA
BAHMANIS
Vijayanaaar
VIJAYANAGAR

MUSLIM INDIA
c. 1400

Miles
0   500

weathered a troubled period of confusion and competition among small states where none could get mastery over all. The last of the Sayyids retired in 1448, two years before his death.

An Afghan called Bahlul, who had previously held the Punjab on behalf of the Sayyids, took advantage of the subsequent confusion to take the throne for himself, thus founding the Lodi dynasty, and reigned from 1451 to 1489, an untypically long reign. A nearby sultanate, at Jaunpur, had effectively set itself up as an independent kingdom, but he was able to subdue it. His successor, Sikander Lodi, lived until 1517, had some success in his empire-building, and extended his influence across most of the North of India. He conducted wars against the Hindus. His son Ibrahim had to deal with a number of rebellions however, notably in Bihar; and one of his governors, at Lahore in the Punjab, intrigued with the Moguls in his own interests, and thus played a part in the circumstances that brought the first Mogul, Babur, through the passes to start a new period of unification and organization in the affairs of the subcontinent.

The Bahmanis and the South

The Muslim kingdoms in the North were not the only places where anything of importance happened. Hindu rulers in the Deccan and the far south, less affected by the Muslim incursions than their northern brethren who, if they kept their kingdoms at all, kept them only as vassals of Muslim overlords, continued the same Hindu pattern of culture and politics as before. The names changed. The old Tamil kingdoms had passed away, and the great Chola power was spent. In the period beginning with the fourteenth century, there are two themes worth noticing: the rise in the Deccan of a Muslim power, the Bahmanis, and the growth of a Hindu empire in the far south, named after its capital, Vijayanagar.

The Bahmani power originated from the activities of a Muslim general of Ala-ud-din, a slave called Kafur, who had an extremely successful military career from 1306 onwards, and from 1347 there was a new Muslim kingdom north of the river Krishna which had grown from two separate Muslim provinces of the Mogul empire whose governors had previously rebelled and established their independence.

The first ruler, Ala-ud-din Bahmani, thus sat at the centre of a second Muslim focus of power, and reduced the area of unfettered Hindu sovereignty to the far south. At about the same time, a new Hindu power came into being: Vijayanagar, previously the capital of a dynasty called the Hoysalas, gave its name in the fourteenth century to a line that gradually extended its power over most of the Tamil South and posed a constant threat to the Muslim kingdom.

Thus India in the fourteenth and fifteenth centuries could roughly be divided into four belts: in the north, the weakening Sultanate of Delhi; south of it, the various Rajput powers and other Hindu kingdoms; south of these, but not extending as far east as the coast, the Muslim Bahmani kingdom; and in the peninsula, another Hindu area, the empire of Vijayanagar.

There were constant conflicts and rivalries in the South, particularly between the Bahmanis and Vijayanagar. There were battles between the two at intervals in the fourteenth century. The Bahmani Firuz Shah (1397–1422) gained victories over Hindus. The fighting between Muslim armies and Hindus was savage and barbarous; enormous numbers of civilians were killed. Muhammad Shah II (1463–82) gained possession of Goa, but his kingdom was weakened by internal conflicts. Eventually, in the sixteenth century, the Bahmani kingdom split up into a number of Muslim principalities.

The same century saw the heyday of the Hindu Vijayanagar. King Krishnadevaraja (1509–30) was renowned not only for his military success but for his humane qualities and his patronage of culture. Vernacular as well as Sanskrit literature flourished under his interest. Trade flourished. Empire was extended northwards by conquests along both coasts of the peninsula. The break-up of the Bahmani kingdom was of great benefit to Vijayanagar. But to our eyes even so liberal and tolerant a king has strange aspects: he would order stern punishments, with every variety of painful death prescribed.

(e) THE EARLY MOGULS

In the possession of the British Crown, there is among other treasures an enormous and magnificent diamond called the Koh-i-noor. It has a rich history behind it, a history which can serve to symbolize for us the flux and variety of mediaeval India. In the course of its life, it has changed hands several times; it has been the booty of war after fierce battles, and it has been a token of peace and friendship. Around it, sultans, rajas and governors have waged desperate wars, and the colourful glories and disasters of Indian history have the story of this diamond bound up with them, so that, for us, it can symbolize the splendour and the extravagance of generations of India's rulers.

It is said to have been mined in mediaeval times in Vijayanagar, the Hindu kingdom in the South that maintained at its court the religion and traditions of Hindu culture while Muslim invaders dominated the North. From there, it came into the hands of the Sultans of Delhi. In the sixteenth century, a new race of conquerors, the Moguls, stormed across the Punjab and built the empire that the famous Akbar inherited. The Mogul prince Humayun received the diamond as a gift from an Afghan family and passed it on to his father, the warrior-emperor Babur, and it became one of his most treasured possessions.

Babur and Humayun

Although this new wave of invaders were known as the Moguls, they were of Turkish race. The word 'Mogul', which is normally used with reference to these people (and sometimes spelled Mughul or Mughal) is an alternative to the word 'Mongol', used to designate Jenghiz Khan and his race of nomadic warriors who roamed central Asia. This name indeed has attached itself to central Asian peoples generally, although they were of several different races. So although the words 'Mongol' and 'Mogul' basically mean the same thing, 'Mongol' normally refers to the nomadic peoples generally, and 'Mogul' normally refers to the particular dynasty in India.

In the area of modern Afghanistan and Iran there were among the Turks various factions and groups in rivalry with each other, and it was natural that, in the general quest for power and dominion, some of them should spill over into India. Babur did so, with his army.

Babur—his original name was Zahir-ud-din Muhammad, and he claimed descent from Timur and from Jenghiz Khan—became a ruler and a general while still a boy, and crammed an incredible amount of military and political activity into a fairly short life. He had a kingdom based on Kabul, and in the contest for power among his neighbours he found that there were good possibilities for expansion south-eastwards into the Punjab. In 1526, after crossing and re-crossing the Indus, he engaged with the army of Sultan Ibrahim, the last representative of the Lodis at Delhi. The battle was fought at Panipat, near the river Jumna to the east of the Punjab—a fateful spot where several momentous battles have been fought. With superior tactics and the use of guns, Babur routed his enemies.

The story of Babur's reign is quite largely a story of wars. A single victory over the declining Lodi power was not enough to make him master of northern India: on every hand there were forts and cities that had to be taken and minor kingdoms that had to be subdued. The most powerful opponent was the grouping of Rajput chiefs, under the redoubtable Rana Sanga who was covered with scars and lacked an eye and an arm. In 1527, artillery and tactics again won the day for Babur against superior numbers.

When he died in 1530, Babur had carved out for himself an empire that extended far across the subcontinent, leaving only Bihar and Bengal in the hands of Afghan lords. The empire was like a wedge, thrusting across from the Mogul homeland in the Hindu Kush.

Babur was followed by his son Humayun, who tried to expand the empire further. Humayun's career was studded with misfortunes, not entirely unearned. His own lack of firmness was perhaps his chief enemy, but he had to contend also with Sher Khan, a masterful Afghan opponent in Bengal, and the jealousy of his own brothers who would not help him when Sher Khan was at his heels.

Important in the story are Humayun's early conflicts in Gujarat, where a lack of thoroughness in mopping up after defeating his opponent, Bahadur Shah, is significant for his later reverses. The attempt to subdue the Afghans in the East failed; Humayun wasted time in Lakhnauti (Bengal) when he had taken the city, giving Sher Khan the opportunity to raise an army and rout him. Getting no assistance from his own family in the Punjab or the Kabul home-land, Humayun was forced to flee ignominiously—to become eventually a friend of the Shah of Persia, who helped him reorganize his fortunes.

From 1540 to 1545 Sher Khan, who took the title of Sher Shah, was effectively master of India. His career is remarkable; with some fortune and much ability he made his way from the obscurity of a local hereditary revenue administrator to the heights of power. In his early career he was successful both as a scholar and as an administrator, organizing the revenue of the district, the *Jagir*, that he inherited. There followed a period at the court of the ruler of Bihar, and a period at the court of Babur at Agra. Not long after he was back in Bihar as chief minister, and succeeded in establishing himself as ruler despite the opposition of the Afghan nobles.

He celebrated the conquests of Gwalior, Malwa, Ranthamborc and Jodhpur. He consolidated an elaborate system of administration, with a pyramid of officials conducting the business of government at all levels. There were stringent rules to govern the assessment of tax that subjects were to pay and to check the corruption of officials. The tax was a standard rate of one-third of the value of crops. Village headmen were made responsible for law and order in their districts. Along the roads, rest-houses were built and trees were planted. Sher Shah was not a Mogul, but it was he more than anybody else who created the apparatus of government that the Moguls used when they returned.

The Moguls returned first of all in the person of Humayun, back after his period of exile to take advantage of the weakening of the Afghan grip after Sher Shah's death. By 1555, with support from the Shah of Persia, he had battled his way back to power in Delhi—only to die a few months later.

The deaths of Sher Shah and Humayun seem to represent the difference between the two men. Sher Shah was fatally injured when some gunpowder exploded; Humayun slipped on a library staircase and fell down it. The man of action and decision, in contrast to the bumbling, opium-smoking man of bad luck? Be that as it may, they both contributed vitally to the following period of Indian history. Sher Shah bequeathed a system of administration. Humayun bequeathed his son, the next ruler and one of India's most famous—Akbar.

(f) AKBAR 1556–1605

Fatehpur Sikri

A man stands on top of the city wall, high up against the clear blue Indian sky in the sweltering heat. Far beneath him is a lake. If his assistant down on the ground can collect enough money from the tourists, he will dive into it. And the tourists will pass on, feeling satisfied perhaps that India is giving them their money's worth.

They will pass on into the city of Fatehpur Sikri, the capital that the Emperor Akbar built. Unlike ancient cities, it has left us not temples but all manner of other buildings that were inhabited by the dignitaries of the Muslim court. Around elegant cloistered courtyards there are palaces, halls of justice, council chambers, tombs.

It is an impressive place. As you pass through the archways and across the courtyards, you are surrounded by some of the crowning achievements of Indo-Muslim architecture, with all its splendour and dignity. But the remarkable thing about Fatehpur Sikri is that it is a ghost city. Nobody lives there any more. There are no deliberations in the council chambers, no revels in the gaming halls. Tourists walk quietly here and there in disciplined groups. Beggars beg. The diver dives. Fatehpur Sikri, designed as the hub of a mighty empire, has become a museum, an art gallery, a circus.

The world in Akbar's time

The desolation of Fatehpur Sikri perhaps makes Akbar seem very remote. His life and times seem to have no links with the present. The city is there, but it is like a coffin. So it would be as well to remind ourselves that, far from being a remote and vanished oriental culture, the India of Akbar was sharing more and more in the traffic of an increasingly mobile world, and that the world itself was beginning to look more like the world of today. In China there was the Ming dynasty, the last but one that China had, which had many contacts with the rest of the world. In Europe the new age of discovery, of migrations, of world-wide horizons, had well and truly begun. Akbar's contemporary in England was Elizabeth I. This was the time of the opening up of America, of voyages around the world, of Francis Drake. It may seem odd that the court of Akbar, with all its exotic oriental pageantry, was visited by Englishmen with such down-to-earth names as Newberry, Fitch and Leedes.

Akbar and Asoka

Akbar lived in a world that had long known gunpowder (which was indeed invented in Asia), and had recently produced printing, which had yet to make its mark in Asia. It was therefore a different world from Asoka's nearly two thousand years before.

But the two men have much in common. Of all the kings and emperors of India in historical times, Asoka and Akbar are today the best remembered. They both had mighty empires. They both left impressive monuments—impressive by their splendour, or by their sheer antiquity. They were both keenly interested in religion, and took an active interest in many different religious sects and beliefs. They both showed mildness and consideration to their potential or actual enemies. Deservedly maybe, their names stand out above all others.

Akbar's servants

We know much more about Akbar than about Asoka. This is because there is a greater variety of writings about him from his own time. There are several chronicles. There are the reports of Jesuit missionaries, some of whom had plenty of contact with him. And there are the flattering writings of Abul Fazl. Abul Fazl was Abkar's secretary and a scholar of note. He is one of the various personalities around the emperor about whom we know something, and who thus help us to see Akbar in three dimensions. This is an important difference between our knowledge of him and our knowledge of Asoka. We do not know anything about the names and characters of the personalities around Asoka.

The success of Akbar's policies owed much to the skill of one minister in particular, the famous Todar Mal. This man combined in his career the roles of army commander and revenue minister. He was outstandingly capable, though his strictness and orthodoxy made it increasingly difficult for his colleagues to get on with him. It was he who was the chief architect of Akbar's carefully planned revenue reforms, designed to make revenue administration more efficient and fair. They showed a serious attempt to tackle the problem constructively and humanely. Then there was the loyal Bhagwan Das, the Hindu noble, a Rajput, who became one of Akbar's chief generals. He was a most able army commander and a man with a strong sense of honour. Once, it is said, he gave a promise of safe conduct to an enemy, and, over his head, Akbar violated the promise. He then tried to commit suicide. However, it is difficult to assess the truth of the story.

Policy towards Hindus

Rajputs, of whom Bhagwan was one, were as we noticed before a caste of Hindu nobles ruling large tracts of country in the west—Rajputana. Akbar wanted to assimilate the territories of the Rajput chiefs in his empire, and his policy was to get these men onto his side. This did not mean that he never went to war against any of

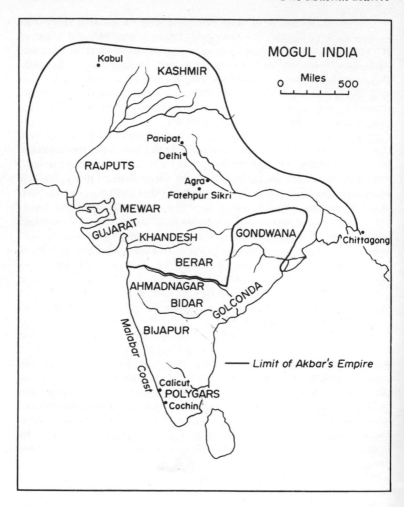

them—he had to, if he was to gain paramountcy in the Rajput area. But he relied as much as possible on making allies of them. He married the daughters of some of them and thus created dynastic links between his own, Muslim, line and the Hindu nobility. His son and successor, Jahangir, was half Rajput; and Jahangir's son and successor, Shahjahan, was also the son of a Rajput princess and therefore three-quarters Rajput.

This sort of policy towards the Rajputs (it didn't always work—

the Rana of Mewar was never brought over to Akbar's side) was typical of his attitude towards the Hindus in general. We have to remember that the Muslims were conquerors with a culture distinct from the Hindu, trying to bring the Hindu Indians into subjection. Akbar realized that it would be much the best for the harmony of his empire if the two cultures, Muslim and Hindu, could be brought together more, and understanding be fostered between the Muslim rulers and the largely Hindu population.

With this in mind he did away with governmental practices that discriminated against the Hindus, such as the levying of special taxes on non-Muslims. Though he disapproved of some Hindu practices, such as the custom for widows to burn themselves to death, he did not make them illegal, and he supported others, such as the sanctity of cows—it was illegal to slaughter cows. He patronized writers in the indigenous Sanskrit literature as well as in his own Muslim tradition of Persian literature, and supported Hindu artists and musicians. During his reign and under his patronage, a new Mogul style of architecture was perfected which was a combination of Islamic and traditional Indian elements.

Religion

His attitude to religion was an example of this same desire to bring Muslims and Hindus together. In the later part of his life, he became less and less attached to his own inherited Islam, more and more unorthodox. He was not a great theologian or a successful religious reformer, but he found time to interest himself keenly in problems of religion and promoted frequent discussions in his conference chambers among men of religion. To his conferences came Hindu teachers, Jains (an ancient sect, going back even earlier than Buddhism), Parsees (with their own variety of faith from Persia), and Christian missionaries. These missionaries were disappointed to find that Akbar did not really want to study Christianity for its own sake; for him it was one more faith that could be mixed in with the rest, another ingredient in the soup.

Akbar's great idea in all this was to create something new that could serve as a basis for a unified religion in his empire, replacing the divergent faiths that then existed in it. The upshot of the discussions was a new doctrine that Akbar himself thought up, called the Din Ilahi.

The Din Ilahi was a mixture of elements from different beliefs. There was much of Islamic Sufism, from which it took a belief in God, though in a very vague sense. Indeed, its vagueness is perhaps its chief characteristic. It was not intended as a hard and fast set of teachings, only as a personal set of beliefs drawn from various sources.

Some people took it up, chiefly people at court who hoped to gain favour with the emperor, but it never caught on. Perhaps it was too wishy-washy, borrowing a little of the characters of several faiths but having no definite character of its own.

Conquests

Being religious did not stop Akbar from going to war a great deal. In the world of turbulent Indian politics, he needed to. It was impossible to stand still, to lead a quiet life: those rulers who did not move forward slipped back. Akbar is renowned as a far-sighted and amicable ruler, but, like all the Muslim rulers, he could be very cruel when the passion seized him. It was the nature of the age he lived in. There seemed to him nothing immoral in a career of conquest in all directions; his father Humayun had been deprived of a large Indian empire, and he had to win it back. Humayun, we may recall, had lost his vast dominions to Sher Shah, and only at the end of his life, after getting help from the Shah of Persia, had Humayun won his way back to power over a part of the Punjab. From this base, Akbar built an empire that consisted of the North of India and much of the South as well.

While he was still a boy, and too young to be in control of imperial policy, Akbar's forces defeated those of the successors of Sher Shah, and he gained Delhi. It was not many years before Akbar had thrown off the domination of palace dignitaries and was conducting his own campaigns. By 1572 he had cemented his control in the west by conquests in Rajputana and Gujarat; four years later he had struck out east as far as Bengal. In 1581 he had to cope with an invasion by his half-brother, Muhammad Hakim, who was dissatisfied with his own share of the Mogul Empire at Kabul and tried to take advantage of Akbar's unpopularity with some Muslims, who regarded him as something of a heretic. Muhammad Hakim was defeated, and by 1585 Kabul was taken. Kashmir, right up north, followed, and in the 1590s Akbar turned his attention to the South. Perhaps, with time and fortune, Akbar could have made himself master of the entire subcontinent; as it was, Berar and Khandesh came under his rule.

Administration

Running the empire, to say nothing of creating it, was an enormous task, and Akbar, with the able assistance of Todar Mal, was assiduous in improving and keeping the administration up to the mark. They had the advantage of the administrative system set up before by Sher Shah, himself an organizational genius, and with this foundation Akbar was able to achieve a more generally effective government than most Indian kings could have. Though even in the best, even in Akbar's, inefficiency and corruption could not be eliminated.

There was established a top level of high officials called mansabdars. Most of these were Muslims, but Akbar relied a great deal on the advice of Rajput nobles and others, and gave high positions to Hindu rulers. The central government was in three divisions: one concerned with a variety of matters such as the mint, household troops of the emperor, and the army's artillery; one concerned with the army generally; and one concerned with the provinces of the empire. Each province was under a governor directly responsible to the emperor. Judges were appointed in all parts to help the governors and the emperor in the administration of justice.

Revenue

One interesting feature of the government was the fact that the collection of revenue was kept separate from the rest of the administration, so that the taxes came in to the central treasury before they were paid out to officials as salaries. The usual system was for officials to take their own salaries out of the revenue that they collected, a system which made it possible for corrupt men— and there were many—to oppress the taxpayers and line their own pockets. Still, even Akbar's scheme depended on the separate corps of revenue collectors being honest. They were instructed to make improvements at the village level by encouraging villagers to develop their agriculture, using tax remittances and money advances to help the farmers. In fact, the tax collectors were more than just that; they were development officers as well. But instructions were no good by themselves; they had to be carried out properly if the policy was to do any good, and too many officials saw their jobs chiefly as a way of getting rich.

Revenue administration was complicated. We should not make the mistake of thinking that Akbar was personally responsible for everything that was done and decided. Obviously, he could not be. Equally, we should not hold him responsible for everything that was done and decided in other matters besides revenue administration— military, social, religious. But it is clear that Akbar had a commanding personality, and, if he had good men working for him, he knew how to find them and how to get the best out of them. This quality may go some way towards accounting for his extraordinary success.

CHAPTER EIGHT

The End of the Moguls

(a) A NEW ERA?

The trouble with history is that it doesn't organize itself neatly into compartments; it is untidy. It is scarcely ever possible to take a particular date as the end of one period and the beginning of another without doing some violence to the truth.

We have an example of this before us. The example is the end of the period of the Muslim rulers and the beginning of the period of European dominance. Now, we have already seen that it is rather misleading to talk about 'the Muslim period' of Indian history, because at all times most of the people were Hindus, and the Muslims never ruled over the whole of India. But apart from this fact, Muslim dominance did not begin and end on particular dates. We have seen that there was no sudden invasion that overwhelmed the whole country: the first Muslim intruders were raiders who came for what they could get and then went back home again. Equally, there was no sudden European invasion that overwhelmed the whole country: there were small groups of traders who did not want to dominate the country at all, but only to trade quietly and peacefully, so long as they could get the terms they wanted.

The Portuguese were the first Europeans to come. With a small fleet, Vasco da Gama sailed around the Cape of Good Hope and came to Calicut, on the Malabar coast, in 1498. A second expedition, to Cochin, followed later. From these small beginnings grew a more and more active European involvement in India. The Portuguese were only the first in a series: they were followed by the Dutch, and then the English. It was eventually the English who gained extensive territorial control, after some competition with the French. At first the interest of the Europeans was not in securing control of territories in India. It was in establishing trading settlements on the coasts and conducting commerce to and from those settlements.

Now, were we to take 1498, the year when this process began, as

the end of the Muslim period of Indian history and the beginning of
the European period, we would be making a ridiculous judgment.
It would be ridiculous because this date is half a century before the
greatest Muslim ruler of them all, Akbar, came to the throne; and he
certainly was not conscious, nor were any of his subjects conscious,
of Muslim rule coming to an end. The affairs of the Moguls and of
the Hindu rulers beneath and around them went on as before without
being vitally affected by the arrival of a few merchants from strange
and distant lands. The proof of this is that we have been able to
discuss the history of India up to the end of Akbar's reign without
mentioning the Portuguese or the other European powers except
in passing.

It is true, however, that—even though the Indians did not realize
it, and nobody at the time would have agreed with you if you told
him—the first coming of the Westerners was in a sense a turning-
point because, from the time that the Portuguese arrived, all the
later developments became, in broad outline, inevitable.

In the first place, it was inevitable that other powers would follow
the Portuguese, because they naturally did not want Portugal to
have a monopoly of the thriving and prosperous trade in spices that
had previously been largely in Muslim hands along most of the route
between the spice islands of south-east Asia and Europe. This made
it inevitable that a number of Western powers should be active
around the coasts of India, negotiating with the Indian rulers for
trading privileges and under pressure from the needs of the competition between themselves to push the rulers as much as they
could.

Then, for reasons that we shall see more clearly later on, it would
be inevitable that the comparative weakness and confusion of the
Indian kingdoms—for throughout history, as we have already seen,
empires were crumbling as well as growing, and there were often
periods of weakness and confusion—would cause the Westerners to
become involved, if only for the sake of their self-protection and the
security of their trade, in the internal affairs of the rulers.

And, finally, because the Europeans had better guns, better
armies, more centralized organization and perhaps a more advanced
commerce—although we should not underestimate the Indian
achievement in any of these things—their involvement in the affairs
of the kingdoms would lead them step by step into a position of
paramountcy in the subcontinent.

There was, certainly, at least one big 'if' in this. These results
would not follow if the Western powers were always weakened by
fighting among themselves. Then the Indian rulers could play them
off against each other. Either they must come together and end their

competition, or one of them must come out on top and the others disappear from positions of influence. What happened in the end was that the British came out on top and the French and the others ceased to be major powers in India.

There are two conclusions from these considerations. One is that the arrival of the Europeans was important in India's history. The other is that nobody was aware of the fact at the time. Things seemed to be, and indeed were, going on as before. The Westerners were not masters, nor were they beggars—they were traders, doing business as were traders from many other countries.

It is therefore necessary to have clearly in mind the idea of an overlap of periods. When Akbar died, the Mogul era still had much of its life and some of its most colourful and successful emperors to come—to say nothing of its cultural achievement. And, in a sense, the European era had already begun over a century before. But it was with the next emperor, Jahangir, that Europeans really began to appear at court.

(b) JAHANGIR 1605-1627

The accounts that were written of the lives of kings and emperors make it appear that for the Indian monarch, the pursuit of expensive pleasures was an important end and preoccupation of life. Pleasure was practised with the most concentrated application, and all efforts were bent to the procurement of the most talented singers, the most beautiful women, the most luxurious silks and shawls and brocades and carpets, the most perfect wine. This impression, if we get it sometimes, is exaggerated: the emperors could not have survived without a great deal of attention to the business of government, and there is plenty of evidence that all the more serious-minded rulers— Akbar for example—worked long hours seeing ministers, receiving reports from ambassadors and messengers, hearing cases in court, giving audiences to subjects who had grievances, dealing with administrative correspondence, inspecting the revenue organization, and so on; and his son and successor Jahangir seems to have had at least the ideal of steady work for much of his reign.

Nur Jahan

Jahangir, however, experienced a conflict between business and pleasure. It seems that he had the habit of drinking too much, which he was able to control only with difficulty, and as time went on he became less effective as a ruler. His Persian wife, Nur Jahan, came to have more and more influence in the running of the kingdom. Whatever the general position of women in Indian society may have been, there have been hen-pecked husbands, and doting ones, all

through history, in every society; and there was every possibility
that a woman could become the power behind the throne.

The empire

The empire suffered territorially too: in the South, a long and
indeterminate war to keep Ahmadnagar in the empire broke out, a
war which Jahangir's successors inherited; and there were losses to
the north-west. Rebelliousness and dissidence were common,
though not necessarily more common than in earlier or later
(including British) periods of Indian history.

The Europeans

It was during the reign of Jahangir that the activities of European
merchants began to involve the Dutch and the English directly
with the emperors. Through the previous century, the contacts had
been made by the Portuguese, with their trading settlements in
Bengal and on the southern coasts. At the end of the century,
England and Holland formed trading companies to carry on commerce with the East, and made attempts to get concessions for
themselves from the emperor. Two Englishmen spent periods at
Jahangir's court, representing the trading interests of the company
and hoping to get good terms from the emperor. For several years,
Hawkins, the first, was kept on at court as an attendant.

In 1615 Sir Thomas Roe came to negotiate for the English king
James I, in the hope of a treaty giving better trading conditions than
the English then had. And from about this time onwards, it is an
interesting feature of the doings and affairs of Indian rulers and
subjects that we have many descriptions from the pens of visiting
European traders. 'After he hath slept two hours they awake him
and bring his supper to him; at which time he is not able to feed
himself; but it is thrust into his mouth by others; and this is about
one of the clock; and then he sleepeth the rest of the night'. So wrote
Hawkins about the routine of Jahangir.

(c) SHAH JAHAN 1627–1658

Monuments

A group of tourists stands in the shadow of the Taj Mahal, the
great white mausoleum at Agra which every visitor to India wants
to see. The tourist guide has been answering questions all the time
so far, but now he has a question for his hearers: why is the Taj
Mahal so beautiful? This question has them rather baffled; they
weren't expecting to be asked the questions themselves. Several
suggestions are rather hesitantly made: the sense of proportion, the

inlay of semi-precious stones, the white marble. But the guide will accept none of these. The answer, he thinks, is a different sort of answer from anything like this. The Taj Mahal is so beautiful, he says, because it was built in memory of a beautiful woman.

It is an attractive answer, and easy to accept, though perhaps it is not very logical. The Taj Mahal was the work of an architect, in one sense—though we do not know the names of the architects employed in the building of the great Mogul monuments. But in another sense it was the work of the emperor Shah Jahan's love for his wife, the queen Mumtaz Mahal, who died in 1631. And it shows something about emperors such as Shah Jahan: that all the resources of the kingdom were poured into the gratification of their private wants, so that they could write their personalities across the page of history in gigantic characters. They could do it in a squalid, wretched way, with gigantic quantities of alcohol or opium. Or they could do it in a splendid way, with gigantic beauty. The Taj Mahal is splendid.

Marvellous though it is, and enormous though the quantities of wealth that went to make it possible were, it is only one item in a considerable programme financed by Shah Jahan, which produced some of the jewels of Muslim architecture. New buildings and re-building at Agra produced fine creations, with a liberal partiality for white marble. A great new undertaking was a fresh capital city, Shahjahanabad, the Old Delhi of today. No emperor was kinder to the architect.

Economic conditions

It is a question whether famines in general were as bad in those times as they were, say, in the nineteenth century, or today. Food could not then be transported freely about the subcontinent, for there were no railways whereby grain could be carried rapidly from an area of surplus to an area of deficit. On the other hand, some of the conditions that aggravate famine were not present then so much as later. Pressure on available land was not so great; family holdings were not so much subdivided; the coming of a money economy (stimulated by European commercial activities) had not diverted much of the agrarian population to growing new crops or following new livelihoods for profit in money, rather than farming for subsistence. These are things that have tended to make famines worse.

Certainly, all was not well with the economy or with the imperial organization of it. Shah Jahan's was a reign in which the salaries of his officers and the taxes on his subjects alike went up, causing hardship to cultivators, who found it difficult to make ends meet and often tried to migrate elsewhere. In the India of those days, a famine, or high taxation in a particular province, or the activities of roving robber bands, or any of various other causes could depopulate whole regions.

The empire

Territorially, Shah Jahan's reign seemed to see an improvement in the condition of his empire. He reversed some of the losses of his predecessor. In campaigns to the south, besides Ahmadnagar, he scored victories over Bijapur and Golconda, though these two, also Muslim kingdoms whose lands had once been parts of the Bahmani domain, kept their rulers. But significant for the future, in a way that nobody at the time could foresee, were some concessions that did not look to him like concessions at all. They looked like good trading arrangements. These were the rights given to European powers to establish settlements on the Hooghly river, on the Ganges Delta.

This followed the destruction of a previous Portuguese settlement there, which was trading slaves and causing trouble, and was over-run with great slaughter. Other powers came to fill the gap. The English and the Dutch built settlements, up the river from Calcutta, and in the following reign the English were allowed to build a fort. This fort, though nobody knew it, was like the thin end of a wedge that was to drive right through India.

(d) AURANGZEB 1658-1707

Aurangzeb was the last of the four great Moguls whose names are often linked together—Akbar, Jahangir, Shah Jahan, Aurangzeb. And in the company of these other three many-hued characters, Aurangzeb usually suffers from a comparison.

He ought, however, to receive more credit than is usually given him, for he was certainly one of the most capable of the Muslim rulers. He was diligent, self-disciplined, thoroughly conscientious, and—in terms of the standards prevalent during his own times—just. If he was hostile to the Hindus (which is anyway controversial), this was his religious duty as he saw it. He had a suspicious mind; but he was quite right to be suspicious, because everybody around him was unreliable. There is something to admire in the spectacle of this seasoned and tireless man, even in his eighties, going about an empire that was collapsing at every point and, by his own skill and almost unaided, holding it up.

Government

At the beginning of his reign, Aurangzeb had to struggle with three other princes for the throne, and imprisoned his own father.

Late in his reign, he had to contend with a rebellion by his son. Such things were common: a monarch could not rest, and there was no security for him anywhere.

We should not wonder then that he showed himself suspicious of everybody, frequently moving people out of their jobs, not letting anybody accumulate much power and influence in any position. Taken to extremes, this attitude could only be harmful to the government of the country. The nobles, in cliques, were at logger-heads with each other, and constructive advice was difficult to get. Policies were therefore inconsistent; administration suffered. Taxation was oppressive, conditions in the countryside were bad. Dacoits (robber bands) were rife.

The Empire

Aurangzeb, like most Muslim rulers, was well occupied during his reign with wars, which he waged in several directions. In particular, he had dealings with some of the Rajput kingdoms in the west of India. Marwar he took in 1678, but he became involved in conflicts on various fronts in the course of which his son Akbar rebelled and took sides with the Rajputs. Fighting in the area continued through his reign, on and off, indeterminately. After 1681 he went south in person to supervise affairs, and wherever he went, things were done effectively, but everywhere else the general atmosphere of apathy and self-interest caused the government to suffer.

The Prince Akbar was no match for his father's ability and one rebellion at least was quelled. Some years later, striking south, Aurangzeb took Golconda and Bijapur, the two kingdoms which his predecessor had also overrun, but which had kept their own rulers.

To the north-east, Aurangzeb made persistent attempts to annex Assam; in 1666 he overran Chittagong. To the north-west, he had trouble in the early 1670s with the turbulent tribes of the Afghan heights who lived by plunder.

An emperor any less fit, alert and energetic than Aurangzeb would never have survived. Unable to trust anybody else, he was leading his army in person, and winning, when over the age of eighty. After his death, however, there was no power to hold together the crumbling empire, and disintegration followed.

(e) THE RISE OF NEW POWERS

The break-up of the empire

Through the eighteenth century, what had been the empire became a confused mêlée of competing kingdoms. There are two processes to note in this development: the transformation of ministers or governors into kings, and the growth of Hindu powers.

The separate provinces of the empire had been under representatives appointed by the emperor. These naturally had considerable powers in the running of government, for Delhi might be far away, and communications were erratic. These people were powerful men, maybe even descendants of former kings who had submitted to the Moguls, and if they were not influential and wealthy when they became governors or ministers, they used their positions to become so. These positions tended to be hereditary, the office passing from father to son. And so when the empire was weak, with no great change beyond their ceasing to pass on large quantities of revenue to Delhi, these men turned into kings.

The Hindu powers

For long, the rulers of most of India had been Muslims. Yet by the time the British began to penetrate inland, they found an India that was like a patchwork quilt of powers, some Muslim, some Hindu.

There are three groups of Hindu powers to notice: the far South, the Rajputs, and the Marathas.

There had always been Hindu rulers in the far South. The empire of Vijayanagar had given way to other powers, notably the Polygars who maintained independence from the empire through its days of power. During the eighteenth century, adventurers and princelings were setting up kingdoms everywhere, and Muslims set up regimes over most of the South; by the end of the century, Travancore (to the extreme south west, the southern part of modern Kerala) and Tanjore (in the south-east of the peninsula) were the only significant Hindu powers left. But further north, by compensation—and perhaps we can see it partly as a reaction against the anti-Hinduism of the later Mogul rulers—there was a great resurgence of Hindu powers.

The Rajputs in the north-west, in the area of Rajasthan, we have already noticed. They were various small kingdoms under Hindu rulers all claiming to be ksatriyas, and many of them were incorporated in the Muslim empires but kept their own governments and other institutions. We have seen how they joined together under leaders to resist invaders at the end of the Sultanate. They were a sort of confederacy.

Adjoining the area under Rajput domination, by the end of the eighteenth century, was a vast segment of India, stretching across to the east coast, under the Maratha confederacy.

The career of the Marathas was one of the most important developments of the period between Mogul and British domination. They started some time before, in quite a small way. Several things held them together, even when they had spread out and become a major part of the Indian political map: the Hindu faith, the Marathi language—in which there came to be a cherished literature, notably the songs of Tukaram—and the successful career of the founder of Marathi power, Sivaji (1627–80), an adventurer who took advantage of the troubled times to become effectively a ruler. He began as a sort of tax-farmer—a local man of influence collecting the revenue for the empire and passing on the stipulated amounts—in a region on the west coast, south of Bombay, from which the area of his power, and that of his followers, steadily grew. He engaged in wars against the Muslim power of Bijapur, and suffered a defeat at the hands of the Mogul forces; he went to Agra, fell into disfavour, was arrested, and escaped. In 1674 he had himself crowned king, and died some years later after further wars.

As the Mogul empire crumbled, a gap appeared, a power vacuum, from which Sivaji and his followers and successors benefited. The empire was not able to secure law and order for its subjects; the Marathas were: and even while the empire was still present in the area in substance and collecting its taxes, the Marathas were collecting their own in the same villages, customarily demanding for themselves a quarter of the sums due in official taxation. After Sivaji's death, the Marathas continued to be a growing menace, and Aurangzeb's attempts to quell them met with only very partial success; they carried on small-scale warfare, ambushing here, skirmishing there, and never facing up to the imperial troops in large numbers with a risk of being crushed. Through the eighteenth century the area of their territory increased enormously, and they ceased to be just one power: they became a confederacy of small-scale rulers, keeping order in their own areas and bringing extreme disorder to adjoining areas, such as (eventually) Bengal, where they raided and plundered savagely. The original line of Maratha rulers lost their power, but their prime ministers—Peshwas—became hereditary, the office passing from father to son. Eventually, they were the real leaders of the Marathas.

The end of the Moguls

This was the India into which the Mogul empire disintegrated, with its long history of Muslim rule behind it and its memories of past glories. It would not be quite right to say that it actually came to an end at any particular point, unless we take the story right up to 1858 when the British put the last emperor on trial for his part in the Indian Mutiny, but it turned into a ghost. In 1739 there was a Persian invasion, as a result of which large north-western provinces were lost. The empire was vastly weaker than it had been for a long time, and though it was able to cope, to some extent, with attacks from Afghans (now unified under a single leader), it was now not the master of all kingdoms but one of them, intriguing with the rest for the purposes of war and friendship. In 1761 the overmighty Marathas were defeated at Panipat. But the emperor, Shah Alam, was destined to lose the powers of government and become a guest or pensioner of the British, the most important new power.

CHAPTER NINE

The Origins of Empire

(a) THE PORTUGUESE

The trade motive

Among the new powers in India were some who did not at first interest themselves very much in the politics of the Indian rulers. Their territories, if they cculd be called territories, were small bits of land on which they erected settlements. There were two developments which made them less like visitors and more like local powers: they started building forts at some of their settlements for the purpose of self-defence; and they were in some cases given the revenues from a few surrounding villages to meet the costs of running their establishments. But even with this they were not really local powers: they had to get permission to build forts, and the revenues from villages were not taxes that they levied as rulers; they were grants made by the local ruler, who could take them back at will, in theory.

These newcomers were of course the Portuguese, the Dutch, the English, the French, and the Danes—though the Danes do not come into the picture very much. The Europeans were not at first participants in the drama of Indian history; they stood at the edge of the stage, and though they were there from the end of the fifteenth century it was not until the eighteenth that they strode out upon the scene, taking some of the best lines for themselves.

Why was it not until this time that they became important in the affairs of India? Or why did they become important at all?

Because they were traders, they did not want to take part in politics. Some of them came as representatives of their governments, some of them as merchants, as private enterprise, but what both the governments and the merchants wanted from India was profit, not power. The upholding of power is an expensive business. The Portuguese who came first came as a state enterprise, as government servants, seeking to give the Portuguese government control over the Eastern trade. The French who came later were members of a trading company set up on government initiative, largely with government money. The Dutch and the British came as members of

120

associations of merchants. The associations had to get charters from their governments to allow them to seek a part in Asian commerce, but they were nevertheless private merchants. But all of these alike came with the idea of getting some of the profit from the trade that had previously been taken by others such as Arabs who handled it along the route, and all alike had the interest and backing of their governments. Like the Portuguese and French, the Dutch and British governments became intimately involved in the affairs of the subcontinent. Considerations of national prestige and military strategy increasingly attracted European rivalries into new theatres of activity. Power and trade were inseparable. So the company merchants, of various nationalities, were also the representatives of their countries' interests.

Increasingly, however, the Europeans came to take a greater part in the affairs of India, taking part in the intrigues among princes and supporting their own candidates for this or that throne. And from activities of this sort grew the eventual dominion of the British over most of the subcontinent.

The Portuguese traders

The Portuguese were well placed to take advantage of the new discoveries and inventions of the fifteenth century which made possible the exploitation of fresh trade routes previously unknown Their position on the Atlantic and their traditions of seafaring stood them in good stead when America was discovered and voyages of discovery, trade and settlement began. It is worth remembering that, when the Portuguese and others first started exploring seriously to the West, what they hoped for was that they would find a new route around the world to the spice islands of south-east Asia—not realizing that the American continent and a great ocean stood between the Atlantic and their objective. That was why the West Indies were so called: they were at first believed to be part of the same group as the islands of modern Indonesia.

Exploration to the East was also pioneered by the Portuguese. Diaz sailed south and rounded the Cape of Good Hope in his historic voyage of 1486–88. In 1498 Vasco da Gama reached the Malabar coast, the south-west coast of India, by the same route. 'What have you come for?' they asked him. 'Christians and spices' was the reply.

This reply points to the two main motives that brought the Portuguese across the seas to Asia. Trade was the essential one, but the keen missionary spirit of zealous Christians was the driving force behind much activity. Jesuits were among the first European visitors, and Akbar himself met them, and invited them to his religious conferences along with representatives of the other faiths.

But spices and some other commodities were what the Portuguese government wanted most. They were anxious to create a new seaborne trade by which the jewels, silks, pepper, cloves, nutmeg and so on of Asia would be carried in their ships round the south of Africa and to Europe.

Previously the trade had passed by a partly overland route, across the Arabian Sea to the Persian Gulf or the Red Sea ports, from where it was carried through Arab lands to Egypt or Syria on the Mediterranean; the last part of the route was dominated at the end of the Middle Ages by Italians. West of India, the trade was largely in Arab hands, and it was the Portuguese ambition to break the Arab domination. This meant getting possession of the chief ports on the route—in India, and in the Persian Gulf.

Albuquerque

The renowned Albuquerque was the first Governor in the East appointed to conduct Portugal's affairs in Asian waters. He held the office from 1509 to 1515, and succeeded in taking Ormuz, at the entrance to the Persian Gulf, Goa, on the west coast of India, and Malacca, on the Malay Peninsula—a particularly important port controlling the collection and distribution of spices in the south-east Asian islands. India was thus, for Portugal, valuable chiefly as the site of trading posts on the route from further east, and as a base from which to enforce the monopoly that Portugal desired.

Trading posts were established in Bengal and on the Coromandel coast—the south-east coast of India. Chittagong, by the Ganges delta, and Daman and Diu, on the Gulf of Cambay in the west, were among other settlements set up by the Portuguese. Both their missionary spirit and their desire to break the power of Muslims handling the international trade brought them into conflict with the Muslims, though relations with the Hindus were usually amicable. In general, though the ideal was peaceful trade, the quest for complete Portuguese control of it led to many conflicts, and their career in India was marked by violence—sometimes provoked by themselves, sometimes provoked by ambitious or capricious governors or rulers. The zeal of the Portuguese to win Christian converts led to friction and conflict, and did not serve the ends of peaceful trade. In this the Portuguese may be contrasted with the Dutch and British, whose activities were not inspired by the same missionary spirit and who therefore did not provoke conflict in the same way.

As relations with the Indians were not always peaceful, the habit of building forts at trading settlements began. The Portuguese built, or sought to build, quite a number at their south-east Asian settlements, for the islands there were the chief scene of their activities;

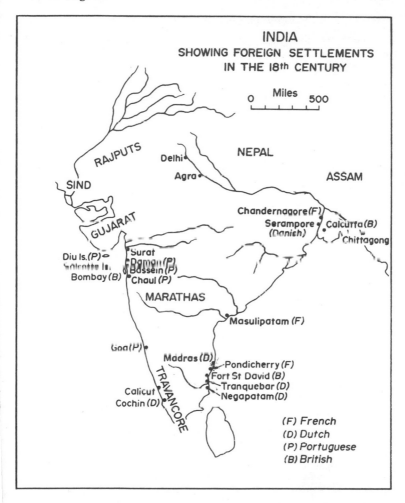

INDIA
SHOWING FOREIGN SETTLEMENTS
IN THE 18th CENTURY

0   Miles   500

RAJPUTS   Delhi   NEPAL

SIND   Agra   ASSAM

GUJARAT

Chandernagore (F)
Serampore (Danish)   Calcutta (B)
Chittagong

Diu Is. (P)   Surat
Salsette Is.   Daman (P)
Bombay (B)   Bassein (P)
Chaul (P)

MARATHAS

Masulipatam (F)

Goa (P)

Madras (D)
Pondicherry (F)
Fort St David (B)
Calicut   Tranquebar (D)
Cochin (D)   Negapatam (D)

TRAVANCORE

(F) French
(D) Dutch
(P) Portuguese
(B) British

in India also the building of forts seemed desirable, not necessarily
as a defence against the ruler of the territory in which it was placed,
but chiefly as a defence against local marauders against whom the
ruler might well have too little power to defend the traders. As
competition between European powers developed, the Westerners
came to need forts as defences against each other. There was no idea
of setting up governments in them and becoming territorial rulers.
But nevertheless the forts and settlements became the seeds from
which territorial dominion grew.

(b) THE DUTCH, BRITISH AND FRENCH

The sixteenth century belonged to the Portuguese. They established themselves at settlements placed in commanding positions all along the routes to the spice islands. With their fleet they could exact submission from a raja in India or a sultan in the Indies. But their heyday could not last, for various reasons: their numerical weakness, which told against them in the end in the competition with other European powers; their oppressive policies in Asia; their over-anxiety to get a monopoly of the trade; their union in 1580 with the kingdom of Spain, after which Portuguese interests in Asian waters took second place to Spanish interests. In the seventeenth century it was the Dutch who made the running, and after them the English.

The Dutch came into existence as a separate country by rebellion against Spain, and the English were traditional enemies of Spain also. The two countries ought to have been natural allies, having a common enemy; but as the century wore on, there was more and more friction between them. In Asia, they were both after the same thing—trading power; and as competitors the Dutch and English in Asia were increasingly hostile to each other, more so sometimes than their home governments who were nominally allies for a great part of the time. During at least the first half of the seventeenth century the chief rivals for power in Asia were the Portuguese and Dutch, but by the eighteenth century the importance of the Portuguese had waned and the Dutch and English jostled for the position of major power.

India and the spice islands

The chief focus of interest for the Portuguese, Dutch and English alike was at first the Indonesian islands. Two things led to a continuing interest in having Indian trading settlements, however: the need for bases in the area from which to conduct naval activities if necessary; and the Indian export of (among other things) cloth. Yarn, sugar, saltpetre used for gunpowder, indigo in large quantities, calico for the markets of Europe—all these things came from India, and more besides, but the merchants, intent on the island spice trade, were especially interested in the fact that from India they could obtain all manner of cloths which they could exchange in south-east Asia for the spices that they wanted above all. It was a very profitable and convenient arrangement.

Another reason why the English became especially interested in India was simply that the Dutch beat them in the competition for trade monopoly in the spice islands of south-east Asia, and India was second best. In the course of time, the spice trade declined in value, and India became much more profitable, so that it was perhaps a blessing in disguise for the English that the Dutch were ahead of them in the islands.

Factories

Various settlements were established by both countries in India. These were called 'factories', but are not to be confused with factories in the modern sense of the word. They were not places of manufacture. They were centres where goods were assembled for shipment. Agents of the companies who lived at the factories were able to buy the goods at their leisure, choosing the times when they were cheapest, and store them for loading when the companies' ships called.

In the early years of the seventeenth century, the Dutch obtained permission to build factories at a number of places in India, in Gujarat and on the Coromandel (south-east) coast. Inland, at Agra, a subsidiary establishment was set up to conduct trading. Not far behind them were the English. Permission was obtained for a factory at Surat, and another followed later at Masulipatam, north of Madras. In the Bay of Bengal, Portuguese freebooters, unsupported by the Portuguese government, were pursuing remarkable careers of piracy and brigandage on the high seas, and the Portuguese settlement in Bengal was, it appeared, co-operating with them in the slave trade. This led Shah Jahan to destroy the settlement, and in its place came English, Dutch and Danish settlements on the Hooghly. In 1639, the English gained permission to have a fort at Madras.

Two developments in the middle of the century were of importance to England's interests—the war between England and Holland which broke out in 1652, and the acquisition of Bombay which came as a dowry from Portugal when the king of England took a Portuguese bride. This was an outright possession, not a concession from a local ruler, and together with Madras and Bengal, Bombay was to be one of the three presidencies from which the British government of India was to develop. It was not long before Charles II transferred Bombay to the British East India Company in exchange for money.

The French

Portuguese strongholds were lost one by one through the early and middle part of the century, and after the Anglo-Dutch war the situation in India was clearer: a straight-out conflict between the Dutch and the English. But a third competitor soon came to join the fray: the French, with a government-inspired company formed to trade in the Eastern seas founded in 1674. Three years later, a French settlement was started at Pondicherry—a snippet of coastline on the Coromandel coast which, like the Portuguese possessions on the west, was to remain a colonial possession right through the days of

British expansion, right through the era of the British raj, and into the time of Indian independence.

Bengal

In the confused condition of India, particularly in the latter days of the Mogul empire, an agreement with a ruler that a factory could be set up was not enough to guarantee the factory's security. The king might be unable to prevent raiders from outside, or robber bands, or even his own officials, from harassing the factory, looting it, maybe even destroying it. It was no wonder then that the European trading companies with settlements in India often sought the right to build forts at the sites of their factories. An attack in 1686 by the Mogul governor on the British settlement on the Hooghly, in Bengal, led to a war with the local powers, following which agreement was reached, and eventually the European powers with settlements on the river all obtained the right to build forts. The assignment of the revenue of some villages for the maintenance of the fort made possible the expansion of the British settlement, which, as Fort William, was to become the hub of administration for the Bengal presidency. This was the beginning of the process by which the merchants increasingly became territorial powers with an interest in securing control of the land around their settlements and an involvement in local politics. They were not given sovereign control over pieces of land, but they were awarded local grants (firmans or perwannahs), usually by the Mogul emperor but sometimes by Nawabs, semi-independent officers of the emperor, by which revenue from land passed into European hands.

The Company, as time went on, was to become less and less like an association of merchants, and more and more like a government: its soldiers were its own, and not soldiers of the British king, and it had its own judges and magistrates and policemen.

(c) CLIVE AND THE FRENCH

The eighteenth century

At the beginning of the eighteenth century, there were thus several European countries interested in India, the chief among them being Britain and France. Each was represented by a company. The European powers were concerned chiefly to make profits from the trade between different parts of Asia. Their activities were merchant activities; they wanted to make profits because their representatives were merchants, and it is part of the business of a merchant to make profits. We should not blame the British and French and the others for doing what all merchants do, or for not doing for the Indians what governments are today expected to do.

The behaviour of the Europeans cannot be properly understood unless we take into account the fact that they were not there as regular well-paid civil servants securely in control of a British possession. They were, on the contrary, very badly paid. They were in a strange land that they often did not understand, and in which they were foreigners who were distrusted. They were afflicted with fearful diseases that gave every one of them a substantial chance of early death. They lived then in a precarious situation where it was natural, praiseworthy or not, to seek ways of making money that were rather dubious. At any rate, whatever standard we judge them by it should not be the same that we apply to their more secure nineteenth-century successors.

This is not to say, of course, that the British and others lived in poverty. Many of them learned how to make fortunes and those that did were able to live like kings. An extract from a book of travels published towards the end of the eighteenth century, describing the life of an Englishman in Bengal, will show something of the quality of their life:

'About the hour of seven in the morning, his durwan [doorkeeper] opens the gate and the viranda [gallery] is free to his circars, peons [footmen], hurcarrahs [messengers or spies], chubdars [a kind of constable], houccaburdars and consumahs [stewards and butlers], writers and solicitors. The head bearer and jemmadar enter the hall and his bedroom at eight o'clock. A lady quits his side and is conducted by a private staircase, either to her own apartment, or out of the yard. The moment the master throws his legs out of the bed, the whole force is waiting to rush into his room, each making three salaams, by bending the body and head very low, and touching the forehead with the inside of the fingers and the floor with the back part. He condescends, perhaps, to nod or cast an eye towards the solicitors of his favour and protection. In about half an hour after undoing and taking off his long drawers, a clean shirt, breeches, stockings, and slippers are put upon his body, thighs, legs and feet, without any greater exertion on his own part than if he was a statue. The barber enters, shaves him, cuts his nails, and cleans his ears. The chillumjee and ewer are brought by a servant whose duty it is, who pours water upon his hands and face, and presents a towel. The superior then walks in state to his breakfasting parlour in his waistcoat; is seated; the consumah makes and pours out his tea, and presents him with a plate of bread or toast. The hair-dresser comes behind, and begins his operation, while the houccaburdar softly slips the upper end of the snake or tube of the hucca into his hand; while the hair-dresser is doing his duty, the gentleman is eating, sipping and smoking by turns. By and by his banian presents himself with humble salaams and advances somewhat more forward than the other attendants. If any of the solicitors are of eminence, they are honoured with chairs. These ceremonies are continued perhaps till 10 o'clock.'*

At the end of the eighteenth century, the British were firmly entrenched as one of the major powers in India, along with the Marathas, who were the major Indian power. Others, such as the Rajputs and Mysore, also competed. There had been great changes during the century. The British—the Company, not the British government—had possessions in Bengal (the largest), Madras and Bombay, and these three, in the north-east, west and south-east of India were the presidencies from which the British territorial power grew. They had armies and courts and tax collectors in all three places. They had the British government watching over the activities of the Company and a High Court in Bengal administering English law as well as the Company's own courts. What had happened to make this change possible?

Two conditions were necessary before the British could become the paramount power in India. One was that India should be weak and divided. The other was that Britain's rivals should not be strong enough in India to hinder the development of British influence. The eighteenth century provided both these conditions. We have seen how the Mogul empire, the one force that could have kept Europe out on the fringes of power, gradually fell apart. India reverted to a state of weakness and division. And as for Britain's rivals, the Portuguese were nowhere, the Danes didn't count, and the Dutch were preoccupied with their possessions and the spice trade in south-east Asia, so that it was left to the British and French to fight it out.

On the French side, Dupleix, Governor of Pondicherry from 1742, outmanoeuvred his opponents time and time again, and dreamed of a French empire in India. On the British side, Robert Clive was an outstandingly successful soldier as well as a skilful politician, and his country owed more to him than to anybody else for its success in the contest with the French. But it was more than a matter of individual abilities: the French were handicapped by their government's involvement in affairs elsewhere and lack of determination to win in

* Quoted in Percival Spear, *The Nabobs* (London, Oxford University Press 1963), p 53.

India, by lack of funds, and by lack of ships. These handicaps left Britain in a strong position to begin her climb to a paramount position in the whole of India.

The first war

In 1744, the War of Austrian Succession in Europe brought England and France to war with each other. In India, the gloves were off, and from 1746 to 1748 there was war between the British at Madras and the French at Pondicherry further south along the coast. Dupleix as the French Governor was in control of strategy on the French side; on the British, Clive was not yet prominent. Fleets raced between Pondicherry, Madras and Bengal, as if in musical chairs, and the French were getting the upper hand when the war was called off. The chief significance of the war is in what followed it.

In the first place, it became obvious to the Indians that European (or at least French) armies—or armies of Indians trained by Westerners even—were very much more effective than Indian armies. The army of the Nawab of the Carnatic had been unable to save Madras for the British. This point was not lost on the Indians, who were increasingly to turn to the Europeans for alliance, so involving them in Indian affairs. In the second place, when the war finished, Dupleix was left with troops on his hands who could be used for other purposes. These purposes, in line with his ambitions for French empire, were to show French power among the rulers of the land and, by skilful diplomacy, to extend French influence over Indian territory.

The second war

His method was to intrigue with the state of Hyderabad; as was common, there were disputed claims to the throne. The French backed one candidate against another; their candidate naturally won, and for their trouble the French were rewarded with nominal powers over part of the ruler's territory—the Carnatic, which contained the British settlement of Madras. More significantly, in 1753 the Frenchman Bussy gained control over the Northern Sarkars (or Circars). The British were not content with this situation, and the years 1751–54 saw renewed fighting among the British, the French and the local powers, in the early part of which Clive distinguished himself by gaining and holding Arcot. Honours were balanced when Dupleix was recalled to France and his successor made peace.

Calcutta

After two years in England, Clive returned to India as an officer in the King's army (previously he had been in the Company's) in 1755, and was therefore in a position to take a hand after the notorious incident of the Black Hole of Calcutta.

What happened was that in 1756 the new ruler of Bengal, the Nawab—theoretically an official of the Mogul emperor, but actually independent—set upon the British fort at Calcutta; those who had not fled were imprisoned overnight in a dungeon of the fort; they were fantastically overcrowded, and most of them died. There has been much debate among historians about the truth of this incident, and it has even been denied that it took place. It seems quite likely that the Nawab personally was not responsible for the deaths. It is possible to see the attack on the fort either as a piece of unprovoked villainy, or as a reasonable precaution to take against a nest of foreigners who seemed to be getting very arrogant towards the Nawab, refused to take any notice of what he said, and in constructing fortifications were probably, in his eyes, planning mischief against him. It depends on one's point of view. Either way, the treatment of the prisoners was particularly inhuman. It brought a force from Madras under Clive, who defeated the Nawab and recovered Calcutta. The Seven Years' War had broken out in Europe, making France and Britain enemies once again; in Bengal, Clive scored a victory by overrunning the French settlement at Chandernagore, north of Calcutta.

Mir Jafar

Further involvement with the Indian powers in Bengal followed. Playing the same game that the French had initiated in Hyderabad, the Company gave its support to a candidate for the position of Nawab in Bengal—a courtier named Mir Jafar, who saw a chance for himself in the confused situation in Bengal and the unpopularity of the present Nawab, who was not showing sufficient favours to the great men of the land. It was a rather doubtful piece of intriguing, but quite in line with the conduct of political affairs in India at the time. Clive's part in it came under attack later: for one thing, he was said to have accepted a fortune as bribe, and for another he was said to have brought round one influential Indian, Ormichand, by showing him a false document leading him to believe that the Mir Jafar plot would benefit him. The case against Clive is that he was unscrupulous and corrupt. The case for him was that, for the benefit of the Company's affairs, he was using methods that everybody else in India was using. 'When in Rome, do as the Romans do'. But his critics in England thought otherwise. At all events, good or bad, the strategy was successful; at the renowned battle of Plassey, in 1757, Clive led a small army of 3,000 against a large one of 50,000, under the Nawab. Much of the Nawab's army took no part in the fighting, being commanded by Mir Jafar, for whose benefit Clive was undertaking the adventure. The result was that the Nawab was routed and Mir Jafar installed in his place. Clive became Governor for the Company from 1758 to 1760.

The Company did not then stand aside from the affairs of the Nawab. Mir Jafar was distrusted and suspected of intriguing with the Dutch, who in 1759 attacked the British in Bengal. The Dutch were thwarted and Mir Jafar was ousted, to be replaced as Nawab by Mir Kasim.

However, Mir Kasim was no more congenial to the British than his predecessor had been. Trouble was caused by his attempt to end the position of privilege enjoyed by the British Company employees, who had the right to carry on trade without having to pay internal customs dues. This right was known as *dastak*. Mir Kasim tried to abolish the privilege, not by removing *dastak*, but by extending it to everybody, so that the British lost their advantage. This move created tension. In 1763 there broke out the Patna war, in which British forces from Calcutta were involved in the defence of the British settlement at Patna, in Bihar, and in 1764 defeated the Nawab of neighbouring Oudh as well as Mir Kasim. An unlooked-for embarrassment was the presence of the Mogul emperor among the defeated Indians at the battle of Buxar. In the settlement that followed in 1765 he was given a piece of territory containing Allahabad in which to maintain his dignity. Mir Jafar was re-installed as Nawab of Bengal.

The North-East was not the only scene of involvement. In the South-East, war had started again with the French in 1758, leading to French defeats at Wandiwash and at Pondicherry itself. Clive attempted to extend British influence by bargaining with local powers, and eventually the Carnatic was gained for the Company.

Years of confused fighting and intriguing in the South followed. The fighting and intriguing do not matter to us: all the parties involved changed sides according to the advantage they saw for themselves in this or that combination or alliance, and succeeded in bewildering each other. What is significant is that, starting from a desire for secure settlements, an attachment to its privileges, and anxiety to forestall the French, the Company had become deeply implicated in the politics of the Indian rulers, and could not escape the responsibilities of being itself an Indian power. If this were a history of the British empire, the work of Clive would deserve detailed study, because he was one of the chief architects of that empire in India. In a history of India, however, it is the work of Warren Hastings that must get most attention. More than anybody else in the early period of British influence, Warren Hastings helped to mould the form of government and administration that was to affect the lives of millions.

(d) WARREN HASTINGS, GOVERNOR-GENERAL 1774–85

Warren Hastings was Governor of the large territories held by Britain in the North-East of India and Governor-General of the British possessions in India as a whole. His career in India marks the beginning of the process by which the British government took firm control over the administration of the Indian possessions. Hastings was the first Governor-General appointed under the terms of an Act of Parliament designed to regulate the running of the East India Company. That is, the government was taking an important step towards supplanting the Company as the effective authority.

Further, the career of Hastings is important because it marks also the beginning of a process by which the administration was reformed and made more efficient. For the Company, profit-making was the main concern; governing the territory it controlled was incidental. Therefore, when Warren Hastings arrived, the administration was not streamlined, or efficient, or particularly honest and public-spirited. When he left, he had done a great deal to root out the abuses and create a workable government machine. But it was only a beginning, as he himself acknowledged.

Again, his career is important because, while he was Governor-General, it really became clear in India that the British were the most powerful force to be reckoned with—not masters of the entire subcontinent, certainly, but an active power that could, and did, use force to settle the conflicts between other powers to its own taste. Accordingly, many of the Indian rulers looked to the British for support in their dealings with each other.

So it is not surprising that this man, Warren Hastings, should have been the subject of such close attention by historians, or that his career should have been dissected and assessed from all points of view. But the controversy about him stems not only from his political achievements but also from the passions he stirred in those about him. Antipathies were brought out into the open. Private thoughts were spoken. Cut off from the cultural life of the England they had left behind, people occupied themselves with forming groups and plotting against each other.

The result was that the story of India's early British rulers is a splendid and complex narrative of intrigue and eloquence, conflict and invective, a game where careers and reputations were the stakes. And when the personalities included men with the genius and character of Hastings, the story takes on a special grandeur. It is not the bare achievements of Hastings' governorship that give to it its flavour. It is the skill with which he planned his reforms, the difficulties he had to overcome, the opposition he had to face from men all around him, his patience, his ability, his integrity and his moments of weakness, his arrogance and haughtiness with their compensating charm. It is the fierce conflicts of men deeply committed to their objectives. It is the struggle for honour and the fight for survival.

The beginnings of Hastings' career

Warren Hastings began his career in the employment of the Company as writer, a fairly humble position. By the time he was forty years old, he was Governor of Bengal. This success he owed to the ability and honesty that he showed in the Company's service.

He was honest, certainly, but this does not mean that he did not take part in the various practices by which the British in India were able to make a lot of money on the side, though legally. He started with a salary of £5 a year. When, in 1765, he returned to England for a spell, he had amassed a fortune of £30,000, most of which he lost in the next few years. Government service does not offer such opportunities nowadays.

In his first position, as writer, he was in charge of warehouse organization, a job he did efficiently. Later, he had political experience as resident of Mir Jafar, the ruler set up in office after Plassey. In 1761 he joined the Presidency Council at Calcutta. After his spell in England, he returned to the Company's service and went to Madras, where his administrative ability was recognized. In 1772 he was brought back to Calcutta to take on (after a short period as second-in-command) the arduous governorship of Bengal. It was arduous particularly because conditions were very bad at that time in the Presidency of Bengal. Poor organization, much dishonesty and corruption, and a recent famine, had seriously impaired the administration and the finances of the Company. Hastings was expected to put the organization of the administration on a sound footing, in firm control of the revenue, and stamp out the various dishonest practices that were all too easy for Company servants to engage in.

Early reforms

Hastings made a vigorous start on the task of re-organization. He was able to achieve a great deal in the first two years, but from 1774 onwards he was preoccupied with the difficulties created by the establishment of a new Council, under his chairmanship, to stand at the head of the Bengal government. However, the reforms that he was able to effect, though they did not give the government the complete overhaul it needed, were a good start. Something was done to abolish the abuses that went with private trading by the British officials. Something was done about the monopolies of trade in some commodities enjoyed—and abused—by various Company men.

The collection of revenue in Bengal was complicated by the fact that there was not just one legal authority in the territory. There were three. These were the Company, the British government, and the native ruler (the Nawab). In theory, the Mogul emperor was the sovereign ruler, the legal head of state, with the Nawab as his representative. Therefore, in theory, the taxes were collected on his behalf. Payments were indeed made to the emperor until 1773, when he came under Maratha influence. The British government did not yet claim any sovereign power in India. The Company could not, because it was basically a commercial organization, not a government.

This meant that the revenue collection was not something created and controlled by the British. It was an Indian system, rooted in Indian customs and institutions. The taxes were collected in practice by the wealthy zamindars, Indians who had the hereditary right to collect the taxes from their areas and passed on agreed sums to the Company. This whole system was difficult, or indeed impossible, to unscramble or to put under entirely British administration. Only men on the spot could know whether the right amount was being paid in each particular village, and there were not enough British officers to staff the entire revenue system. It therefore remained largely in Indian hands, and it was difficult to tell how much of the taxes collected was actually passed on. It is likely that a lot stuck to the hands of the zamindars.

Further, it was difficult to ensure that the treatment of villagers was fair. However, Warren Hastings did what he could to build safeguards around the collection system. For a time, English collectors were established in charge, though it was found necessary to revert to Indian officers (*amils* and *diwans*). Steps were taken to prevent abuses by the English staff. Private trading and landholding were forbidden. Zamindars held their tax farming rights for limited periods only.

Another source of inefficiency and injustice was private trading by the Company's servants. They had the right to carry on trade in India without paying any local customs dues on their goods. Therefore they could carry goods for other people, and charge money for doing so. (This was the practice called *dastak*.) Hastings abolished it.

Monopolies were another source of abuses. Various Company servants held the sole trading rights in certain commodities. This

SCENES BY NINETEENTH CENTURY ARTISTS

Government House, by James Fraser, 1824

River and shipping near Smith's Dock. One of Fraser's
views of Calcutta

The terraces (ghats) on the Ganges at Benares. They look
similar today

Colonial arcl:
ture: the lodg
the Governor
General at Sir
It now houses
research instit

Trichinopoly: Rock fort and lake by Clive's house

meant that they were the only people able to distribute and sell their goods, and they were able to ask high prices because there was nobody in competition with them. This was an unhealthy situation, which Hastings did much to improve.

The Regulating Act and the new Council

From 1774 onwards Hastings was not only Governor of Bengal but Governor-General of the British territories in India. This meant that he had supervision of the presidencies of Bombay and Madras as well as Bengal. This position did not, however, give him much power in the other territories—his responsibilities there did not go beyond the authority to make war or peace on their behalf. And his new position made things more difficult for him in his dealings with his colleagues.

The position of Governor-General was set up by the Regulating Act of 1773. This was an Act of Parliament in Britain designed to bring the affairs of the Company in India more under the supervision of the British government. The Act contained quite a number of provisions rearranging the power structure of the Company and establishing the form of its administration in India; but the Act did not go so far as to bring the day-to-day running of the Company under the control of the Crown. It merely required that the financial correspondence of the Company between England and India should be made available to the Treasury. This meant that, in particular, the government should be able to inspect the Company's financial affairs.

The Act did not only lay down what should happen in the Company headquarters in England. It laid down also a new form of Council for Bengal, where Hastings was named as the first Governor-General. This Council was what gave Hastings most of his difficulties in the next five years, because he needed to co-operate with it, but co-operation was rarely forthcoming. The difficulties were caused by the fact that policy could be decided only by a majority of the four-man Council, with the Governor-General as fifth, with a casting vote. He could not override it. In all matters he needed the support of at least two members of the Council. But if three of them teamed up against him, he was powerless.

And this, unfortunately for Warren Hastings, is exactly what happened. Three of the four members of the Council were sent out from England, and these three formed a group that, right from the start, voted against the Governor-General most of the time. This put him in a frustrating and humiliating position. For two years, until one member died, he could scarcely move hand or foot.

One councillor in particular gave Hastings his worries: Francis, the most junior member, but the most active and purposeful of the four. His purpose was chiefly to destroy Hastings' power and position. Historians usually single out Francis as the demon who was really responsible for preventing Hastings from going ahead with his policies. It is easy to find unlovable characteristics in Francis. He was ambitious for himself, and admitted to wanting to be Governor-General, an office which he prized very highly. He was incredibly persistent, vengeful and callous in pursuing his campaign against Hastings. Two other councillors came under the sway of his personality and followed his lead. He was thus able to hound his adversary day in and day out, and only in 1780, when his supporters were dying off, and when Hastings wounded him severely in a duel, did he give up the struggle and return to England.

There are dangers, however, in making heroes out of some men and devils out of their opponents. Francis had certain sincere ideas about what should be done for the good of British India. It happened that the means he used strike us today as ruthless. But ruthlessness was in the air.

Foreign policy

When we talk about foreign policy in the India of the time, we need to remember once more that India was not a single country that happened to be partly under the domination of foreigners. It was an arena of jostling, competing rulers; and the British in Bengal, Madras and Bombay were simply one of the competitors. And this was the arena where Hastings was able to take some initiatives hoping that the Council, for the honour and security of the Company in India, would follow his policies. But taking initiatives did not mean declaring wars for the sake of conquest. This was not a motive either of the directors of the Company in England or of Hastings. Wars were fearfully expensive, and ruling Indians for the sake of ruling Indians was not an attractive proposition to the Company.

The official policy, then, was non-interference. The neighbouring Indian states were to be allowed to go their own way, and the British were not to meddle in their conflicts. When in fact Hastings did so, he got into serious trouble for it afterwards. Non-interference meant not taking sides in Indian wars and not using British troops except in the defence of the British territories.

But, as men on the spot found out, it was not as simple as that. Any Indian state that took no interest in the affairs of its neighbours, not lifting a finger to see that neighbouring territories did not come under the domination of powers hostile to itself, was asking for trouble. In Bengal, for example, it was convenient to have to the north-west a buffer state, Oudh, with which good relations were maintained and which would act as a barrier between Bengal and possible hostile powers beyond. If Oudh should come under the domination of one of its enemies, that spelled danger for Bengal. It was difficult, it was even impossible, to be neutral in the conflicts of the subcontinent. If the British were inactive, there were always the French, and other European nations, to take advantage of a situation. One reason why, in 1774, the British attacked Salsette (an island near Bombay) was that, otherwise, the Portuguese might have beaten them to it.

Oudh and Rohilkand

The major powers in India were: the Maratha Confederacy, a fairly loose grouping of aggressive Hindu rulers occupying a great part of India; the British, with large territories in Bengal and Bihar and settlements at Madras and Bombay; the Mogul territory in the North, a shadow of its former self; and, in the South, the territories of the Nizam of Hyderabad, and Mysore. Now the Maratha Confederacy did not at first seem a serious threat to Bengal, because after its defeat at Panipat in 1761 it was not a power in the North. But when the Marathas reappeared in the North—and in 1771 installed the Mogul sultan as a puppet emperor of theirs in Delhi—the threat was revived, and it seemed wise to strengthen Oudh as a buffer state.

This was the background to British participation in the affairs of the rulers of Oudh, with their territory adjacent to the British controlled territory. When the Mogul sultan accepted the position offered him in Delhi, the British no longer felt obliged to let him keep the territories that they had let him enjoy. These territories included Kora and Allahabad, to the North-West of Bengal, and Hastings' solution was to sell these territories to the Nawab of Oudh. Hastings himself regarded this as a cunning move. It gave the Company the proceeds of these territories without the worry of running them. It helped to bind Oudh to the British by a debt of obligation. And it would deflect upon Oudh the hostility of Delhi and the Marathas, who might in the future make claims on these places.

At the same time that they were sold to the Nawab, in 1773, an agreement was made with him that the Company would help him in his dealings with the Rohillas, a class of nomadic warriors, dominating a territory next to that of the Nawab of Oudh. At first, Rohilkand (the land of the Rohillas) and Oudh were in an uneasy alliance, because both of them felt threatened by the Marathas. In fact the Marathas appeared in Rohilkand in 1772 and again in 1773, but retreated without giving battle, deterred by the presence of forces from Oudh and also Bengal. The Nawab of Oudh, Shuja ud

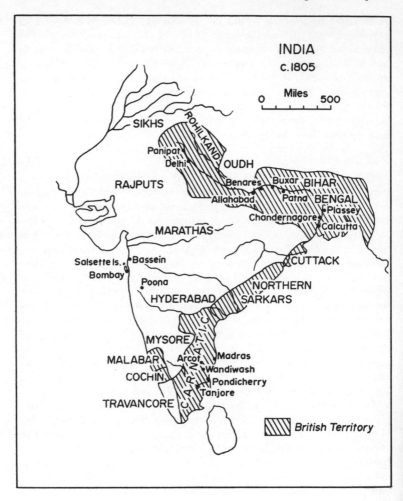

INDIA
c.1805

Miles
0   500

SIKHS

ROHILKAND

Panipat
Delhi   OUDH

RAJPUTS   Benares   Buxar   BIHAR
                 Allahabad   Patna BENGAL
                          Chandernagore   Plassey
                                          Calcutta

MARATHAS

Salsette Is.   Bassein
Bombay
          Poona   CUTTACK
          HYDERABAD   NORTHERN
                       SARKARS

MYSORE
MALABAR   Arcot   Madras
COCHIN   Wandiwash
                    Pondicherry
TRAVANCORE   Tanjore

⧄⧄⧄ British Territory

Daula, then claimed payment from the Rohillas, because he had
made an agreement with them that they should pay him for helping
them against the Marathas. They refused payment, and then it was
that Shuja ud Daula turned to the British to help him conquer
Rohilkand.

Hastings was very reluctant to do so, having had second thoughts
about the agreement under which the help was to be given, but now
the thing was done, and in 1774 with British assistance the Nawab
of Oudh, Shuja ud Daula, overran the Rohillas with a great deal

of bloodshed. The direction of the fighting, and the following atrocities, were out of British hands. Hastings could not fairly be blamed for the cruelty shown by the Nawab to his enemies, although he was later blamed. He was also blamed for interfering unnecessarily in the affairs of these states.

The affairs of Madras

Through much of the seventies and early eighties, the Company was involved in other expensive wars to which it was committed by the dealings of Madras and Bombay with their neighbours. There was hostility to the Company at this time, not only from various Indian powers, but also from the French, who, after 1788, were committed to hostility towards Britain by their alliance with America. Little help for British India was forthcoming from England, where the government had its hands full with France and America. But at the end of it all, the British presence in India was, if anything, stronger than ever. This strength, or consolidation, did not come about as the result of any clear and consistent policy of self-assertion and aggrandizement. It came about piecemeal, as the result of a multitude of petty involvements that pulled the presidencies willy-nilly deeper and deeper into the tortuous politics of the subcontinent.

Madras became involved in the tortuous politics of its neighbours, neither from any particularly creditable motives, nor from any greed for conquest. The nearby Indian ruler, the Nawab of Arcot, owed the Company a great deal of money. The Council at Madras contained men who wanted him to be able to pay it back. They therefore involved the Company in his affairs; but in doing so they were not launching a policy of colonization. They became entangled in Indian politics simply because they were there, and because the Company was a power in the land.

But the dealings of some of the local Company men in Madras with the Nawab of Arcot were only one element in the political complications. Another element was the British government, which had its own line to follow. The Governor-General in Bengal, Warren Hastings, also became involved in the wars and treaties that were made. So there were several fingers in the pie. The result was confusion—confusion for which the Regulating Act of 1773 was largely to blame, because it did not establish the responsibility for government clearly enough.

First of all, Sir John Lindsay was sent out from England with some naval ships. He was concerned to have good relations with the Marathas, the largest Indian power, and was opposed to another Indian ruler, Haider Ali of Mysore.

The Council, however, was interested more in the affairs of the

Nawab of Arcot, and in 1773 helped him to defeat the Raja of
Tanjore. This line of policy was very unpopular in England. A new
Governor, Lord Pigot, was sent out to take over the direction of
affairs in Madras. However, just as Warren Hastings had difficulty
with his Council in Calcutta, so Lord Pigot had difficulty with his
Council in Madras. In fact, the difficulty led to a bizarre episode.
This was the action by some members of the Council, led by Benfield
and others, against their own Governor. In 1776 they imprisoned
him, feeling that their rights were threatened. Most of them got
away with fines. The fines were heavy, but then the Company men
in India were wealthy.

In this way, then, the government of the settlement at Madras was
divided and confused. Nor did the trouble end there. War with
France, war with Haider Ali, and hostility with other Indian princes
complicated the position further. In 1780 Hastings sent one of the
top commanders, Sir Eyre Coote, to help in the action against
Haider Ali. As commander Coote did much to redeem the Company's
position, but in general the British commanders could not and did not
score swift decisive victories in the confused and shifting politics of
India. It was indeed fortunate for the Company that in 1783
France made peace with England, and the French commanders in
India accepted the peace. But the troubles were not over.

One was Mysore. Haider Ali was dead, but his son Tipu was very
active. Another was the management of the administration in
Madras, particularly the finances. This was a bone of contention
between the Governor, Macartney, and Warren Hastings, which
was removed only when the Governor resigned in 1785. A third was
the conflict in Madras between the King's soldiers and the Company's
soldiers. This was one example of the troubles following from having
two authorities in one place, each with its own officials, soldiers and
servants generally. In Madras, there were regiments from the
regular British Army, the King's troops, as well as Company's
troops. When a Company officer was appointed commander-in-chief,
many officers from the King's regiments refused to take orders from
him. This highlighted the problem of divided authority and divided
loyalties in the Indian possessions, a problem that would not be
solved for some time to come.

The Affairs of Bombay

Madras is in the south-east of India, and was chiefly involved with
the powers in that area—Haider Ali in Mysore, the Nizam of
Hyderabad, the French in Pondicherry. Britain's other presidency
was Bombay in the west, and the involvements of Bombay were
chiefly with the Marathas, a confederacy of Indian rulers under the

general authority of the overlord, called the Peshwa of Poona.

The British territory of Bombay consisted of the port, with its trading settlement, and the area around it. This area was surrounded by the Marathas. Therefore the foreign affairs of Bombay revolved around the problem of dealing with the Marathas. As with other parts of India, it was a case of too many cooks spoiling the broth. First the authorities in Bombay, then the Council in Calcutta, then the British government—all at different stages took a hand, each with its own view on which Marathi leader to deal with and how to deal with him. As for the Marathas, it was by no means always clear who was really in control, if anybody. This is what made possible some of the inconsistencies in British policy. For most of the 1770's, there were two main contestants for authority in Poona, the seat of the power of the Marathas. One was Raghunath Rao. The other was Nana Phadnavis.

On the whole, British policy favoured the first of these, but not consistently, and ultimately British dealings came to be with another Maratha leader altogether—Sindhia—who came to be friendly towards the British, and with whom a treaty was made in 1782. This treaty laid down that Raghunath Rao should retire and live on a pension. Thus the British abandoned their former ally.

The Courts

We have already noticed how the division of authority between the British government and the Company could cause discord and inefficiency in military and political affairs. There is another example of this division of authority in the way justice was organized.

The organization was split between the Company, which had its own revenue courts and provincial courts, and the Crown, on whose authority the Supreme Court in Calcutta functioned.

This meant that there were two sets of officials. One set was employed by the Company and operated the Company's courts; the other owed no loyalty whatsoever to the Company, and was anxious to maintain the dignity and independence of the law. Naturally, there were jealousies and clashes between them.

The officers of the Crown, represented by the Supreme Court in Calcutta, complained that the local courts of the Company were not properly organized and did not give proper justice. The officers of the Company complained that the Supreme Court did not have authority over the Company's servants, and was perpetually interfering in other people's business.

An example of the jealousy between the two authorities is an episode that occurred in 1780. The Supreme Court sent officers to arrest an Indian zamindar. The zamindar collected taxes for the

Company, and therefore in the Company's eyes came under its own jurisdiction, not that of the Supreme Court. So the officers who were sent to arrest the zamindar were themselves arrested.

This shows the tension that existed between the Supreme Court and the Company. Fortunately, however, each organization was headed by a reasonable man—Warren Hastings, the Governor-General in authority over the Company servants, and Sir Elijah Impey, the Chief Justice of the Supreme Court. Although Warren Hastings tended to see things from the Company point of view, he was anxious for a sensible re-organization of the courts. In 1776 he proposed that the two sets of courts should be combined, a proposal that was unacceptable. In 1780 he made Sir Elijah Impey head of the central Company court. This meant that one man headed both authorities. It was a blow struck for co-operation. But it was not popular with either side. The Company men complained that it was allowing the Supreme Court even more interference in their affairs. The Crown officers, in England as well as India, complained that by accepting a paid office from the Company Sir Elijah Impey was surrendering the independence of the law. In fact, when he later returned to England, he was impeached; but he defended himself successfully against the charges.

In 1781 there was an Act of Parliament which had the effect of protecting the Company's privileges. However, Hastings' action in appointing Sir Elijah made possible a good improvement in the organization of the Company courts.

Some dubious episodes

From 1776, there was no longer a majority against Hastings on the Council at Calcutta. In 1780, his bitterest enemy, Francis, left India after being severely wounded in a duel with him. But with that, the opposition to him did not disappear for good. In 1785 Hastings resigned and returned to England, where his enemies impeached him. An impeachment was an accusation before the House of Lords. At the end of the proceedings, which lasted thirteen years, the charges fell to the ground, and Hastings was acquitted. But there were certainly some dubious episodes in his career, which his opponents brought up against him.

One of these was the affair of Chait Singh, the ruler of Benares. Chait Singh was administering Benarcs on behalf of the Company, and paying the Company a certain sum each year. In 1780 Hastings called on him to demand higher payments. He refused; Hastings' bodyguard was attacked, and retired; British forces were called up; and Chait Singh fled. Hastings was high-handed in dealing with him like this, but the need for money was desperate.

Another was the affair of the Begams of Oudh. These were the mother and grandmother of the ruler of Oudh, two ladies who had charge of the treasure of the previous ruler (Shuja ud Daula). In 1782 the current ruler (Asaf ud Daula) was unable to pay the Company all he owed, and then with Company encouragement he put pressure on the Begams to give up to him some of the treasure. This pressure involved torturing their servants. A complaint against Hastings in this affair was that he accepted a ten lakh (1,000,000 rupee) bribe from one of the Begams that was intended to stop him from making further demands. However, he did not use this money for private purposes—it was spent on the army.

There were other complaints against him; and it is difficult to separate truth from falsehood in assessing his career. Hastings can be blamed for accepting presents, Francis and his friends for conspiring against him, his enemies in England for their intrigues. Nobody involved in the Hastings case seems entirely blameless. And this, in a way, is how we could perhaps look at the affairs of Hastings' career as a whole. The point is not that everybody was bad, however. The point is that everybody had special problems, special pressures on them, that made them act as they did. If we were to look at things from the point of view of each of the personalities in turn, we would see that each of them had a point of view that made his own policy seem reasonable—particularly when the general standards of conduct were so different from those of today.

CHAPTER TEN

The Government of India, 1800-1900

(a) UNDER COMPANY AND CROWN

It has been said that Britain acquired her empire in a fit of absent-mindedness. This simply means that the British government did not set out in the eighteenth century to take over India and govern it. Each extension of British control was not part of a plan of conquest but something incidental to some other purpose, like putting an end to raids that were interfering with trade, or doing a good turn for a friendly Indian ruler. Sometimes the motives for taking over each part were selfish, sometimes unselfish, usually something of each; but the point is that there was not an overall plan to conquer India.

The Company

The first British possessions in India were not run as conquered territories to be assimilated into an empire. They were run as spheres of action for traders. It was not the British government that ran India. It was an organization of traders, the British East India Company.

The position of the Company in India was rather peculiar, and needs some explanation. It would seem, on the face of it, that traders could perfectly well carry on their trade peacefully, and leave the government of India to the Indian rulers. But it did not work out like this; the traders, as representatives of a strong foreign power, and of a foreign culture, became increasingly involved in the political affairs of India and the rivalries between rulers, which could not be kept apart from trade. The Company, because it had resources that compared well with those of the Indian rulers, found itself turning into an Indian power itself, running the affairs of some rulers for them, collecting taxes and so on.

The British government did not want a commercial concern to interfere like this in the affairs of foreign lands without supervision, and so the government gradually took steps to bring the activities of the Company under its eye. As we saw in the previous chapter, the Regulating Act of 1773 was the chief step. And right up to 1858, after the mutiny, the actual government of India, or the parts that that were under British control, was carried on by the Company as an outgrowth from its business of trading and making a profit.

At the end of the eighteenth century there were three British possessions in India, from which the rest of the Indian empire gradually grew. These were the large and important presidency of Bengal and the smaller presidencies of Madras and Bombay. Madras and Bombay had Governors in charge of them; Bengal had a Governor-General, who had general supervision of all three and powers of making peace or war. Hastings, as we have seen, was the first. The Governor-General was paid by the Company, but was appointed by the British government. This, then, was one way in which the government supervised the Company.

Another was by the right to demand that the Company should show its accounts to the Treasury. A third was the establishment of a Supreme Court, which was responsible to the Crown and administered British law. Further, the Company was able to operate in India by being given a charter by the government. This charter had to be renewed every twenty years, and at the time of renewal the affairs of the Company were scrutinized by Parliament and any reforms that seemed necessary were written into the new charter. Finally there was a Board of Control in London, consisting of members of the government, which had a final say in the political and military affairs of the Company. This put the Company effectively under government supervision.

Important to notice here is Pitt's India Act, 1784. This was the Act of Parliament which set the pattern for nineteenth-century Company rule. It established the Board of Control, which contained six Privy Councillors. The Governor-General was to be nominated by the Company, but the appointment had to be endorsed by the Board, which exercised considerable control over the affairs of the Company by sending directives straight to India. The political and military correspondence of the Company had to be shown to it. Further, after Hastings the Governors-General were not Company men with a background of service in India; they were ministry men representing the point of view of the government, who were thus amenable to the influence of the Board of Control.

Under the Company, the British possessions were divided into districts run by magistrate-collectors, officials with responsibility for law and order and for collecting revenue. These were the chief functions of government; there was little idea of education, health, agricultural improvement and so forth as responsibilities of government. The Company's other activities were largely commercial. It employed a large staff, the members of which were often out to make money for themselves by private trading activities alongside their ordinary duties. Warren Hastings, possibly one of the more honest, made a fortune in his early days with the Company, as we saw. The money-making opportunities were not all illegal, but they were not very healthy for India. In the nineteenth century, however, things changed. Company servants were forbidden private trading, and higher standards of conduct came to be accepted among them. There was more idea of service to the country.

The Crown

India could not be run indefinitely as a commercial proposition, however, and after the Indian Mutiny of 1857 it seemed that things were due for a change. In 1858 and in laws passed in later instalments, India was effectively taken over by the British Crown, and the Company disappeared from the scene. The Governor-General became also a Viceroy, representing the Crown. He carried on the government with an Executive Council. Laws for the country were made by the Legislative Council, which consisted of the Executive Council and other members. Bengal, Madras, Bombay and later other provinces had their own Councils.

In the Governor-General's Council there were a Law Member, a Military Member, a Financial Member, some civil servants, some others who were not members of the government (later, from 1862, including some Indians), and the Commander-in-Chief. The Governor-General had a veto over the Council's decisions. In London, instead of a Board of Control, there was a Secretary of State for India—a minister in the British government with a ministerial department to look after Indian affairs and a team of advisers to help him. This system did not, however, result in the sort of earnest scrutiny of Indian affairs that the renewal of the Company's charter had provoked.

(b) Growth of the Empire

While Warren Hastings was Governor-General, the Company was established as one of the major powers in India, if not yet obviously the strongest.

With the rise of Congress and its growth into a major political force as the vehicle of Indian nationalism, the stage was set for the last period of Indian history before independence—the demand for self-government and the development of political institutions to give Indians more representation.

The period between these two stages, corresponding, though

imperfectly, with the nineteenth century, was a period of British dominance in India, and the story of the times is in some measure the story of British activity. But it was not wholly the story of British activity. Though more and more territories in India came under direct British rule, even at the end a large proportion of the population of the subcontinent lived under Indian rulers who had wide powers of government.

Nevertheless, in order to understand something of the story of India during the period of the British rule, or raj, we need to look first at the government and its affairs. Some of these affairs can be considered by looking at the whole of the century at once. Others, such as the growth of the British possessions in India, need to be considered by starting at the beginning and going through to the end of the period. In this section, we can take a brief glance at the way in which the territory and the preoccupations of government expanded in the course of time.

Cornwallis, 1780–1793

Cornwallis was the Governor-General after Hastings. He was given the job of putting into operation the recent regulations designed to bring the operations of the Company more closely under the supervision of the British government, and establishing the administration of the Company's territory on sound lines.

He was a conscientious man, and tried hard to bring more efficiency and honesty into the business of the government of Bengal, the chief presidency, the one where he himself as Governor-General was stationed, and the one over which he had direct control. His significance in the development of government is therefore that, while the Company was used to acting as a set of merchants, Cornwallis tried to make it act like a government.

The officials employed by the Company to collect taxes, to keep law and order, to administer justice, and to do all such other things as the Company's position as an effective government of various territories required, were in the business to make money. After all, they were in a commercial Company. And they used their positions in all ways possible to make private fortunes. Their salaries, high by Indian standards, were not particularly impressive by British; but the opportunities they had to carry on trade privately and the privileges they had as government servants made it easy for them to earn many times their annual salaries every month, with a little bit of luck. What Cornwallis did was to try to keep the enforcement of justice separate from the collection of revenue, so that there would be an independent judiciary to act as a check on the administrators, and to attempt a reform of the civil service. He established the

Covenanted Civil Service, which consisted of all the highest positions
in the administration, and in which all men on being appointed
were to promise not to carry on private trade or in any other way
abuse the authority and privileges they had. From the time of
Cornwallis onward, a determined attempt was made to keep the
administration clean. The fact that Cornwallis kept all the top
administrative posts in British hands should be seen as a part of this
attempt. Previously it had been possible for Indians to hold high
offices, notably in revenue collection, but Cornwallis distrusted
Indians and kept them out of the most responsible positions.

Wellesley, 1798–1805

Lord Wellesley was Governor-General at a time when Europe was
in turmoil. The French Revolution had upset the old order of things,
and not unnaturally Wellesley was very much concerned in his
policies with the threat that could be seen in a French presence in
the area. This sort of preoccupation led him to intrigue in the South
with the Nizam of Hyderabad. Tipu, the ruler of Mysore, tended to
favour the French, and brought retribution on himself from British
hands. Deeply involved in the political manoeuvring of the southern
kingdoms, Wellesley also took the Carnatic. In the North, on the
borders of the Company's sphere of influence in Bengal and Behar,
he extended British power by taking Oudh, which had previously
been left independent as a convenient friendly buffer state between
the Presidency of Bengal and the turbulent Indian powers beyond,
but now gave trouble because of the confusion and incompetence
of its governance.

By such actions, in spite of the official policy of not interfering in
the affairs of Indian kingdoms, Wellesley embroiled the Company
further in the politics of the land. If it had been possible before to
regard the Company simply as a foreign trading venture, it was so
no longer.

The Marathas

One other involvement of Wellesley's belongs to a separate chapter
of Indian affairs: the Maratha Wars. The Marathas were a group of
Hindu chiefdoms or royal houses, under the at least nominal leadership of a ruler called the Peshwa, who controlled large tracts of
territory in the north and west. We noticed before their origin with
the adventurer Sivaji and their growth as a territorial power.

A conflict between the Maratha families, contesting for power
among themselves, gave Wellesley an opening: taking sides with one
of the contestants, he succeeded in turning the situation to the
British advantage and leaving the Marathas with a Peshwa compliant

to the British, and extensive new territories in the north-west in the Company's hands. These were known as the ceded and conquered territories. Matters did not rest there. War with one of the Maratha powers followed in 1804, but Wellesley was withdrawn the following year, and matters were not pressed to a conclusion.

So long as the Marathas were a large and effectively independent force in the land, as they still were, there was bound to be trouble. Raids by marauding tribes called Pindaris from Maratha territory were a constant menace to the British possessions in the north-east, and the Marathas were not willing to stop these raids. In 1817 war broke out again, with the British taking on the Marathas and the Pindaris, and the following year the power of the Marathas was broken; further slices of territory were added to the British possessions—this time joined to the presidency of Bombay—and the Peshwa was set up harmlessly with a pension in Cawnpore, to become another figurehead ruler with little or no power.

Bentinck, 1828–1835, and reform

Lord Bentinck is worth noticing here, though we shall be looking at some of his work later on, as a representative of a trend in British thinking. This trend was to a keen interest in the welfare of British subjects in the empire.

It could take different forms. There were those who wanted to see the culture and traditions of the Indians respected and protected. And there were the reformers, the men who wanted to do away with those aspects of Indian life that seemed backward or barbarous, and teach Indians things that would be useful to them in practical affairs—trades, professions, the English language which would be a gateway to profitable careers under the government.

Usefulness is the key idea here. There was a school of political thought in England favouring government that was designed to do the greatest possible good to the greatest number of people. It held that good should be measured by its practical usefulness. This sort of idea was known as utilitarianism. The writings of a leading utilitarian, James Mill, who produced a history of India (published in 1817), influenced the men who came to take part in the government of India. The reformist ideas of Governors-General such as Bentinck and, later, Dalhousie, whether or not directly influenced by Mill, belong to the same climate of opinion—a readiness to interfere for the good of the Indians, an assumption of responsibilities to them that went beyond the collection of revenue and the maintenance of law and order.

Some Indians themselves were caught in the same current of thought, and wanted the British to take an active hand in social regulation, to do away with evils like *sati*—the custom of suicide by a widow, which Bentinck tried to abolish. One Indian in particular deserves mention—Ram Mohun Roy, mild-natured, progressive, a student of religions, an enthusiast for all that seemed to him best in English culture. He was in favour of the spread of English education, and of the reform of Indian customs, at a time when the British themselves were very hesitant about interference in Indian society. Roy lived long before the rise of nationalism as an active force—he died in 1833—but with the later nationalists he shared a zest for modernization, for practical benefits to the people, for progress. Unlike them, he saw the British as allies in the process rather than as foreign tyrants who must first be removed.

But reform was not the inspiration of the raj as a whole; it was merely one tendency, shown by some people. There were others, just as representative or more so, with a conservative outlook. Against reformers like Bentinck and Mill can be set conservative viceroys like Lytton and Curzon, conservative administrators like Lyle. There were those who saw the British role in terms of consolidation of power, defence against outside threats (and in some periods the Russian threat seemed very real), and respect for Indian traditions.

Burma

Burma is not part of India, and its history—like that of other regions of south-east Asia—does not belong to India's. Yet its affairs in the nineteenth century are very much tied up with India's, because of the troubles of the frontier between Burma and Assam which helped to pull down British wrath on Burmese heads, and because Burma, on being taken over by Britain, was governed from India and treated as if it were another Indian province.

It was a mysterious country; its rulers at their court at Ava were far inland and knew little of the world outside; they cared less. The ignorance of the Burmese about the wide world, and the ignorance of the British about the Burmese, only aggravated the troubles that led to the subjection of the country to British rule.

This subjection came in three stages, with wars beginning in 1826, 1852 and 1885 respectively. The first ended with an exchange of Residents: that is, a British official was posted to live at the Court at Ava and a Burmese official went to Calcutta. The second ended with the British annexation of lower Burma—the provinces on the coastline—Arakan, Pegu, Tenasserim. The third led to a final takeover of the crumbling kingdom.

These wars were mounted from Indian soil, and the British officials who took over the government of the new provinces went out from India, with Indians to help them as clerks, soldiers and so forth. All

Two camels with Sindhi riders. By Henry Ainslie, *c.* 1805-79

Terracotta horses at a temple in Coimbatore, Madras, 1834

Nepalese villager smoking a hookah. Dung on the wall behind is drying for use as fuel

Villager with a bullock, by George Chinnery, 1784-1852

Madras: farmhouse, courtyard and stock

the decisions affecting Burmese government were taken in Calcutta, and the Indian pattern of administration was imposed ready-made on the country. Being tied to India in this way was probably harmful to Burmese interests in the long run.

The North-West

Throughout India's history, invaders came through the passes of the north-west, and it is understandable that the security of the north-western frontier was a major preoccupation of the British in India. The danger was not from the Afghan tribes who lived in the area, though they could be a nuisance to the Punjab. What was especially feared was an attack by Russia. Today, as far as we can tell, the danger of a Russian invasion through the passes was never really very serious; but the rulers of India certainly seem to have thought it was, and their sometimes foolish-seeming policies towards Afghanistan were dictated by an earnest desire to establish British dominance in the area. Such policies were foolish in the circumstances, because the Afghans were not willing to tolerate British dominance. In 1878, after a series of earlier interventions, an expedition to Afghanistan secured a treaty giving British India control over Afghan foreign policy.

Meanwhile, disorder in the Punjab led to the takeover of more territory in the North-West. Sind, on the mouth of the Indus, was annexed in 1843. Sikh unrest led to invasions by Sikhs of Company territory, and in consequence the British annexed part of the Punjab and separated from it the state of Kashmir in the far North, which was to have British protection.

Dalhousie, 1848–1856

Afghanistan was never annexed. The last of the annexers had been Dalhousie, the mid-century Governor-General who propounded the doctrine of Lapse by which rulers without heirs lost their kingdoms to the Paramount Power—Britain. Following this doctrine, several smaller states were brought into the British fold. And thus, by the various means that we have noticed—not as part of a planned campaign of territorial gain, but as a result of all sorts of local fears, provocations, misunderstandings, underhand deals and altruistic motives in all combinations—the British traders in India found themselves turning into the governors of an empire.

The nineteenth century falls into two parts, and the Governor-Generalship of Dalhousie is significant for both.

In the first part, before the mutiny of 1857, the government was run by the Company, and the Company was embroiled in the politics of the Indian kingdoms. By degrees, most of India fell into its hands.

Dalhousie's administration, just before the mutiny, marks the high point, and also the end, of the empire-building phase.

In the second part, after the mutiny, the government was run by the British Crown, and the Crown was embroiled in a different sort of politics—the politics of progress. By degrees, India progressed—Indians played a larger and larger part in their own political affairs, and nationalism grew. Dalhousie's administration marks the beginning of this phase of progress also, in a sense, because Dalhousie more than any other Governor-General was keen on progress, on telegraphs, on railways which he started in India, on all the facilities of modern civilization. His career, and the measures he took will be detailed in a later chapter, but they do mark a crossroads in the development of British India.

CHAPTER ELEVEN

The Mutiny of 1857

(a) THE CAUSES OF THE MUTINY

In a way, it is dangerous to talk about 'the causes' of the Indian Mutiny, as if we knew exactly what they were. It is true that we know what kinds of things made the soldiers rebellious, what they complained about, what they tried to do when the mutiny was under way, what the grievances of Indians against the government were, and what some reasons for the support mutineers received from the rest of the Indian population in areas affected by the mutiny were. To talk about 'the causes', however, might suggest a known, precise list of things bringing about the mutiny, amongst which we can distinguish the really important from the simply incidental. Although we might have ideas about these things, there is still room for different points of view.

Some might regard the mutiny as purely an army affair, and claim that the rest of the population did not really support the soldiers who mutinied. Others might see the events of 1857 as a full-scale revolution against British rule, with the Indian soldiers simply taking the lead. Some might see the mutiny as an expression of religious grievances; others, as a movement for political freedom.

Just giving a list of 'causes' is not good enough. We would like to know which ones were important and which were not. Suppose we imagine that some things had been different—that the soldiers had not been issued with greased cartridges that offended their religious scruples, for example. This was the issue which started the mutiny off. If the cartridges had not been issued, would there still have been a mutiny anyway, because of the other reasons for it? Or again, suppose that British policy about the village taxation system had been different and people had not had the same grievances over taxes: would that have been enough to stop the mutiny from spreading as it did? It is not easy to give answers to such questions.

The question of causes, then, is rather complicated, and the best way of tackling it is by making a few distinctions between different aspects that must not be confused.

153

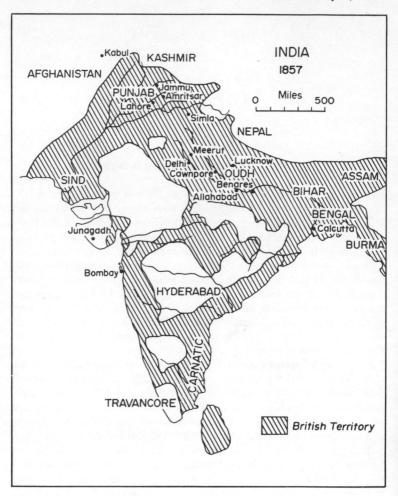

Revolt or mutiny?

The first distinction we must make is between a revolt and a mutiny. The 'Indian Mutiny' is so called because it was started by Indian soldiers disobeying the orders of their British officers and becoming rebellious. This is not the same thing as a revolt, in which the civil population takes part. If we find that the Indian mutineers were joined by the civilians in the areas where there was trouble, it might be better to call the whole movement a revolt, because it was not limited to the army. Indeed, this is what happened in Northern

India, especially in Bengal, in Oudh, and around Delhi. Over a great area, the mutiny sparked off riots and anti-British rampages in which princes, landowners, peasants and miscellaneous caste groups were alike involved. But it would be a mistake to regard the movement as a general rising against the British. It was not. What people did was determined by all sorts of local reasons, and there were plenty even in the worst affected areas who did not help the mutineers, and even helped the British who remained there.

Revolt: willing or unwilling?

So we know that many, but by no means all, people joined the mutinous sepoys in opposition to the British. But why they joined is another question. They doubtless had grievances against the British government; but were these grievances enough to make people join in, and raise revolt, with enthusiasm and spontaneity? They might have taken sides with the sepoys—Indian soldiers—because they thought they had to. Sympathy with the mutiny need not have had very much to do with it. It could be that, when the mutiny broke out, government broke down and in some areas British authority disappeared. When this happened, the sepoys were the most powerful force in the land. Then the civilians, peasants and aristocrats, thought that the British raj was over and accepted revolt because their bread seemed to be buttered on that side. To resist was dangerous.

So far as the mutiny was a revolt, it seems to have been very much like this. British power disappeared for a time in a number of places, and the power of the mutineers took its place. Whatever people actually thought or wanted, it was safest to join the mutineers. For many, any other line of action would have been foolish, even suicidal.

This does not mean, however, that nobody was really willing to join in, that there was no real anti-British feeling. There was a great deal, among most classes of people, though it would perhaps never have led to anything like a revolt if the mutiny had not started, and appeared to be succeeding.

Political or religious?

This makes it necessary to draw a further distinction, between political and religious objectives among those who joined the mutiny out of conviction rather than necessity. It was not a movement for political freedom like the nationalist movements in African and Asian countries in the present century. The supporters of the mutiny were certainly bent on getting rid of the British government—at least in the early stages. They rallied to the descendants of the Old Indian ruling houses: the Mogul emperor at Delhi, the Maratha heir at Cawnpore. These scions of earlier dynasties were not real rulers; they kept their titles and lived on incomes from sources allowed to them by the British. So when the mutiny came, it was understandable that they should seek to regain the power that their families had lost, and that Indians looking for an alternative to the British should regard one or other of them as sovereign. This gave the mutiny a political character to some extent. But this is not the same thing as joining the movement in the first place for political reasons.

The reasons why some gave willing support to the movement, and why it started in the first place, were not chiefly political. The motives were motives of caste or religion rather than anything else— certain actions of the British authorities and the British army officers made it seem that the Hindu religion and the Muslim religion were in danger. This makes quite an important difference between the mutiny and modern nationalistic movements, which are intended right from the start as programmes for political independence and for the development of a new sense of national identity amongst a colonial population. The rebels of 1857 acted first in defence of their religions, as they understood them.

Against the British or against each other?

Many, then, wanted to protect Indian religions, and to do this by restoring pre-British native Indian empires. But this was not the only sort of reason that people had for taking part in the disorders. Once the disorders had started, there was an opportunity to settle all sorts of old scores that could not be acted on while there was law and order in the country.

Without an effective government authority to keep the peace, it was possible for debtors to rise against creditors, peasants to rise against landlords, Hindus to rise against Muslims (for they could not trust each other and make common cause), and bandits to terrorize everybody. In some parts, the British came to be almost forgotten in a welter of anarchic conflicts. It may have been mutiny, it may have been revolt, but it was also civil war.

What sorts of causes were there?

It follows that there were many sorts of causes for the things that happened in 1857. Some people rose up against authority because they saw a chance of escaping the tyranny of their landlords. Some rose up because they hoped to get back rights to revenues that the British had taken away from them. Some rose up because they saw others rising up also, and wished to protect themselves against the enmity of rival religious or other groups. Some rose up because they saw possibilities of plunder and loot. But these reasons do not provide a complete explanation of the mutiny. They were the conditions which made it possible that it should spread and become a serious problem, but they were not the things which sparked it off. If we think of the mutiny as an enormous fire, then we must think of the grievances and rivalries that kept it burning as the fuel; we still want to know what was the spark that set the fuel alight, and this distinction between fuel and spark is one more that needs to be made.

The spark was the famous affair of the greased cartridges. The army was issued with a new sort of cartridge for its rifles, which were themselves of a new type, the Enfield. These cartridges had to have the ends bitten off them when they were put into the breech. There was nothing wrong with this; what gave offence to the soldiers was the grease with which the cartridges were treated before being issued. The grease was, at least in the case of some early issues of cartridges in 1857, made from the fat of cow or pig. And it was dead against the religious prejudices of Hindus and Muslims to put to their mouths something that came from the sacred cow or the impure pig. It was the religious objection of the sepoys at Meerut and elsewhere to using such cartridges, or any that they imagined as such, on parade, that sparked off all the troubles, and led to the spread of them when the initial outbreak was not quickly checked.

Would there have been trouble on the same scale even if there had been no greased cartridge incident? We cannot say with any confidence. Perhaps the grievances and tensions would have been enough to produce an outbreak eventually, from one spark or another. Or perhaps if the cartridges had never been issued, or if the trouble at Meerut had been quickly damped down, there would never have been the mutiny as we know it.

Economic and religious grievances

What were the particular grievances that impelled people to act? In the first place, we need to notice the importance in the mutiny of the state of Oudh, formerly a princely state but now taken over by the British. It was the chief recruiting ground for the army, and in fact many if not most of the mutineers in the main outbreaks came from Oudh. It is therefore easy to understand that the troubles of this state had a lot to do with the mutiny as a whole. The effect of the British takeover of Oudh was to make nearly everybody involved thoroughly disgruntled. Previously the collection of land revenues here had been in the hands of wealthy and powerful tax farmers, *talukdars*, who had dealt with the villagers. The British, however, when they took the government of Oudh into their own hands, did without the *talukdars* and dealt directly with the villagers. This naturally brought upon the government the hostility of a powerful class in society that was thus deprived of a source of income. But the villagers were not satisfied either, because the revenue demands made by the British were clumsily worked out and oppressive. And the ruling families felt they were treated brusquely and with injustice by the government, which thus got the worst of all worlds.

Apart from the discontent in Oudh, taxes were generally a source of real distress in many areas. In 1833 the British government had made a survey of agricultural land to assess the value of the fields as a basis for taxation. The result in many cases was heavy demands that the villagers could not meet, and that compelled a lot of them to borrow money and get into debt from which they could not escape. Everywhere there were creditors who had taken possession of farmland when the farmers defaulted over their debts, and thus became tenants on their own property.

Landlords were often unpopular among villagers who felt that they were being exploited. In many villages, tax farmers also were an alien class and a butt of resentment and dislike. There were areas where the old aristocracy, the zamindars, were still living in villages where they had once been masters, but the revenues were now collected by city-dwelling tax farmers who had bought the right to collect the taxes and were only seen by the villagers on the occasions when they came for money; in such cases, when the mutiny came, villagers rallied behind their former zamindars against their present tax collectors.

Among the princes, the ruling houses of former times, there was smouldering resentment of the government, also. Many had been deprived of revenues and powers that their fathers had held, though they still held their titles, which now seemed to them empty. Such dispossessed rulers made natural rallying-points for mutineers and rebels, whatever motives prompted these to rise up.

Religion and caste had a lot to do with the hostility that was felt towards the government, particularly among some of the soldiers. It is worth recalling that the mutiny itself was the work in the first place chiefly of soldiers from Oudh. These people came from a place where there was considerable discontent anyway. Further than this, many of them had been through the Afghan wars, in which they experienced novel and unpleasant conditions of life in a strange country where they could not live all the time according to the rituals and requirements of caste. For example, they had to violate caste in their eating habits. Now the sepoys were usually men of high caste—rajputs and brahmans—however junior they were in rank, and caste rules were important to them. Anything that worked against caste was quick to make them antagonistic towards the British army authorities.

There was considerable distrust of the motives of their British officers, who were thought to be trying to convert them to Christianity. Some officers, in fact, were anxious to do what they could to win converts, but it was official policy not to engage in religious propaganda among the Indians. The distrust, however, was enough to magnify every little sign in the eyes of suspicious soldiers who were jealous of their own beliefs and religious practices. Unfounded rumours spread. For example there was a rumour that soldiers already in the army would be forced to travel overseas for spells of service, and it was against caste rules for brahmans to travel over water.

The truth was that an order was made in the army to the effect that future—not present—recruits would be liable for overseas service, and these future recruits would know what to expect when they decided whether to join the army. But once the rumour had spread that serving soldiers would be forced to violate their caste, there was no checking it. It was the same with the greased cartridges— soldiers suspected that they were being issued with them, even when a decision had been made not to, out of respect for their religious scruples, and with the rumour spread hatred. These conditions added up to a formidable array of fears, suspicions and discontents, some against the British, some between Indians. The chief thing to notice is that there was such a confusion of different reasons that people had for joining in the disorders of the mutiny.

(b) The Course of the Mutiny

The mutiny was not a single movement, a planned rising that started and finished in one place and at one time. It was a string of related events, sparking each other off. It was a whole set of mutinies in different places and times. But the story of the mutiny is virtually confined to the events of one year, 1857. Little overflowed into 1858, except some of the mopping-up operations by the British authorities. It is one year, one minute part of India's rich and extensive history. What is it about the mutiny that makes it bulk so large?

We cannot say that it is important because it was the beginning of the nationalist movement. It was not. It was simply a mutiny, or a series of mutinies, that fed on the various discontents that people had. It does not very greatly help us to understand the nationalist movement that came later. Nor was it a paroxysm that convulsed the whole of the country; only parts of the North were affected by it; the presidencies of Madras and Bombay were left calm. Its importance lies elsewhere. Its importance lies in its effects on people.

It affected the people of India at the time, great men and peasants, British and Indian, soldiers and civilians. It affected them by tugging at their passions, stripping off the veneer of civilization and everyday behaviour, and leaving bare the rougher natures and the blind instincts. It has affected the people of India and Britain since, because it is a story that cannot be read without prompting some feelings in anybody who identifies himself with either country. Anger, shame, pride, despair at human nature, self-delusion—one reaction or another inevitably shows itself in anything that is written about the subject.

For a substantial part of 1857, the city of Delhi was in the hands of undisciplined mutineers, who roamed the streets and terrorized everybody. A diary of the time says, for just one day: 'Buldeo Sing, the brother of Lachman Sing, Thanadar of Alipur, was seized and brought to the Kotwali. He was accused of sympathizing with the English. He was shot, and his body suspended from a tree. Thirteen bakers residing at the Kabul Gate were dragged from their houses and killed, on being suspected of supplying bread to the English. The shop of Jamna Dass was plundered because he sold *attah* at a high price.'*

At Lucknow, women and children were massacred by the mutineers. When British troops took the city and crushed the mutiny, they knew this, and themselves subjected all kinds of Indians, innocent and guilty alike, to every variety of cruelty and undeserved punishment. A British officer wrote: 'At the time of the capture of Lucknow—a season of indiscriminate massacre—such distinction was not made, and the unfortunate who fell into the hands of our troops were made short work of—sepoy or Oudh villager, it mattered not—no questions were asked; his skin was black, and did not that suffice? A piece of rope and the branch of a tree, or a rifle bullet through his brain, soon terminated the poor devil's existence.'†

Dum-Dum and Meerut

The first flare-up was at Dum-Dum, Barrackpore, in Bengal near Calcutta. It occurred in January. One British officer was killed. There was no immediate widespread consequence, but in April a more serious mutiny occurred at Meerut, not far from Delhi. The trouble in both cases was a fear of using the cartridges that were greased with fat from cows and defiling to the touch of a high-caste Hindu. At Meerut, about ninety sepoys refused to use the cartridges on parade and were arrested. Like a stone falling into a pond, this incident sent ripples pulsing wider and wider across the face of India.

The few score mutineers at Meerut could be handled without too much difficulty; what sparked the explosion was a rumour that,

* Metcalfe, Sir I, *Two Native Narratives of the Mutiny at Delhi* (Westminster 1898)
† Majendie, Major U. D., *Up among the Pandies* (London, 1859)

following the first disobedience, the British were going to disarm the infantry stationed there. The sight of British soldiers who were actually going on church parade seems to have started this. In no time, the Indian cavalry and infantry alike were running amok; and, once they had started, there was no turning back. Meerut was the scene of fearful rioting and massacre. Thinking that he did not have enough British forces at his disposal to cope with the disorders, the general did not take energetic steps to quell them or to pursue the mutineers, and he has been blamed since by many people for not being more active. It has been suggested that, with more decision, the whole mutiny could have been nipped in the bud then. However that may be, the Indian units made off overnight for Delhi where other Indian troops joined with them. Europeans were hunted out and killed and the Mogul Bahadur Shah was declared emperor in place of the British authorities.

Delhi

Delhi was the chief bastion of the mutiny. It was not then, as it is now, the capital of India. The fact that mutineers overran the city did not mean that the source of British authority in India was eclipsed or that the government was made ineffective. Nevertheless, it became the focus of the mutiny, and when it was re-taken by the British, the back of the mutiny was broken. The reason for this was the presence in Delhi of Bahadur Shah, scion of the great Mogul emperors. He served as a symbol of the rising. With him at its head, a lot of random disorders without any clear purpose could be made into a programme of action—the restoration of an Indian regime, the protection of Indian religions and customs, expulsion of foreigners who were a threat to the religions and customs.

The city was for long a scene of confusion and random violence. There was serious disagreement and suspicion between the mutineers who had come from Meerut and the mutineers who had joined them from Delhi itself. The princes from old Indian families who put themselves at the head of the rebel soldiers were not competent as army commanders. And the emperor's heart was not in the rising, although he couldn't very well refuse the position at the head of it assigned him by the mutineers. It afterwards turned out, when he was put on trial for his part in the affair, that he had been secretly in contact with the British.

News of the mutiny reached Lahore, the centre of British authority in the Punjab, on 13 May, and only in June did a force reach Delhi. It was not strong enough to act at once, and had to wait until September before reinforcements allowed it to move in and clear the streets.

This did not by any means put an end to the mutiny. Much of the North and North-East of India was aflame, and both during and after the siege of Delhi there were widespread rioting and breakdown of government in a large number of cities.

Lucknow

As has been mentioned, Oudh was the principal scene of discontent among both the general population and the army. In Lucknow, it was clear that trouble could be expected, and preparations were made for a siege. But it did not come at once. There was a mutiny of most of the troops stationed near Lucknow, and this triggered off risings in many other cities; from the end of June the one British battalion and several hundred British civilians, including schoolboys, with a number of sepoys who had not mutinied, were besieged in the Residency. The siege lasted for a number of months, even after reinforcements came. Only in November did a large enough force arrive to disperse the mutineers, and they were not finally crushed until early the next year, 1858.

There are two lessons in this episode. One is that the mutineers could not score swift decisive victories. There were very many of them, and they were up against a comparatively small number of defenders in a weak position; but the sepoys were too disorganized to take full advantage of the situation. The other is that, although the British were better organized, and had a core of British soldiers and loyal Indians who in the end were enough to quell the mutiny, they had to move very carefully in a precarious situation, they had to concern themselves with the disarming of potentially mutinous Indian troops in places where risings could be forestalled, and they took time to move their armies about the country and assemble them in sufficient strength at the places where they were needed.

Authority could only be restored when an ample force arrived to restore it at the point of a gun.

Other centres

In the Punjab, there was little trouble; but native battalions there had to be disarmed as a precaution, and this contributed to the delays that arose before a strong force could be despatched to deal with the mutiny at Delhi. In Benares, there was mutiny when General Neill of the Madras army arrived to disarm the local Indian soldiers. In Allahabad, there was mutiny when the news came that the British were on the way there to take control of the situation. In Cawnpore, there were serious disorders centring on Nana Sahib, the surviving representative of Maratha royal authority and therefore the rallying-point for the mutiny (in the same way that Bahadur Shah was, in

Delhi). The British commander surrendered, seeing that his forces were too small, and one of the most unpleasant episodes in the mutiny was the treachery and cruelty shown to the British by Nana Sahib and the mutinous leaders. No more pleasant was the savagery with which the mutiny was later suppressed by British troops. They were angered by the knowledge that women and children had been massacred in that place; but their own reprisals on the Indians were as random and vicious.

Thus, when the mutiny was finally quelled in the course of 1858, there was a legacy of hate on both sides, and terrible damage had been done to the morale of the country. It was obvious that things could not go on as before, and indeed it was the mutiny which prompted the British government to take away the authority of the East India Company and assume direct responsibility for the government of India—instead of sharing the responsibility awkwardly with an originally commercial organization not fitted by its nature for the increasingly complex and delicate business of governing a large country. In the circumstances, the surprising thing is, not that there was a mutiny, but that India was able to develop so peacefully and constructively in the decades which followed it.

CHAPTER TWELVE

The British Raj

(a) ADMINISTRATION

Indianization

Right through Company days and well into Crown days, almost all the people involved in the apparatus of government were British— in practice even if not necessarily in theory. The highest positions in the administration all belonged to what was known as the Covenanted Civil Service, because its members made a covenant or promise not to engage in trade or do such other things as would be inconsistent with the ideals of their duty to the country. To obtain positions in this service, it was necessary to have connections among important people in England, and this meant that Indians could not get in. The Covenanted Civil Service did not contain all the government officials in British India, but it did contain all the highest and best paid, and being a member of it carried much more honour as well as salary than being a member of the ordinary, provincial civil service, which contained many more people.

Efforts were made from time to time to get Indians into high positions, because after all this was their country. One Governor-General, Bentinck, took steps in this direction; while he was in office, in the early 1830s, Indians were admitted to the positions of civil judge and deputy collector. The Company's charter came up for renewal while he was in office, and the Act of Parliament renewing it set out that there should be no discrimination between races in appointments to the Company's positions. Appointees still needed influence in England, however, to obtain senior posts; and in practice, this fact told against Indians.

The next charter, twenty years later, set up examinations for entry into the Company's service. This meant that from now on Indians could get positions on the strength of their performance in examinations. But for various reasons, such as age limits, only a handful entered the Indian Civil Service, as the senior branch of the administration was now called. In 1892, by the Indian Councils Act, steps were taken to involve Indians in the process of government, as non-official members of the Councils. But, as we shall see later on, there was by now a rising demand among Indians for representation in the government, and what the British gave them was always a few steps behind what some of them wanted.

So, although the word 'Indianization' was not heard a great deal until the twentieth century, the process was under way in the nineteenth.

Revenue Problems

At the beginning of the nineteenth century, it was considered that the chief business of government in the country was the collection of revenue and the preservation of law and order. The subjects gave up the one, and got the other in exchange. This was a traditional Indian idea of government. By the end of the century, the needs of the modern world meant that the government was concerning itself with a wide variety of other matters which had not existed before, or had been left to others: road building, education, agricultural modernization, and so on.

The chief source of revenue was the land tax, because most people lived on the land and did not have large money incomes. Income tax, and other taxes, were introduced more and more, but the collection of land tax by the Collectors or others was most important and raised the biggest problems. It raised problems because the British possessions were vast and it was difficult to get in touch with all the peasants and landholders individually to decide what was a fair amount of tax to levy. The problems can be divided into three: who should pay the tax to the government? should the amount of tax be fixed once and for all or adjusted from time to time? and what amount should be charged anyway?

Who should pay?

There were millions of peasants with small holdings of land everywhere. Should the revenue officers go round all of them individually for the tax? This obviously would involve a great deal of work and a large staff to measure land and assess the amount that it would be fair to levy in each case. Or should somebody else pay? It was much simpler to collect the tax from one person for a large number of landholders, but this left open the possibility of dishonesty and oppression. This one person might well take more from individual peasants than he was required to pass on and might retain the balance for himself.

If the peasants in an area did not own their land, but paid rent for the land they worked to a single landlord who owned it all, obviously the tax should be collected from him. He would see to it that the rents he charged gave him enough to cover the tax and left him enough for his needs.

Or it might be that the peasants really did own the land they worked, but traditionally paid their land tax to a tax farmer (called a *zamindar* in many parts), a person appointed by the ruler to collect the tax in an area and pass it on to the government. The position of zamindar might be hereditary, passing from father to son. When the British took over a region, they had the choice of continuing the system of collecting the tax from the tax farmers (who had previously collected it from the peasants), or of collecting the tax straight from the peasants.

Now, the important thing to notice is that the same sort of thing happened in either case. The peasants paid money to a single individual, and the government could then collect tax from him.

The problem was this. To the British, unfamiliar with the customs of the country, it was difficult to tell whether the single individual was a landowner collecting rent, or a tax farmer collecting taxes to pass on, or a petty king or chieftain levying his own taxes, or even a moneylender who had gained possession of the lands of peasants who were in debt to him. In fact a mixture of different methods was worked out by British officials in different places, usually after a lot of unsatisfactory experiments. In the North, especially Bengal, tax was collected from zamindars, or whatever they were, who were treated as landlords. This meant that many of them, being treated as landlords though they were really tax farmers, gained rights over the peasants' land that they should not have had. In some parts, taxes were collected from villages, which had worked out among themselves who should pay what share of the set amount. In the South—in Madras, and later Bombay—the system was to treat the peasants as the landowners and collect from them individually. This required the drawing up of records to show how much land each peasant had, and it required a large staff.

What sort of settlement?

A further problem was that of deciding whether the tax demands should be adjusted from time to time to take account of changes in conditions. In bad times, it would not be fair to ask as much as in good times. Or if the land was improved, or prices of grain went up, it would be fair to ask the peasant to pay more tax. But it was much simpler to set a fixed rate to be paid each year.

What happened was, again, a mixture. Lord Cornwallis at the end of the eighteenth century was in favour of a permanent settlement, a fixed demand. This was enforced in Bengal. Elsewhere different methods were tried. Many administrators felt that, even if for the

sake of simplicity a permanent settlement was made, it was only fair
to the cultivators to let them go free, or pay less than was required,
in bad years when they could not afford it. They could make it up
in good years.

How much should be paid?

Even when it was known how much land a particular individual
peasant had, and whether it was good land or not, this was no
guarantee that the tax levied would be fair. The British officials
concerned then had to decide what proportion of the value of the
land should be paid, and at first there was no reliable guide to show
what the proportion should be.

From ancient times, the convention had been that a cultivator
should pay a share of the value of his crop. The Hindu scriptures
usually state that the share should be one sixth of the value of the
crop. The British however tended to overcharge through not
understanding the situation. When they consulted local brahmans
to find what rates had been levied by the Muslim rulers before them,
they were told rates that had not actually been levied by the
Muslims, but had been officially declared as a sort of bargaining
counter; the actual rates had worked out at much less than the
official ones. Not realizing this, the British tried in some places to
levy the full official rates, with the result that cultivators could not
live, and migrated elsewhere. Great areas became depopulated.

Gradually, with experience, realistic rates were worked out.
Starting by charging a half of the gross value of the produce, the rates
gradually came down to something more like the economic levies.

(b) THE ECONOMY

Effects of British rule

It was not originally regarded as part of the government's business
to interfere with the actual methods and processes of cultivation.
In spite of this, the presence of the British in most of the subcontinent had a pronounced effect on agriculture, in ways that were
partly beneficial, partly harmful, and, either way, largely unintended.

Improvements

Some of the benefits were certainly intended. In ancient times,
governments may not have bothered much about fertilizers and
improved methods, but they certainly bothered about irrigation on
which the whole livelihood of the peasants depended; and, after a
slow start, the British bothered about irrigation too. An irrigation
department was set up in Madras as early as 1819. In the North,

important work was done in canal building and restoration, largely by British army engineers. By 1830, the Jumna river canals were restored. The great Ganges Canal was finished by 1854.

Benefits that were not quite so directly intended came from the spread of modern trading methods into the market. Railways made it possible to sell crops not just in the local market but far away; and railways thus brought merchants from far away into the market to buy. With them they brought more efficient methods of dealing that were fairer to the cultivators who had crops to sell. So modern trading and the improvement in communications—not just railways but hard all-weather roads—went hand in hand to make things better for the farmer, and contributed to the little profit he was able to make.

Harmful effects

Paradoxically, some of the advantages of British rule had a harmful and unintended effect on agriculture. They contributed to a rise in population and an increase in the pressure on land. This was the beginning of a problem that is very much with India today. Nowadays, the chief reason why population is growing too fast is that standards of public health are higher, and fewer people are dying at birth or in infancy. In the nineteenth century there were other reasons.

It is always difficult to know just how great were casualties from brigandage and anarchy in pre-British times. Gangs of armed robbers, 'dacoits', roamed about the countryside from time to time spreading terror. There were of course large and peaceful empires for much of the time in the old India; and even under the British, dacoity has been a serious problem in living memory. Nevertheless, with the extension of Company's rule in the nineteenth century things were much more peaceful and one of the checks on population— war—was diminished.

Famine also was diminished. The government did not promote the growing of more food; but it did promote the building of roads and railways, which made it possible to transport food rapidly from one place to another.

For both these reasons especially, the population grew, and pressure on land increased. The average holding became smaller and smaller. True, while there was less room for everybody on the land, there was more room in the growing cities: industries eventually developed, and new jobs were available. But the process was too slow. Emigration, to places such as Trinidad and South Africa, began. In spite of the good intentions of most government officials towards Indians—and even because of them—it would be difficult to prove that the average Indian peasant was appreciably more prosperous at the end of British rule than at the beginning. He might be more secure, less likely to die violently, better able to get medicine for himself and education for his children, but he might also be hungrier, less through the fault of his rulers than through the unkind workings of fate.

Industry

The growth of towns, and of industries in them, was something that could assist in a redistribution of the population as land grew scarce. Industries meant new jobs, and exports which could pay for some of India's extra food requirements. But, in a country where even today the bulk of the population lives in the countryside, urbanization and industrialization had no immediate and dramatic effect on the society and economy of India.

Generally speaking, the effects of industries on India were partly beneficial but largely disruptive in the first half of the nineteenth century, and largely beneficial in the second half.

They were disruptive in the first half because India did not have modern textile mills, and her millions of cottage workers sitting at handlooms could not produce cotton cloth, silk and so forth as quickly or cheaply as could Lancashire. This meant that imported cloth from Britain was bought in preference to locally produced cloth, and many weavers were deprived of a living. So although imported manufactures meant lower prices, they also meant disruption to some traditional village crafts, and more people looking for a means of gaining a living.

The reason for India's slow start in industrial development was partly that she lacked the means by which industry, raw materials and markets could be easily and cheaply linked together. To some extent, the development of industry waited on the improvement of communications. This got its biggest boost in the middle of the century, especially under the Governor-Generalship of Dalhousie. There was then a jute mill set up in Calcutta in 1854, and in the next twenty years or so many cotton mills sprang up: by 1895 there were 144 of them. Other manufactures included paper, woollens, and leather goods. Bombay became a great centre of industry. Plantation industry, particularly tea in Assam, became a big export business by the 1880s.

Communications

From facts such as these, about both agriculture and industry, it is clear that the development of communications was a vitally important feature of the country's history. India was entering the world in a way that had not been possible before. Places far apart, previously ignorant about each other or indifferent towards each other, were eventually linked by post, by telegraph, by all-weather roads, by railways. Efficient systems of postal contact had been established at the end of the eighteenth century, chiefly for the purposes of government and Company business, and the system developed into a national service available to everybody at progressively cheaper rates. An Indian Post Office was established in 1854, and letters could be sent for the equivalent of a penny. Telegraph communication with Europe was started in 1865, after having been used within India for ten years. The Suez Canal was opened in 1869, making the voyage to Europe vastly shorter. Railways, originally suggested for India in 1843, were slow to come because many doubted that they would be profitable, not realizing how much new traffic the railways could create simply by existing. But Dalhousie was an enthusiast for railway construction, and work on an Eastern Railway was begun. By 1862 Calcutta was linked by rail to Allahabad. Bombay became the centre of a network in the South.

These developments, along with programmes of roadbuilding in all states undertaken by new public works departments, had several repercussions. It became possible, as we have seen, to create new profitable industries, because raw materials could be taken to them and finished products carried from them to markets or customers at low cost. Trade was given a great boost; local products could be cheaply carried to distant markets, in India or abroad—foodstuffs or craft work—and with the intensification of trading activity, modern methods spread. International trade was made possible on a new scale. And with the telegraph the links with the government in Britain were much closer; the government in India was no longer left to its own devices so much.

Alongside these particular effects was a general broadening of horizons. It was easier for Western culture to spread, and for old traditions to crumble under the impact of new ideas.

(c) Justice

Law

Laws in India were the responsibility of the Governor-General and his Council. When the Legislative Council was created by adding members to the Executive Council, the passing of laws was its responsibility; the Executive Council as such was concerned with running the government, not with making laws.

The first Law Member in the Governor-General's Council was the famous Thomas Babington Macauley, who was appointed in 1834. He did important work in drawing up a code of law, which India lacked. His work was not immediately put into practice, but it formed the foundations of the Indian Penal Codes which came into effect between 1857 and 1861.

Originally, in the earlier part of the century, there were two types of court to administer the law: the Company's courts, staffed by appointees of the Company to hear cases involving Company servants, and Crown courts, which were independent of the Company and administered regular English law. As we have seen there was friction between the two; but in 1861, the old High Courts (one in each of the three presidencies) were abolished and new ones were set up which included the previous Company courts. Later, other provinces besides the three presidencies came to have their own High Courts or Chief Courts administering the Indian codes of law.

In Britain, it has been a traditional principle that the judiciary— the legal profession—shall be separate from the executive —the government. The legal profession owed its loyalty to the law or the Crown, not to a particular government, and held itself ready to judge the government or any of its members or servants if they broke the law. Governors-General like Cornwallis wanted to see a similar separation of judiciary and executive in India. Cornwallis established such a pattern in Bengal. But in general, in Indian conditions, it was more natural to combine judiciary and executive.

In most parts, the local officials were collector-magistrates, who were both running the revenue system on behalf of the government and hearing minor cases on behalf of the law. Such people, constantly going round hearing grievances and meeting cultivators, were more in touch with the people than judges in their courts or tax inspectors in their offices. There was a tendency for some degree of compromise to be worked out between the two ideas. The magistrate-collectors operated the revenue system and kept law and order as well, but there was a separate set of courts independent of the government where all major cases were heard.

How much interference?

This was the machinery of justice. What sort of justice did it dispense?

The answer 'British Justice' is not enough. Laws in Britain had been designed to suit conditions very different from those in India, and could not be transposed abruptly from one scene to the other without raising endless problems. The forgery case in Warren Hastings' time is a case in point: in England forgery was a very grave crime; in India it was almost taken for granted.

We must remember too that the Hindus with their sacred texts had a well developed system of justice going back to antiquity, and many customs which had behind them all the force of religion. There were many who were in favour of interfering with the society and the customs of India as little as possible, for fear of upsetting something that had stood the test of centuries, and that worked well enough for those who had evolved it. On the other hand, there were those who wanted to see change, who wanted to put an end to the practices that seemed like injustice in English eyes, who wanted to see reforms that would be of practical use to the Indians. Macauley, with his zeal for a new code of law, was one of these. Governor-General Bentinck, and later Dalhousie, were others. This debate was important, and we will not understand the behaviour of the British administrators unless we can see both points of view.

Those who wanted as little interference as possible had the utmost respect for Indian culture, and did excellent work in promoting the study of Indian languages and literature; and they opposed change on the ground that the British were in a strange civilization which they did not properly understand, and in which they should not rashly meddle.

Those who wanted to interfere were not necessarily arrogant imperialists anxious to put everything into a British mould and have change just for the sake of change. Many of them were humanitarians concerned to benefit the Indians as much as possible, to put an end to the more barbarous customs and to promote progress and prosperity. Though British rule tended to be conservative and reluctant to interfere with native society, in the end the reformers came to dominate the thinking of successive Indian governments.

Reforms

It was this reformist thinking which lay behind a number of steps taken by the government at different times to curb Indian practices that offended British ideas of justice and indeed civilization. Slavery was abolished. From 1843, slavery was not recognized by law. This meant that slave-owners had no legal rights over their slaves. From 1860, slaveholding was an offence. The argument against abolishing slavery was that slaves were not necessarily worse off than other people, and did at least have security from their owners, who had to feed them and look after them. But to the reformers slavery was a clear social evil.

It cost money to have a daughter married off; sons were preferred, who would stay with their parents and look after them in their old age. For these reasons baby daughters were unwelcome, and there

was a custom in some parts of killing them. This was prohibited.
One particularly notorious custom was called *sati* (or *suttee*).
The word itself means 'good woman'. What it entailed was that when
a woman's husband died she should commit suicide by throwing
herself upon his funeral pyre. Reluctant to interfere at first, the
government was eventually pushed into action by some particularly
nasty cases. The reformer Bentinck abolished the custom in 1829.

It is one thing to declare a thing illegal; it is quite another to stop
it, especially when most people approve of it. These reforms did not
put an end to the practices overnight; but in the course of time the
desired end was achieved.

Government Activity

We can see from all these things that in the course of the nineteenth century the government, originally interested only in law and
order and revenue as adjuncts to commercial activities, became
more and more entangled in the affairs of the society it governed,
it could not keep aloof. This development is symbolized by the
change after the Indian Mutiny from Company rule to direct rule
by the British monarch. It is a development embodied in the government's impact, intended or unintended, on agriculture and industry;
in the preoccupation of the reformers with justice for the Indians;
in the abolition of certain customs; in government activity to promote communications, irrigation, forestry (a department was created
in 1889), famine relief (a commission studied the question in 1880),
and other areas of activity. But what perhaps, more than anything
else, made inevitable the birth of a new India, was the spread of
Western ideas and Western education.

(d) Education

In the days of the British raj, education was a precious thing that
conferred great benefits upon its owners. It could give them positions
in the government service, make them village accountants, or
teachers, or lawyers, or other professional men who were looked up
to in society. Therefore education under the British is an important
part of the study of Indian society, and one which has given rise to
different points of view among those who have written about it.

Was the British achievement in the education of the Indians a
good one or a bad one? There has been bitter disagreement on
this question. So much depends on the point of view with which we
look at the period. If we consider the need felt for education in India
nowadays, we find ourselves complaining that in the eighteenth and
nineteenth centuries far too little was done for education far too

slowly. If we consider the position of the governments of the time—
and they could not see into the future—we can understand their
caution.

More or less education?

This is one question that people did not disagree about much:
everybody thought there should be more, because it was a good thing.
Of course, it is another matter whether there actually *was* more
education under the British raj than before it. Some people argued
at the time, and some have argued since, that the Company with its
high taxes took away from the Indian rulers and wealthy classes the
resources that had previously been used to maintain village schools
almost everywhere. These people have claimed that the Indian
villagers were actually better off before the British came. But,
anyway, most officials, missionaries and Indian men in public life
wanted to see education develop: the disagreements were about
what sort of education, and who should provide it.

Private or public schools?

There was certainly disagreement on this question. Governments
preferred for a long time to encourage initiatives by private
individuals in the setting up and maintenance of schools, without
committing themselves to public intervention on a large scale.
Many complained that too little was being done by the governments.
In the earlier part of the nineteenth century, grants-in-aid were
given to help a number of local village schools. After 1850, some
village schools were actually set up by the government. As for
secondary and higher education, a few colleges were set up from
early times: Warren Hastings' college at Calcutta in 1781, Duncan's
college at Benares in 1791, the Sanskrit College at Calcutta in 1821,
and others. The universities of Calcutta, Madras and Bombay were
created in 1857. But, by 1882, there were as many as 1,341 secondary
schools in existence established by private agencies, usually Indian.
This was far and away in excess of the state activity in the field. In
the year 1901–02, there were about 55,000 private schools and only
about 17,000 state schools. Those who urged the government to do
more felt that the resources of these private schools were inadequate,
and that the methods were not modern enough, and that things
would be much better under a government programme.

Religious or secular education?

Governments moved slowly in the matter of education. The
entreaties of eighteenth century reformers like Wilberforce, that
more should be done for the Indians, did not at first have very much

effect. The reason was not simply that governments did not like to spend money. The reason was partly that governments were always reluctant to interfere with Indian institutions. They did not want to ram something strange and unwelcome down Indian throats.

Now this reluctance was particularly marked in the matter of education, because education was associated with the spread of Christianity. During their early development, the schools were all run by missionaries, who very naturally wanted to convert the Indians. But the government was unwilling to make itself responsible for a movement that seemed designed to disrupt the Hindu and Muslim beliefs and practices which were fostered by indigenous tradition. It wanted to appear strictly neutral in activities that affected religion.

Sanskrit or English education?

The same respect for Indian culture and traditions made governments reluctant to insist on Western style education. This was quite a thorny question for educators and officials.

There were two points of view. One was that the Indians should be educated in their own culture. Their ancient classical language, Sanskrit, was the language of many works on law, mathematics, astronomy, religion and so forth, and it was felt that it would be disruptive, and cause hostility, to thrust Western education upon them—even though many prominent Indians in the cities were all in favour of the spread of it.

The other point of view was that to confine Indians to education in their own culture, based on works in Sanskrit, would be to make of them second-class citizens. They would be cut off from all the advantages and opportunities that a knowledge of English could bring. According to this point of view, the British government ought to justify British rule by giving the Indians the benefits of British culture—by allowing them to study English, by setting up schools for them where the actual language of instruction should be English, and where Western medicine, sciences, engineering and so forth could be studied.

This was the point of view of many Indian educators such as Ram Mohun Roy early in the nineteenth century. People like him disapproved of the government's policy of providing education in the local Indian languages and in Sanskrit, and they set up various schools on their own initiative to give a modern education centred on English. The government slowly followed their example. In 1829 an English section was established in the Calcutta college. In 1835, following the urging of Macauley, it was decided that English should be made a medium of instruction in colleges.

Primary or secondary education?

But decisions such as these affected only a few favoured people in a few secondary colleges, where education was expensive to provide, and the government had to spend a great deal to educate a few people. In 1891, out of a population of 262 million people, only twelve million were literate and only about half a million knew English. Government activity in the field of education was obviously not producing very striking results out in the villages, where primary schooling was necessary.

There was agitation about this; many thought that much more should be done for primary education. In 1892, under Lord Ripon—who was very interested in the problem of state education—there was an Education Commission, a body that made a thorough study of the crisis in India's school situation and recommended among many other things that, though secondary schooling should not be sacrificed, a lot more should be done to promote government schools in villages everywhere and thus do for primary schooling what British rule had so far failed to do, and what perhaps Indian enterprise had tried more successfully to do in the days before the British came.

Looked at from the modern standpoint, progress in education was therefore not very impressive at all, and there was no real idea of it—until late—as something that should be available for everybody. But it did not need a very wide diffusion of Western-style education to cause important repercussions in Indian society. If even only a few Indians, an elite, were keenly aware of what Western culture and technology had to offer, had the benefit of these things themselves, and wanted them spread to their fellow-Indians, the raw material was present for a great change in Indian society. Following the lead of its elite, vast numbers of people came to want the benefits of modernization, and the political advancement that seemed to be the means to it.

CHAPTER THIRTEEN

The Rise of Congress, 1885-1929

(a) 'POLITICS' 1885–1907

Beginnings of Congress

The government of India was centred on London, where the Secretary of State for India was assisted by a Council. Many Indians thought that this Council was not sufficiently in touch with India to take part in running it. In India, there was the Viceroy, who was assisted by a Legislative Council. Further, the country was divided into provinces, each of which had its own council. Most of the people in this pyramid of councils were British officials. The Indians were not expected to take part in politics.

But the times were changing. In 1885 there arose an organization called the Indian National Congress which took a very strong interest in politics from the start. In the course of time it came to make certain very specific demands for the reform of the constitution of India, giving a voice to Indians in the running of the country. It wanted the Secretary of State's London council abolished. It wanted the central Legislative Council in India expanded, to include a good number of non-official Indians. And it wanted a re-organization of the examinations for the Indian Civil Service. The desire was that the examinations should be held simultaneously in England and India, giving an equal chance to Indians and Englishmen who wanted to become high officials of the government in India.

These demands for greater Indian representation in the running of government were not very popular with the senior British officials. But Congress stuck to politics, and in spite of some reforms of the sort that it wanted, it became more and more demanding, more and more insistent on the importance of giving increased representation to Indians in their own country. Eventually Congress became the chief voice of nationalism, became an implacable antagonist of the British regime, became at last the government of an independent

India; so it is today. It is well worth while, then, to examine the beginnings of this movement and the circumstances in which it grew.

Political or social problems

Various complaints about the Indian National Congress were made by its British opponents. The claim that it should not meddle in politics was only one of these; but an important one, in the minds of those who made it. The Viceroy, Lord Dufferin, wrote:

'It is true that a considerable number of highly educated, intelligent, and I believe perfectly loyal, honest, and well-meaning Native Politicians have conceived, though in a vague and hazy way, the idea of the introduction into India of political institutions of a far more democratic character . . . It will be sufficient to observe that the principal subjects which they have brought forward as constituting the grievances of the people of India are of singularly trivial importance in comparison with the many momentous administrative problems which have been already dealt with by Government even during my own tenure of office, or which are still pressing for solution.'

His argument was that having democratic institutions, with Indians playing a more important part in government, was less important than social problems like overpopulation or waste of money by the Indians on ceremonies and unproductive activities. And he thought that Congress was being trivial in neglecting such problems and clamouring for political changes.

Did Congress represent India?

This was one complaint then; the belief that the Indians in Congress were bothering themselves about unimportant things. In a way this complaint arose from another, the belief that the Congress members were not really representative of their country and were therefore not really important.

Not all Indians, of course, were interested in politics, or wanted more Indian participation in administration. The meetings organized by Congress were attended, and studied, by a very small section of the population only—the Western-educated city dwellers. These were Western-educated in the sense that they had received a British style of education, using the English language, and most of them had had university training. But there were only a few thousand of these people. The rest of the population, all the many millions of them, lived as if in a different world, a world by and large of poverty and ignorance. Maybe it was a rather unkind idea, but it was the idea of people like Dufferin that the Indians behind the Congress were unrepresentative, separated from their own countrymen by their education, greedy for their own power, and ignorant of the real problems of the country—problems caused by social evils that the British administrators were daily grappling with.

Differences within Congress

One of these social evils was the division of the country into regional and religious groups which were jealous of each other. Congress itself could not escape the consequence of this division. Its members could not agree with each other all the time. They belonged to different groups that were often hostile to each other. The leaders of Congress were aware of the dangers of disunity. It was important that the organization should speak with one voice if it was to have influence in the land. Therefore it was made a rule that it should make pronouncements only on matters about which most members agreed. This meant, for example, that nothing should be said about matters on which Hindus and Muslims disagreed. There was much antipathy from time to time between Hindus and Muslims, and the leaders of Congress in the early days wanted to avoid anything which might exacerbate the distrust between the two religions. But as time went on, there came to be more and more extremists in the movement, people who wished to promote the Hindu religion at the same time as they were promoting Indian representation. And in promoting Hinduism, they could easily give offence to the Muslims.

As early as 1882, B. G. Tilak formed his cow protection movement. The protection of cows may seem an odd political programme outside India, but even today it is a subject which plays an important part in the agitation of Indian politicians. The reason for this we have noticed before: in Hinduism, cows are sacred.

Eventually Congress came to be divided into the extremists and the moderates. The extremists, men like Tilak, were keen Hindus anxious for rapid political reforms. The moderates, men like Gokhale (who became president of Congress), wanted co-operation between all groups, and did not want to antagonize either the different Indian religions or the British government unduly. The rift between extremists and moderates widened. In 1905, the same year in which Gokhale became president, a separate Muslim League was set up. In 1906 there was a split between Gokhale and Tilak. There were disagreements over the Congress programme: the moderates were aiming at Indian participation in the government, without cutting off India from Britain, but the extremists wanted India to be independent. In 1907 there was an outright struggle for control of Congress between the two groups, in which the moderates were victorious. But the unity of the movement was ruined.

Relations with the government

When we read the statements and speeches by Congress leaders, the most striking development we notice as the years passed is the increase in antagonism towards the British government. When the movement started, it was entirely friendly to the government; but before very long it came to be regarded by some senior British officials as mischievous and positively dangerous.

It is fascinating to compare the tone of speeches at the first meetings of Congress with what came later. In 1886 the president, Dadabhai Naoroji, said:

> 'It is under the civilizing rule of the Queen and people of England that we meet here together, hindered by none, and are freely allowed to speak our minds without the least fear and without the least hesitation. Such a thing is possible under British rule and British rule only.' (*Loud cheers*)

Thirteen years later, at the end of the century, the government was making enquiries through the police to find out who were the supporters of Congress, with a view to bringing pressure to bear on them and weakening the movement. Lord Dufferin, as we have seen, had described Congress in 1888 as well-intentioned but trivial. By 1900 the Viceroy of the time, Lord Curzon, was almost contemptuous of the movement. This change of attitude was caused largely by the increasing extremism of some of the movement's members.

Reforms

This extremism and hostility of some Indians seemed to the British to be especially ungrateful, because in fact several reforms of government were undertaken, with the effect of giving Indians more representation. The India Councils Act of 1892 enlarged the councils in India, both at the centre, under the Viceroy, and in the provinces, giving increased non-official Indian membership. The scope of these councils was broadened, also: they could discuss all manner of business and give advice on a wide range of subjects. But the British did not realize, and in the circumstances they could not be expected to foresee, that as a sop to nationalism such measures were too little, too late. We should not see Tilak and the other extremists as unmitigated villains and wild men bent on destroying good government and communal harmony. They were straws in the wind, a wind that was to blow away the British era and much of what went with it, good and bad together; and men, like straws, were controlled by circumstance, being thrust by their own conflicts and their own frustrations into more and more uncompromising attitudes.

(b) THE ACTS OF 1909 AND 1919

The Government of India Act of 1909 had the effect of giving substantially increased representation to the Indians in the councils, and introduced indirect elections. In 1919 a new reform went much further. It introduced a new idea of government to India, the idea of dyarchy—double rule. The Indians shared the running of the country with the British. It was an experiment, and it was intended only as a temporary measure. It did not work, because Congress would not co-operate in making it work.

The growth of nationalism

Things had changed a lot since the days when Congress leaders could heap praises on the British, and be cheered for it. Antagonism was now increasingly widespread, and there was no longer any idea that Indian politicians would act meekly as yes-men for the government. But the change had not been sudden, nor was it ever total. There was no one point at which the government became an enemy in the eyes of the Indian educated classes. At all times, there was a complex mingling of different attitudes: those Englishmen who regarded the Congress politicians as wild and mischievous could point to their hostile language and hostile actions; but those who regarded them as responsible men, deserving of a greater share in the government, could point to other things—the spread of education, the friendship that many Indians had for the British, either collectively or as individuals, the apparent loyalty and enthusiasm with which Indians supported Britain in the Great War, the displays of excitement and affection when King George V came with Queen Mary to Delhi in 1911. There was not a straight-out contest between rulers and ruled. Most Indians anyway were not interested in politics, and it was only a small number of professional men—officials, lawyers, teachers, and so forth—who opposed the government. Moreover, the conflict was complicated by the antagonisms within the nationalist movement; between moderates and extremists, Muslims and Hindus.

Of course this does not mean that Congress was not important, or that its leaders did not deserve to be heard. It means that the small number of professional men was a harbinger of what was to come. They were not typical of all Indians; but in the course of time nevertheless they came to be leaders of Indian opinion, and in the course of time the mass of the people—Hindus at least—was prepared to follow.

The Government of India Act, 1909

However strong these forces may have been, there was not yet, and there was not to be for a long time, any sense of panic in the government's actions. The Government of India Act was a carefully considered reform to give more representation to Indians in the councils.

Two Indian members were added to the council of the Secretary of State in London, and one to the Viceroy's Executive Council. The Legislative Assemblies in the provinces were strengthened in several ways. There were to be Indian members elected to them— chosen not by a single general election but elected indirectly by various local organizations. New countryside constituencies were created, so that the members should not represent only the cities. Also there were special constituencies for groups such as Muslims. The scope of the provincial councils' powers was enlarged. So although there was nothing like a move towards real self-government, nothing that would make the extremists happy, yet something was done to give the Indian politicians a louder voice.

Dyarchy

Dyarchy is the name that came to be given to the sharing of authority between British and Indians brought in by the reforms of 1919. These represented a great advance in the handing over of responsibility.

Share in responsibility was given by bringing a majority of elected or non-official members into the councils at the centre of government, and by splitting the work of government in the provinces into two parts, one run by the British and the other by Indians.

In the central government, the Council of State was to have sixty members, thirty-four of them elected. The Legislative Assembly was to have 140 members, 114 of them elected or non-official. The provinces were to have a new status, under governors instead of lieutenant-governors. Two classes of ministry were established, one consisting of what was called reserved subjects, under British officials, and the other of transferred subjects, to be run by Indians. The reserved subjects were things like defence, law and order, and these were the powers that the British felt they should keep in their own hands. The transferred subjects consisted of such things as health, forestry, local administration and so forth—routine affairs that would give the Indians a training in self-government. It was understood that if the experiment worked, more self-government would be given later.

But it was too late. The nationalists were too committed to opposition, and in the 1920's dyarchy was virtually wrecked. The leaders of Indian opinion were not co-operating. Tensions between the two races became more acute; troubles multiplied. In 1919, the very year of the reforms, there was ugly rioting at Amritsar, and the British army commander sent to the spot, General Dyer, ordered his troops to shoot, causing many casualties. This incident helped to inflame racial feelings. In the next few years there was more rioting— not only against the government, but between the rival nationalist groups.

(c) Non-Co-Operation 1920–1929

It was largely in the 1920's that crusading leaders appeared who were to steer the nationalist movement through its most turbulent period. Gandhi, a lawyer who had lived and worked in South Africa, rose to proclaim the policy of passive resistance to the British, a policy that served as a banner for a successful campaign. Jawaharlal Nehru, son of a Congress president, followed his father as nationalist leader: but he belonged to a new, uncompromising generation.

Gandhi

No name figures more prominently in the history of modern India than Gandhi's. No man's memory, perhaps, is held in greater honour in India today. For many millions he represented, and still symbolizes, all things that were or seemed good in the struggle for independence, the dignity of self-government, the sanctity of a crusade for righteousness. This element of sanctity is important in the mystique of Gandhi. He was more than a political leader. There was a strong religious flavour to the doctrines that he preached and the appeal that he had for his followers. He was something of a priest as well as a politician. He came to be identified with honour and righteousness, until, after his death, criticism of him came to seem something like sacrilege.

He appeared, then, first and foremost as a holy man, and that is one important element in his career. But by itself it would not be enough. He needed to be a shrewd politician too, and this element he was well able to supply from his past experience in politics and his instinct for understanding the psychology of his opponents. Before entering the Indian nationalist movement, he had been a lawyer and a political leader in South Africa, working for the Indians there. He had gained experience in organizing nationalist groups and starting strikes. And he had gained an understanding of the British government and its ways.

His contribution to the nationalist cause in India was a carefully worked out doctrine of passive resistance. This was called *satyagraha*—literally, maintaining the truth. It involved also the doctrine of non-violence, a feature prominent also in Indian religions. Thus what Gandhi preached combined the dynamism of a political movement with the pacifism of Indian religions, and it enabled his followers to feel that they were at once good nationalists and good Hindus.

Passive resistance

This quality of holiness is only one part of Gandhi's success. Apart from this, the particular means he adopted were well suited to his ends. The ends were to oppose British rule and establish an independent self-governing India. The means were to embarrass the government at every turn and bring it to a standstill, not by violence, not by revolution, not by mutinies or rebellions, but by passiveness, by turning the other cheek, by refusing to co-operate in any way with the government and thus making it ineffective without turmoil or bloodshed.

These methods could be very effective, because if they were properly used the government would be made impotent without being given the excuse for using force to crush its opponents. A mutiny could be put down with as much energy as the situation required, and the mutineers punished, as past Indian history showed. But passive resistance did not offer the government a clear target for reprisals. People who simply lay down in the road could not very well be executed or sent to prison for many years.

But what happened in practice was not quite like this. Not all followers of Gandhi had his standards of restraint and integrity. Indeed, few of them had. Although Gandhi's leadership cast its imprint deep on the nationalist movement, the spirit of his teaching was too little understood, or, if understood, abused by those who professed to be following it. There is no getting away from the fact that passive resistance, conceived of as an honourable and peaceful struggle with an honourable opponent, was all too often made into a seemly label for hypocritical, violent and squalid actions.

Congress in the 1920s

There was more and more violence. Rioting was frequent, particularly between Muslim and Hindu crowds. 1921 and 1922 were bad years. But violence was entirely contrary to the official policy of the Congress movement, which was to make the constitution unworkable by non-co-operation. The 1920 assembly had decided on a Gandhian line, urging its followers passively to resist the government in all its forms.

But some of the chief pre-occupations of the leadership were with rivalry between Indians rather than opposition to the British. While everybody had accepted the authority of the British regime, conflict between Muslims and Hindus had been put into cold storage, as it were. But now that Muslims and Hindus were actively making plans for a future in which the British were expected to disappear from the seat of power, all the antagonism between the two religious persuasions flared up.

In 1928 Motilal Nehru (the father of Jawaharlal) made a report setting out the form of constitution that Congress wanted for the country. One of the chief features was the re-arrangement of the provinces so that there would be a balance between Hindu and Muslim provinces. This measure was designed to get the confidence of the Muslim community. But the report also favoured abolishing the separate constituencies for the councils, and it was these separate constituencies which assured for the Muslims much of their representation. The report did not much appeal to them. Other measures proposed included a strong government at the centre—not leaving very much scope for the provinces to run their own affairs—and dominion status for the country. That is, India was to remain a dominion of Britain, although self-governing; outright independence was not demanded.

Now this report was no more than a statement of what the Congress leaders would like. It was not acceptable to many of the younger nationalists, who were more extreme in their demands. Motilal Nehru belonged to an older generation which was more ready to compromise. But the Simon Commission, sent out by the British government in 1927 to recommend ways in which India could have peaceful constitutional evolution, had been met by resolute non-co-operation on the part of the Indians. It had not included any Indian members, which gave offence. And from now on Congress was not doing business with the government.

In 1929 Jawaharlal Nehru became president of Congress, and a policy of working for complete independence was adopted. It was a policy that was carried through until it succeeded, and Nehru became the first Prime Minister of an independent India.

CHAPTER FOURTEEN

Nationalism

(a) THE MEANING OF NATIONALISM

From 1929 onwards the Congress movement was squarely and firmly committed to getting complete independence for India without delay and without half-measures. There was no turning back and there was no compromise: Congress had to win, or break. It won.

There is a world of difference between Congress as it now became and Congress as it had started, late in the nineteenth century. Then, it had been a sort of debating society for cultured gentlemen—there had not been in its deliberations the earnestness, the urgency, the bitterness that impelled its members increasingly in the twentieth century. Now, it had entered the real world of politics with a vengeance. It had to justify itself to supporters who took a greater interest in politics and had clearer expectations of their leaders than before. And it had to contend with rivals and opponents. It was struggling for power now, not simply discussing what the government of the country ought to do.

Among the Hindus at least, Congress was the main repository of nationalism. As such, it represented a force that had long been stirring in India but now gathered momentum like a bus running downhill, with the brake off.

Similar forces were at work in other parts of the world, and have been ever since, until today 'nationalism' has become a thoroughly familiar word in the newspapers. What does it mean? What does nationalism mean to the people who profess it? Why has it seemed to affect so many different parts of the world at almost the same time?

Attitudes to nationalism

For Gandhi, the spiritual as well as political leader of the nationalist movement in the eyes of many millions of Indians, one of the most important ingredients in the programme was that the educated leaders of the movement should use spinning wheels.

'The spinning wheel is an emblem of human dignity and equality in the truest sense of the term. It is the handmaid of agriculture. It is the nation's second lung. We are perishing because we are using only one lung, and yet only a few Congressmen have a living faith in the India-wide potency of the wheel.'

He admitted that not very many of his colleagues in the movement shared his enthusiasm for the wheel, but he was convinced that it was of potentially enormous value for the nationalist cause.

'The general body of them have no faith in it and yet, if I could carry their reason with me, I would substitute the four-anna franchise by personal, daily, hand-spinning'.

What is the connection between spinning and nationalism?

Nationalism can be all things to all men. If we want to understand what it meant to Gandhi, we have to think of it in a special way. For him, it meant getting rid of the British, but it meant far more than this. It meant the building of a nation.

It is easy for Westerners to think of themselves as belonging to this or that nation, but it was—still is—a comparatively new idea in the countries of Africa and Asia. For most of the teeming millions of Gandhi's India it was by no means natural to think of themselves as members of the Indian nation. We have to remember that most could not, and still today cannot, read; that most rarely moved outside the little world of their own villages; that they were divided from each other, not only by the fact that they lived in fairly static groups, but also by caste, by religion, by enormous differences in wealth and education. They did not, and still do not, have so much in common with each other as do the citizens of a Western country. Therefore we can see why they are more ready to think of themselves, and act, as Hindus or Muslims, brahmans or untouchables, Bengalis or Punjabis, and so on, rather than as Indians. And we can see why the leaders of the nationalist movement were concerned to build up a loyalty among the people to the idea of 'India' on top of all the petty loyalties to their groups by which they were inspired.

This is where the spinning wheels come in. Gandhi's idea was that simple pursuits like spinning should serve as a bridge between different classes of people and keep the educated and Westernized in touch with the life of the common people.

Not all the nationalist leaders wanted to do this in the same way. They were not all interested in sharing in the life of the common folk by pursuits such as spinning. Jawaharlal Nehru, president of Congress, was more interested in helping the common folk to share in modern developments like industrialization than in getting the leaders to share in old ways. But what the nationalist politicians shared was a desire to cement the people of India into one whole. This proved to be impossible. There was too much distrust between the Hindu and Muslim religions. In the end, India was carved into two, one part keeping the name of India and the other part becoming Pakistan. So for some purposes it is useful to talk of two nationalisms: Indian, or Hindu, and Muslim. In the eyes of Congress leaders in the decade or so before independence, however, the Muslims were not true nationalists because they had their eyes set on one group within the nation, a religious group, and not on the nation as a whole.

The world context

When we talk about things going on in one country, it is easy to forget that there are other countries in the world as well. When we ask questions about the development of nationalism in India, we should remember that nationalism developed in many other places, notably in south-east Asia and Africa, and we should also remember that in Britain itself there were changing ideas about the empire, with some people wanting to see the colonies brought to independence. What went on in India, from the end of the nineteenth century onwards, was part of a process going on in the world at large.

It would therefore be wrong to try and understand Indian nationalism entirely by looking at the particular events and circumstances of India. We have to recognize that something was afoot in the world, something good or bad, or more probably both (being mixed with the good and bad motives of the men who represented it); but something inevitable and something very widespread.

Aspects of nationalism

The spread of Western education, the spread of Western industries, the spread of Western ideas brought not only to India but to all the other poor countries of the world where there were colonial powers a new sense of purpose and a new loyalty. The sense and the loyalty were born first in a select few, in some of the educated; but somehow, in the course of time, the movement of nationalism became more like a mass movement, became a political reality. Workers in the towns came to want higher standards of living that had seemed unattainable to their fathers, and looked to the nationalist politicians for leadership. The local heads of caste and religious groups realized that the British might not be there forever, that one day there might be Indian rulers. And it seemed naturally important that any future Indian rulers should not be oppressive towards their various castes and religions. So these communities became actively interested in the politics of nationalism. These developments acted on the nationalist leaders, who found themselves dragged into an earnest world of competition and bitter realities. The new loyalty and the new sense of purpose were things to be fought for, not just talked about.

In India, as in other places, these things expressed themselves in different and partly contradictory forms. There was a negative aspect (which does not necessarily mean a bad one) and there was a positive aspect (which does not necessarily mean a good one). There was a forward-looking aspect and a backward-looking aspect.

The negative aspect was the anti-government character of the movement. It seemed to be necessary, for the purpose of building a new Indian nation, to get rid of the foreign government. From 1929 Congress was committed to complete independence from Britain. From 1930 to 1934, with an interruption in 1931, there was a programme of civil disobedience launched by Congress, by which people were urged not to obey the government or have anything to do with its activities. When World War II broke out, Congress demanded a new constitution, giving effective Indian independence, immediately and not at the end of the war, as a condition of supporting the war effort. When this was refused, Congress launched another disobedience campaign.

To say that these policies are negative, for the purpose of classifying them, is only to say they were concerned with removing something— the British government. They can be compared with other policies, which can be described as positive, the setting up of something new— an independent Indian nation. This meant doing away with the barriers between different groups of Indians and helping them all to develop in harmony with each other.

Two of the problems of promoting unity may be mentioned here. One was the problem of communalism. This is a word that has come to be used a great deal in India with a special meaning. It means the spirit of opposition between different religious groups. Congress professed to represent no particular religion and no particular caste; it claimed to represent all Indians. However, it failed to get the support of large numbers of Muslims, whose rival organization, the Muslim League, eventually became powerful and had a large basis of Muslim adherence. Therefore, in spite of the professed policies of Congress, there came to be a split between two political movements which corresponded with religions: the Muslim League with Islam, and Congress with Hinduism. It was the conflict between these parties and these religions that made impossible the creation of an independent and unified India.

The other problem, which has still not been satisfactorily solved, is the abolition of caste barriers. From early times, especially under Gandhi's influence, it was the policy of Congress to remove the disadvantages of the Depressed Classes—the large numbers of people who are regarded as impure by the caste Hindus. But you cannot change human nature by an act of parliament: it has been one thing for Congress governments to legislate against barriers between caste and caste, or between caste and outcastes, quite another to get people to abandon the age-old customs of discrimination and privilege among themselves. The problem continues today.

These are ways in which the movement represented by Congress was negative and positive at the same time. Taking another view of its characteristics, we can say that it was both backward-looking and forward-looking.

The leaders were mostly Western-educated men—men brought up in Western-style schools where the instruction was in English, or who had even been to England for their schooling. In spite of being intensely Indian in their aspirations, they had in some ways a Western outlook, and it was part of their nationalism to bring India into the modern world, to industrialize, to spread education, to spread liberal ideas, to give all men equality of opportunity. Jawaharlal Nehru said:

'Personally, I owe too much to England ever to feel wholly alien to her. And, do what I will, I cannot get rid of the habits of mind, and the standards and ways of judging other countries as well as life generally, which I acquired at school and college in England. All my predictions (apart from politican plans) are in favour of England and the English people, and if I have become what is called an uncompromising opponent of British rule in India, it is almost in spite of myself.

'It is that rule, that domination, to which we object, and with which we cannot compromise willingly—not the English people'.

What this shows is that, to people like Nehru, nationalism was not a purely anti-Western thing.

Nationalism meant getting rid of Western political domination, but it also meant adopting Western ideas of government and the like in India; it meant modernizing, improving the standard of living of the poor, using the State as a means for bringing to everybody the facilities and advantages of the twentieth century.

There were others for whom nationalism meant something different: getting rid of Western ideas and ways of life as well as Western political domination. For these, it meant a return to purely Indian things. For example, the Arya Samaj (founded in 1887) was an organization which wished to use the Hindu religion as a path back to a state of purity and simplicity which was thought to have existed before there was any Western influence.

This strain in the nationalist movement, this conservatism, helps to explain why there was so much conflict between rival nationalisms, why distrust between Indian leaders and their communities prevented the emergence of a single nationalist programme (although Congress would claim that theirs was a single nationalist programme, representing all Indians including Muslims). In harking back to traditional Indian culture, the religious movements (Arya Samaj was simply one of the more extreme) were harking back to a pre-British condition of rival religions and communities that were jealous of each other.

It is clear that the ideas of the men who rose up against British rule, and eventually brought British rule to an end, were varied. Their programme for India can be seen under different aspects, the chief tragedy being that, in spite of their Westernization, they could not override the differences and suspicions between themselves. When independence came, it came in a torrent of blood.

Cultural nationalism

There are several reasons why it would be a good thing to have a look at the cultural scene at this point. One is that twentieth-century Indian culture is rich, varied and interesting, and deserves a mention even if there is no room to do it justice. Another is that it is a pleasanter subject than politics, because when the nationalist spirit breathed through art and literature, with all its varieties of modernity and traditionalism, the result was not—as with politics—strife and trouble, but a multitude of fascinating new forms. Another is that culture cannot really be separated from nationalism.

It cannot be separated from nationalism because none of India's intellectuals in the early part of the century could escape from the tug of political thought and pre-occupation—simply because they *were* intellectuals. The people who wrote, and thought, and painted, were the same sort of people as those who led the fight for independence—the educated élite. And they were all caught in the same tensions and pre-occupations because they were all torn between the same opposing forces: the spirit of traditional India, with its philosophy, its Hindu religion, its age-old ways of life, and on the other hand the spirit of the modern world, with its cosmopolitanism, its quest for progress, its desire for change, its belief in equality.

We can do no more than note an example or two of these opposite trends in art and thought, and notice that in a subtle way they can be synthesized to make something new. The spirit of Indian tradition, the old India, is represented by the rediscovery of ancient wisdom. This does not mean that it was unknown before; but only since late in the last century has the study of ancient Hindu thought been a vital force on the cultural scene. Europeans had a hand in the revival of interest in the metaphysics and philosophy of Indian religions, Hindu and Buddhist.

In the field of scholarship, more and more Indians, infected by nationalism, were turning to the study of ancient Indian traditions as an inspiration and a justification for their political aspirations. People like the lawyer K. P. Jayaswal studied Indian history and reconstructed, with some exaggeration, a glorious past which they discerned in antiquity and which seemed to fortify the demand for political advancement in the India of the present.

In the field of literature, Indian languages came into their own, especially Bengali. Though Hindi is spoken by more people, Bengali is generally considered to have a richer literature. Back in the nineteenth century, Ram Mohun Roy enriched the language with his philosophical writings. Later, Bankim Chandra Chatterji earned a reputation with his Bengali novels. But towering over all is the figure of Rabindranath Tagore (1861–1941), one of the really great names in modern India. Poet, novelist, thinker, he was at home equally in his native Bengali and in English. His songs have passed into the stock of Bengali folk tradition.

The modern trend is best represented, not by naming Indians who have, like astronauts, propelled themselves totally into the world of Western culture—if indeed any such exist—but by mentioning the simple fact that Western ideas, Western methods of education, and the English language are vehicles of much of modern Indian culture. Go to any reputable Indian university and you will find Indian lecturers talking in English (albeit Indian English) about any of the things that are studied in Western universities. Go to any cultured Indian's home, and you are at least as likely to hear pop or classical Western music from his phonograph as Indian music, vital though Indian music is today.

But the greatest achievements of art, music, scholarship, literature and so forth can be reached neither by forsaking the traditions that Indians have inherited and turning themselves into imitation Westerners, nor by burrowing into the past and pretending that the modern world doesn't exist. The greatest achievements come from combining old and new, from breathing the spirit of the East into the form of the West—or vice versa. Rabindranath Tagore and the people round him may be mentioned again to represent this synthesis, this combining. He came of a wealthy and talented family with large landholdings in Bengal. His father and grandfather were renowned writers and thinkers, and their house was thronged by poets, novelists, artists. Rabindranath was no more than the most illustrious of an illustrious family.

Rabindranath's writings are important contributions to English as well as Bengali literature; in 1913 he was awarded the Nobel prize for the English version, written by himself, of his poem 'Gitanjali'. In his lifetime, his house at Bolpur, Santineketan, 'abode of peace', became a centre of writers and, particularly, artists who did much to create a new style of Indian culture that combined tradition and novelty; and after his death Santineketan became the site of a university where the teaching is carried on in the traditional Indian method. In Calcutta, the Tagore family buildings became the nucleus of a Tagore memorial university specialising in Indian song and dance.

We can distinguish, then, between two sorts of Indian intellectuals who were active on the scene in the first half of this century. On the one hand, there were the men of art and letters, in whom the coming together of East and West, of old and new, caused the creation of new forms, caused harmony. On the other hand, there were the politicians, in whom this same coming together, through no fault of their own, but through the nature of politics and the tensions of modern India, caused disharmony, caused strife, caused communalism in all its most virulent forms.

(b) COMMUNALISM

The Muslim League

Early in the twentieth century, when talk of greater representation for Indians, and of greater participation in government, was in the air, the various minority groups in the population naturally wanted to share in the representation and to participate in the greater degree of self-government that the future seemed to hold. The Muslim League was formed in 1905 to act on behalf of the interests of the Muslims. The separate electorates created by the 1909 reforms, which gave special representation to Muslims, were an early success for the organization's programme.

In the period after World War I, the League was not active on the political scene, but it was revived in 1924 and put forward a programme for India whereby the country was to be a dominion of Britain—self-governing, but not completely independent—and have separate electorates to ensure that Muslims would be adequately represented.

The idea of separate electorates was this. If a large number of electorates had more Hindus than Muslims in each of them, then each electorate would probably elect a Hindu to represent it in a provincial or the central legislature—parliament. This would mean that, even though there were a lot of Muslims in the area, they would have no Muslims to represent them in the legislature. But if there were separate electorates, seats in the legislature to which members could be elected only by Muslims, and nobody else, then there would be at least some members to speak up for the Muslim interest and put forward the Muslim point of view.

Though the Muslims were a minority in India as a whole, they were in the majority in the areas where they were chiefly concentrated. These were in the North-West and the North-East. In Bengal, fifty-five per cent of the people were Muslims. In the Punjab, the proportion was fifty-seven per cent. Understandably, the Muslim League wanted any new constitution to ensure that Muslims were in a position to win elections in the provinces where they had a majority, and that they could get adequate representation also in the central or federal assembly, whatever form it might take.

The Communal Award and the elections of 1937

The constitutional struggles of the thirties were not a straightforward conflict between a reluctant British government and a nationalist movement eager for political advance. Rather, the conflict was triangular, with much of the discord being between Congress and Muslim League. The Round Table Conference of 1931 (the second of three) discussed, and failed to agree about, two main issues: the division of power between British and Indian in the central government and the representation of the Indian communities. On this second issue, League and Congress failed to reach agreement.

The British government had to go ahead on its own and lay down what form of representation Muslims and others should have. This declaration, known as the Communal Award, gave the Muslims one third of the seats in the central legislature. Because this award had not been agreed to by the nationalists at the conference, it was not popular at least with Congress.

In the elections eventually held in 1937, the Muslim League fared distinctly worse than Congress. The League won less than a quarter of the seats reserved for Muslims, whereas Congress won over seven-eighths of the seats reserved for Hindus. The League had not yet become a party with overwhelming attraction for Muslims. In the North-West Frontier Province especially, Muslims did not vote for the League. But, on the other hand, Congress did not succeed in getting many Muslim seats.

By the time of the next elections in 1946, the League support among Muslims was much stronger, and it won most of the Muslim seats. This shows that the issue was becoming clear: people recognized Congress as the Hindu party and the League as the Muslim party. From a minority interest on the wings of the nationalist movement, the League grew to be a rival nationalism on its own, and took with it into independence two large sections of the country.

The Muslim attitude to federation

A word is necessary to explain how the British proposals to the nationalists seemed in Muslim eyes. The Muslims were a minority, afraid of what might happen to them if the Hindu majority should obtain power in an effectively independent India with no safeguards against the abuse of this power. At first, the League demanded separate electorates, and was not satisfied with what the British government offered. Later, when the League felt strong enough to challenge Congress, and when it seemed to Muslim leaders that a future under Hindu government could not be tolerated, the demand was for nothing less than the right for Muslim-majority provinces to form their own Union independent of the others. The British proposals during the war on this subject, though they went some way towards this, did not go far enough to satisfy the League.

Communalism, then, was a rampant demon, a spirit of suspicion and distrust (often enough, well-founded) between the followers of the two main religions of India, a spirit that led to the increasing polarization of nationalist politics—a process by which all political ideas were sucked towards two religious extremes, and nothing was left in the middle.

(c) Gandhi and Civil Disobedience

Salt

Gandhi, who came to be known as Mahatma ('high-souled'), has been mentioned in the previous chapter as an organizer of passive resistance against the British. His policy was a policy of non-violence. The idea behind this was that the government could be made unworkable if the Indians refused to have anything to do with it.

Following this policy, Congress ran campaigns of civil disobedience in the early thirties that attracted enough support to cause considerable disruption of the administration.

Civil disobedience was a programme designed to back up the Congress claim for independence made in 1929. It was launched the next year, with Gandhi as its leader. The objective was to coerce the government into giving independence. Dominion status, a form of association with Britain under the Crown, had been thrown over-board; a complete separation was all that Congress would settle for now, and the nationalist leaders were in no mood for compromise.

Mahatma Gandhi wrote a letter to the Viceroy in which he said that he regarded the government salt monopoly as a social evil, one that bore harshly on the poor. He threatened to organize systematic disobedience to the salt laws if nothing was done to reform them.

Salt was a government monopoly. This meant that subjects were not allowed to produce it freely; and this is what Gandhi was complaining about. It seemed to him unnatural and unjust that salt production should be illegal.

Acting on his threat, when the Viceroy made no move to do away with the grievances mentioned in his letter, Gandhi led a march to the coast of Gujarat. There, on the sea shore, salt was picked up and cleaned. This was illegal, and the demonstrators were risking arrest, but no arrests were made.

The real trouble started afterwards, when Gandhi urged everybody to start ignoring the law and producing salt, and teaching others how to produce it. Attacks were made on government salt works. There were massive demonstrations in the streets of Bombay. Police out-posts were burned elsewhere. Gandhi threatened a second march, but was arrested before it came off.

And as it started, so it went on. Salt was the first in a series of matters that were made the subject of boycotts and demonstrations. Despite Gandhi's own desires and expectations, the demonstrations were not always peaceful, and the authorities did not lack an excuse to put them down harshly.

Civil disobedience

Thus the campaign of civil disobedience, though it was inspired by the Gandhian philosophy of passive resistance, was a hectic and violent interlude in the history of the nationalist movement. It was more than a peaceful demonstration, such as those that are familiar nowadays. It was a direct challenge to the authority of the govern-ment, and it aimed deliberately at making the laws unworkable and bringing British activities to a standstill.

Boycotts were an important tool in the hands of Gandhi's followers, who refrained from using or buying anything that came from the government or from the British. Liquor shops were boy-cotted. British goods of all descriptions were boycotted, in an attempt to harm the trade that Britain had with India. People were also urged by Congress not to buy foreign cloth. Imports of textiles were thought to be harmful to the Indian economy, in which there was an ancient tradition of handweaving. Even though the imports might be cheaper, they were at least potentially a threat to the livelihoods of Indian weavers. This then, like Gandhi's concern with spinning and with the salt monopoly, shows an interest in promoting the livelihood and handcrafts of villagers.

More directly political and damaging to the administration were boycotts of government officials and agencies and refusal to co-operate with the legislatures. A ban was also declared on British banks and insurance companies. Many people refused to pay their taxes. This sort of thing above all made it clear that the movement could not be treated lightly.

The movement looked dangerous, not only because of the anti-government character that it professed, but also because of the violence of many who were part of it. It was never Gandhi's wish that his political philosophy should be made the cloak for communalism, violence and bigotry, but that is what happened. Gandhi did not wish evil to any of the individuals in the government personally, and he did not wish to provoke bloodshed; but too many followers wished both, and were ready to engage in the most provocative actions under the name of passive resistance. There was thus an element of hypocrisy in the whole thing, but not in the intentions of Gandhi and those like him among the leaders.

None of this should be allowed to give the impression that the whole of India was at the complete disposal of Gandhi to put into operation whatever policies he thought of. This was not so at all. When civil disobedience was eventually called off, it was called off largely because it had seen its day and people were no longer responding so enthusiastically.

There are harrowing reports of the treatment of people who refused to pay taxes, and of people who came to attend conferences of Congress in 1932 and 1933, which were banned by the government. It seems clear that there were plenty of occasions when police—Indian, Anglo-Indian, and British alike—were thoroughly brutal. It seems clear too that there were plenty of occasions when the principle of peaceful non-co-operation was violated by the demonstrators (though there were occasions when they showed great self-discipline and showed no violence under great provocation). There were riots. Police stations were attacked. Gaols were broken open. The course of events was not what Gandhi wanted.

Gandhi was in and out of gaol through the crucial period of nationalist agitation. The salt march of 1930 put him in gaol. He was out in 1931 to take part in the Round Table Conference with the British and various Indian parties, but was sent back on his return after participating in Congress activities. When the war broke out, Congress asked for immediate Indian independence and started another disobedience movement when this was refused. Gandhi was again arrested. But even from within his prisons he was an inspiration to the nationalist movement, and has since become for Indians the personification of it.

(d) THE CONSTITUTION OF INDIA

The two Indias

In 1935, the British government put before Parliament a bill giving India a new constitution. This bill became the longest statute among the British Acts of Parliament. Its provisions were numerous and complicated. But, for all its length, the whole document was not intended to be more than a temporary arrangement until a greater degree of self-government could be given. It was eventually superseded after the war.

This India Act, like the other documents and agreements in the history of self-government negotiations, shows a stage in the bargaining and manoeuvring between the various interests in Britain and India. The details need not concern us much, because they represent temporary things. But one of the complications requires some explanation, and this is a complication that required careful handling from the British side whenever any sort of constitutional innovation was being discussed. This was the complication that there was not just one India. There were two. Indeed, in a manner of speaking there were more than five hundred.

Usually it is convenient to talk about 'India' and 'the government' as if there were one state, India, ruled by Britain. But it was not as simple as that. As previous chapters have shown, Britain found India, not as one country, but as a swarm of jostling kingdoms struggling against each other; and the British did not take them over in one go, in a single act of annexation, but got control of them piecemeal. The various Indian states became British territory one at a time for different reasons. Eventually it became clear that Britain was the paramount power in the land, and certain rights over the native principalities were claimed.

There were over five hundred of these altogether. Most of them were very small, too small to run a twentieth-century type of government of their own. But still they had their own rulers—kings or princes—and strictly speaking the British monarch was not sovereign in them. And indeed the British could not make constitutional changes in them on their own initiative. They could only advise and try to persuade. If there was to be any new pattern of government, any representation for the people, in a state, the decision had to be made by the ruler.

Local self-government: a village council (*Panchayat*) in Madras

Three Vietnamese
Buddhist monks at
the Pali Institute,
Nalanda—still a
centre of Buddhist
study

Mock-Tudor Post Offic
Simla, in the mountain

Modern Delhi: the Rajpath, showing a military cavalcade, with
government buildings in the background

Nor were all these states petty ones. Kashmir in the north-west covered an enormous area. Hyderabad, in the south, contained a population eight times the size of (for example) Britain's in the time of Elizabeth I. Together the states of the princes contained a quarter of the population of India. They were dotted about everywhere, many completely surrounded by British territory. And they could not be dragged into any arrangement that the British made with the nationalist leaders. The princes had to agree.

The Simon Commission established in 1927 (on which Attlee, later Prime Minister at the time of independence, sat) studied the problem of the states, and recommended that Britain should not hand over her position as paramount power in relation to the Indian states to any other government (such as a nationalist government of a newly independent India) without the consent of the Indian states. This meant that, in the opinion of the committee, nobody else should step into the shoes of the British and take over the British relationship with the princes unless the princes agreed.

Now it was a concern for this principle that helped to delay the realization of the 1935 constitution. The constitution laid down that there should be a federal government at the centre, a government of Indians with representation for the Muslims and other minorities. There were to be two houses, with the Indian states represented in each of them.

But this part of the constitution, setting up a federal government for the whole of India including the states, was never put into effect. And the reason for this was that, in accordance with the 1935 Act, the federation should not be established until a substantial number of the princes agreed to accept the constitution (enough princes to include half the population of the native states among their subjects). And as time went on the princes became more and more distrustful of the constitution and the Congress and the League, and so the federation was never created.

The negotiations

In 1929, the same year in which Congress committed itself to seeking complete independence for India, the Viceroy, Lord Irwin, said that Dominion status was the 'natural issue' of the constitutional progress that the British government planned for India.

Some years earlier, this would have been acceptable to Congress. Now it was too late. This is the irony of the struggle between nationalists and government: that always the nationalists asked for a little more than the government was prepared to give, and as the government yielded a little bit, so they became more demanding. It is the same pattern that we have seen many times in countries on the way to independence. It is almost as if neither side could afford to let the matter resolve itself without a struggle.

A conference in London was promised at which all sections of Indian opinion should be represented. This promise led to the three Round Table Conferences already mentioned, in 1930, 1931, and 1932. At the time, Congress was running a civil disobedience campaign, and Gandhi was in gaol; but by a special arrangement with the Viceroy, he was led out to attend the second conference, in return for an undertaking that Congress would call off its civil disobedience. This pact eventually broke down, but at least it lasted long enough for Gandhi to join with the Indian and British ministers and others to discuss the problems of constitutional advance. The meeting, however, was not very fruitful because of disagreement between Congress and Muslims.

The Communal Award—the declaration by the British government setting out the terms of representation for minorities—and the discussions at these conferences formed the basis for the 1935 constitution under which elections were held in 1937. Several things have already been said about this constitution. It gave a substantial amount of representation to the Muslims, provided for legislatures in all the provinces of British India, and set up a federal government at the centre—subject to the agreement of a number of the princes, which was never forthcoming. What happened was that the rest of the constitution was put into effect, and elections were held for the provincial legislatures, where Congress got convincing majorities in most states. Under the constitution, the Governor-General at the centre and the governors in the provinces had certain powers, which were to be used only in an emergency.

It is difficult to tell how different things would have been had there been no war. In 1940, when Churchill was Prime Minister, it was declared that afterwards there would be a new constitution which the Indians would be allowed to devise for themselves, so long as no large minorities opposed it. In 1942 (after the successes of Japan in the war) Sir Stafford Cripps, a member of the British Cabinet, went to India with further proposals: the states and provinces would be able to frame a constitution after the war, from which individual provinces would be free to withdraw and by which rights of minorities would be safeguarded.

These moves were prompted by the need to get as much co-operation as possible from the Indians in the war effort. The situation was dangerous, and it was important to be able to count on India. But Congress stood out against these proposals, insisting on effective independence. This concession was not forthcoming and there was a breakdown in relations between the British and

Congress, which passed a resolution in favour of non-violent opposition to the government and was in consequence declared an unlawful association.

And so the story of the nationalist struggle headed towards its climax and the dreadful days of partition. It is a story that few historians have been able to tell in a totally calm, dispassionate voice. Even when we are trying to be fair, it is easy to let a hint come here and there that this or that side is really to blame for the troubles and injustices. And it would indeed be unwise to pretend to an impartiality we do not feel.

But the truth is twofold. On the one hand, neither side—or no side (for in India there were several sides)—comes out of the affair with a clean record. In all camps there were violence, treachery, deceit, hypocrisy from time to time. But on the other hand, badly though things turned out in the end, they would have turned out even worse but for the restraint, the wisdom and the compassion of many of the chief actors in the drama both in India and in Britain.

CHAPTER FIFTEEN

The War and Partition

(a) THE CONTENDERS

How many contenders?

On August 15th, 1947, India became independent. The Union Jack was hauled down, to be replaced by two new flags, one for each of the two new states into which India was split. To add to the complication, one of these two states was itself split in two. Pakistan, though a single country, was and is divided geographically into two separate regions, East Pakistan and West Pakistan. Nearly a thousand miles of India separate them.

Why should India have been dealt with in this fashion? Surely the obvious thing to do, when giving independence to a country that has been treated as a single unit for all the purposes of government, is to hand over power to a single government. It seems quite unnecessarily complicated to split the place into three parts with two governments. Even without knowing anything in particular about India, we might well imagine that this procedure would give rise to many practical problems. India's system of railways would have to be broken up. So would her telegraphs. The armed forces would have to be unscrambled. At least one new centre of government would have to be created. All the vast quantities of documents that a modern government needs to organize itself would have to be duplicated. These are some of the obvious problems. Why then did the British and the Indians make life so difficult for themselves by cutting the country up at the moment of independence?

The reason has already been suggested in the previous chapter and is one of the saddest things about twentieth-century India: it is that the Hindus and the Muslims could not trust each other.

The situation was difficult for the British government. If power was handed over to a government representing a majority of the Indian voters, this would be the same thing as handing over to Congress, which was effectively the political party of the Hindu religion. But the Muslims, who were a large minority in the country as a whole, were afraid of what would happen to them under a government run by Hindus, and insisted on their right to run their own affairs. In the end their leaders insisted on the right to set up a separate state. Congress fought against this idea, and accepted division reluctantly only at the end.

Now, this way of talking and writing about the events leading up to partition is misleading. It is the easy way, because it makes things fit into a pattern. The pattern is threefold: the policies of the British government, the policies of the Indian Congress under Jawaharlal Nehru, and the policies of the Muslim League under Muhammad Ali Jinnah. Three contenders, three policies, and a crisis in India's history can be seen as the outcome of the bargaining and policy-making of these parties.

It is misleading, because the history of India during the war and up to partition and independence was not in fact determined by these three contenders. The British government, the Congress leaders, and the Muslim League were all, to some extent, subject to forces beyond their control. The British government was under strong pressure to clear out of India, and any other British government would probably have done the same things. The Congress leadership was under strong pressure to insist on independence under terms that would give a Hindu government effective power over the whole of India. Mr. Jinnah, the leader of the Muslim League, was rather less obviously subject to forces beyond his control; it seemed as if he could have been less stubborn, less insistent on a divided India. But, when we look at the way Muslim feeling and solidarity grew, and at the hatred and suspicion between Muslim Pakistan and Hindu India since partition, it is clear that Mr. Jinnah himself is likely to have been under powerful pressures.

The British government

In 1935 the British government had given India a new constitution which put the day-to-day running of government into Indian hands, with the promise of more power to come later. The eventual aim was dominion status—self-government for Indians in every way, but under the British Crown.

When the war broke out, it seemed hardly practical to grant immediate and complete independence, as Congress demanded. Promises could be made about what would happen after the war, but for the time being Britain would have to keep control.

In August 1940 there was an offer of free and equal partnership with Britain (after the war) in the British Commonwealth, under a constitution which would guarantee the rights of minorities. Like many such offers, this was rejected by Congress because it did not go far enough to meet Congress demands for independence now for a unified state. The rights of minorities could be interpreted to mean an unwelcome degree of self-government for the parts of India with a Muslim majority. In 1942 came the Cripps mission.

Cripps was a well-respected socialist member of the British government who was known to be sympathetic towards India. He made an offer of a new constitution after the war to be drawn up by the Indians themselves, giving representation to the native states, and to provinces the right to withdraw. This would mean that the provinces in which there was a majority of Muslims would be able to stay out of the new India. India as a whole would have the right to stay in the Commonwealth or leave it. When Congress held out for immediate independence, he offered to provide the immediate establishment of a new Executive Council for the country—a team of ministers—that would be entirely Indian except for the Viceroy himself and the Commander-in-chief of the armed forces. But all Cripps' efforts were in vain: Congress wanted immediate independence, and the League would not tolerate any sort of constitution that was designed in the hope of establishing a unified. India. The Muslim leaders now wanted partition.

In 1945 a new offer was made by Wavell, the Viceroy, repeating the points that had been made earlier—the nationalists would have distrusted it, if only because so much of it was a repetition of what they had heard and rejected before—and offering an equal say to Muslims and Hindus in deciding their fate. In London, the Secretary of State for India, L. S. Amery, said that Congress leaders in prison would be released. There was a conference at Simla, which broke down.

This was the situation when the post-war elections of 1945 in Britain produced a new Labour government. It was clear that the problem for India was no longer—and had not been since before the war—British unwillingness to hand over power. The problem was the problem of knowing to whom power should be handed over. Congress? The League would never accept a Congress, Hindu-dominated government and there would be civil war. A mixture of Congress and the League? They could agree on nothing, and would be at each other's throats. Congress and the League as separate countries in a divided India? Apart from the practical difficulties in carving India up, this would be undignified for Britain—an admission that a smooth handover of power to a carefully trained India was impossible. Besides, Congress was bitterly against partition. The problem seemed insoluble.

Congress

It is easy to tell the story in such a way as to make the British government's attitude seem reasonable all the way through, and the nationalists' very unreasonable. The British continued to make offers, and the nationalists continued to reject them. But we should remember that things did not look the same from inside a gaol in the 1940's as they do from the pages of a book twenty or thirty years later. In Congress eyes, the British could not be trusted. Promises had, they considered, been broken in the past. Promises given by Britain in wartime in order to get Indian support were not likely to be fulfilled unless Britain was coerced into fulfilling them.

India had been subjected to foreign rule long enough, and now that the British government said it was willing to see some sort of self-government in India, instead of giving the country its freedom at once, the country was dragged into a war that was not of its own making, without its consent, with no more than promises of future self-government at a date that nobody knew, and made to suffer all the hardships that a war entails. There were rising prices, famine, deaths by the thousand in the towns and villages, to say nothing of the Indian soldiers sent to their deaths in Burma and North Africa in defence of British interests. The British claimed to be fighting for freedom in Europe, which may well have been so: but, if so, why could not Britain first give freedom to India? And then, when the war ended, could even the Labour government in Britain be trusted? Once in power, all these British seemed the same: unreliable and dilatory. This was the Congress point of view

As for religion in India, there was an important difference between the ideas of the masses who supported Congress and those of some Congress leaders. The masses were Hindu and therefore anti-Muslim; and therefore the Muslims naturally would not join Congress in any large numbers. But, though most Muslims were frightened off, Congress was still theoretically a non-religious party with room in it for all religions. Many of its leaders were quite sincere about this. Nehru himself was entirely opposed to the communal spirit—the exclusiveness of religious communities. He happened to be a Hindu, but nationalism for him meant creating a new, modern India in which the old hostilities between races, regions and religions in the country had no place. It therefore seemed to him that the British were being treacherous and obstructive when they paid so much attention to Muslim demands for minority rights and toyed with various schemes that would take power away from the central government and give it to the provinces. This was like going back to the old India of petty kingdoms. What Nehru and his colleagues wanted was a new, strong, unified, modern India.

The Muslim League

Historians have on the whole been unsympathetic in their treat-

ment of the Muslim League in pre-partition days. They see it as
breathing a fierce, communal, crusading spirit. Mr. Jinnah was an
unlovable man. Many Muslims behaved provocatively and bar-
barically towards Hindus (as did Hindus towards Muslims). The
League kept rejecting suggestions that seemed reasonable to the
British government. Starting in the early 1930s from the position of
a small party representing only one of a number of minority groups,
it became a constant thorn in the flesh to the independence discussions, and held out for a form of independence—partition—that was
inconvenient, costly, undignified for everybody, and left India
weaker than it might be thought she need have been.

It has therefore been easy to see the Muslims as an obstacle to a
smooth transfer of power to an independent India. But such an
interpretation overlooks the fact that the Muslims were a minority
which had every reason to fear the consequences of Congress rule.
The Congress leaders may not have been militant Hindus anxious to
pay back the Muslims for real and imagined oppression in the past.
They might indeed have been secular-minded men. But the Muslims
could see perfectly well that the great bulk of Congress support came
from Hindus, and they could see perfectly well that in an India
under a strong central government, which would be a Congress
government, there would be little to prevent the Hindus from taking
advantage of their superiority in numbers and persecuting Muslims.
Congress would not be able to stop it, because Congress depended on
Hindu votes.

At a later stage, the British Prime Minister suggested that the
Muslim League was being obstructive in holding up the progress
of negotiations. Mr. Jinnah replied bitterly that for the League to
accept assurances from Congress would be like a fly walking into a
spider's parlour. To the Muslims, it looked as though Britain was
setting up a parlour with Congress as the spider in it. And Britain
and Congress together, in the interests of a united India, were
inviting the Muslims to walk into the Congress parlour, and be
devoured. So bitter, by the end of the war, was the hostility between
Muslims and Hindus, so deep their distrust of each other, that, it
seemed to Mr. Jinnah, nothing short of outright partition of the
country into a Hindu part and a Muslim part would suffice.

(b) The Effect of the War

Hardship

In 1945, Britain emerged as one of the victors in the war. Despite
the turmoil in India, there had been no real rebellion there of any
seriousness, and Indians had contributed enormously to the war on

Britain's behalf. One might draw two conclusions from this: that Britain and India were now bound together more closely; and that when it came to negotiations with nationalists or anybody else, Britain was in a position of strength. Both these things would make it seem less likely that Britain would hand over power to an independent India. But neither of these things was so.

Britain and India were not bound more closely together. As we have seen, nationalism grew during the war, and at several stages Congress leaders declared civil disobedience, and were imprisoned. Pressures for change were building up. The afflictions that war dealt out, not just to soldiers, but to whole nations in Europe and Asia, brought separation closer.

Moreover, there were scarcities in the shops. Prices rose. Bad harvests brought famine, and many thousands of people died. These were the civilian casualties, not the soldiers themselves.

Britain also, naturally enough, experienced hardship. At the end of the war, people in Britain also were anxious for a change, even though their wartime government had won their respect and their Prime Minister, Winston Churchill, had become a national hero. They were anxious, however, now that the war was over, for a new approach, for the reconstruction of the industry and the welfare services of the country, for an end to scarcity and the promise of benefits to come. For these and other reasons the general election of 1945 saw the return of a Labour majority in the House of Commons.

The Labour government, formed under Mr. Clement Attlee (later Lord Attlee) was not in a position of strength in its handling of colonial questions. This was partly due to Britain's weakness, partly to Labour's traditional opposition to imperialism, and partly to Britain's preoccupation with pressing problems at home. The government did not want to have its time taken up and a part of its armed forces engaged in coping with a nationalist movement in India. Britain was ready to withdraw from India, and wanted only to do this in a way that would not lead to civil war in the country after independence—war between Muslims and Hindus.

Benefits

Certain aspects of the war do not entirely fit into this picture: some of its side effects were of positive benefit to India. For the purposes of the war, industry was developed rapidly. In the years 1940–41, the production of pig-iron rose by about twenty-five per cent, of steel by nearly fifty per cent; armour-plating began to be manufactured; factories manufactured munitions and other necessities of war. Industrial development meant work and pay for many Indians, better pay than they had been used to. A hundred thousand people were employed in these factories. Largely cut off from Europe early in the war, India had to develop a war industry quickly, because it was difficult or impossible now to import things from England. Pressed by a sense of urgency, the authorities established industries producing much the greater part of the range of manufactures needed for war purposes. These were not just weapons: they included everything that an army needs, from shirts to warships, and obviously many of the industries could be useful in peacetime as well. A vast amount of cloth was made which was exported to America for the American army.

There were benefits also in the way that (again, pressed by the urgency of war) Indians were increasingly being given training and skills that gave them careers and which they would not otherwise have had. The development of the war industry required a lot of skilled labour. In the army, Indians were given higher ranks and more responsibility; the training of Indians as officers was taken seriously. And in the administration of the country, Indians were now occupying virtually all the civil service posts in the administration of the provinces and most of the posts in the central service—the I.C.S. (Indian Civil Service).

Oddly enough, despite shortages and famines, India benefited financially from the war and emerged from it as a creditor of Britain. At the beginning of the war India was materially in Britain's debt, but at the end of the war (as a result of British wartime expenditure in India) the debt was paid off and it was now India which had a considerable credit in London.

Dissatisfaction

Dissatisfaction with the existing state of affairs was a natural consequence of both the hardships of war and its benefits. Shortages and sufferings meant that people were ready for change and prepared to back a nationalist party, or determined in other ways to express their grievances. The new jobs of the war years and the new training they made possible for some people meant that more Indians were becoming—if only slightly—Westernized and anxious in consequence to increase the country's rate of economic and social development. Many Indians had travelled as soldiers to Africa or south-east Asia and were no longer able, at the end of the war, to return to the conditions of life they had formerly accepted. It was not surprising therefore that the end of the war should see a great deal of unrest.

In Delhi some Indian army officers were put on trial for having fought with a rebel group against Britain. This was the Indian National Army, an extreme nationalist organization. It had been formed during the war under the leadership of Subas Chandra Bose (who later became famous as an Indian patriot), to fight against Britain and on the side of the Japanese. Bose was killed in an air crash, but some of the Indians who had been with him returned to their country and were arrested.

The trial revealed the presence of a great deal of sympathy for the accused persons who, against the background of the new hostility to British rule, seemed like heroes. There were violent demonstrations in favour of them.

In 1946, further signs of serious unrest appeared in Bombay where a naval mutiny broke out, and spread to units of the armed forces elsewhere. Riots occurred in Calcutta. Police went on strike in many places. The situation was gradually brought under control, but it was very worrying to the government.

(c) THE LAST STAGES 1946–47

The elections of 1946

In 1946 elections were held in India for the various provincial and central bodies. Some seats were reserved for Muslims only, and others for Hindus only. Interest focused upon the performance of the Muslim League, which at the last elections in 1935 had appeared only as one of a number of minority parties. Everybody knew that Congress had overwhelming support among the Hindus, and even a few Muslim adherents as well. Therefore it was clear that Congress would emerge the most powerful party, but it was not clear how strong the League would turn out to be.

During the war, Mr. Jinnah, the leader of the Muslim League, had worked very hard to build up the organization, and, quite apart from his efforts, Muslims had been realizing more and more clearly that British rule would not last forever and that one day they would have to face the consequences of independence for an India that had a majority of non-Muslims. The result was that, in the provinces, the League won nearly all the seats reserved for Muslims, and, in the Central Executive, all of them. This showed that Muslim support was solidly behind the League.

Congress won absolute majorities in all the provinces where there were not large numbers of Muslims. The League won enough seats in Bengal, Sind and the Punjab to be the chief element in the government. The two parties were now facing each other squarely, the League demanding a separate state for some provinces, to be called Pakistan; Congress demanding a unified India in which there would be one strong central government. The problem for the

British government was that of finding a solution that both parties could be persuaded to accept.

The Cabinet mission

In March, 1946, a mission of British ministers came to discuss the problem with the Viceroy and the Indian leaders, and to make clear to them that the British government was serious in its intentions of granting independence. The Cabinet was opposed to the idea of a Pakistan, but it could not afford to take sides with either of the main nationalist parties, because this would instantly cause violent disturbances and make it more difficult than ever to secure agreement between them. At this stage its aim was to devise some sort of constitution which would make India a single country with a single government but still give the Muslim provinces (Sind and the others) control over their own affairs and freedom from interference by a central (and presumably a Congress) government in Delhi. Perhaps this had been impossible for some time already; but the effort was made. The Cabinet put up a scheme. For a time it seemed that agreement was within reach and steps were taken to elect a new Constituent Assembly of Indians to work out the terms of independence in detail.

After the Cabinet mission had left however, the whole scheme broke down. Congress declared that, in sending representatives to the Constituent Assembly, it would not feel bound to accept the Cabinet's scheme. This would mean that Congress could use its majority in the Constituent Assembly to create instead a different sort of constitution from the one the Cabinet mission had proposed. And the League, regarding the Assembly therefore as being like the spider's parlour, refused to walk into it.

Direct Action

From this point things began to move forward with increasing momentum. Mr. Jinnah declared that the League had acted peacefully and constitutionally long enough, and would no longer co-operate constructively in the independence arrangements. There was, in fact, a threat of direct action against the authorities by Muslims. Mr. Jinnah may not have intended to start violent demonstrations that could obviously lead to civil war, but certainly many of his followers behaved as if they interpreted his statement in that way, and in Calcutta there were terrible developments. Calcutta had long been an explosive place, with its poverty and its large under-employed population. The riots there were for a time utterly out of hand. It was calculated that 4,700 people were killed. Rioting spread to other parts of India—East Bengal, Bihar, the Punjab— wherever there were large numbers of Hindus and Muslims living side by side. Twelve thousand people had lost their lives by February 1947.

In December 1946, the Constituent Assembly opened. Its purpose was to devise the constitution under which India was to become independent. In February 1947, against a background of violence in India, the British Prime Minister, Mr. Attlee, announced that independence would come by June 1948. Lord Mountbatten was appointed as new Viceroy, charged with the task of handing over British power on agreed terms to the Indian leaders.

Mountbatten

Earl Mountbatten, the last Viceroy of India, a relative of the King and a businesslike naval officer with a great gift for getting on with people, had the difficult task of negotiating the end of British power in India, the end of an era. It was difficult, for the same reasons that it had been difficult for his predecessors to arrange for constitutional changes to be made; but it was no longer impossible.

It was no longer impossible because it was now established beyond all doubt that Britain was going, and a definite date had been fixed as the latest for the departure. Those who had eyes to see could not delude themselves that Britain actually enjoyed having India, and was dreaming up ways of hanging on to her imperial possession.

After seeing the nationalist leaders and exploring the possibilities, Mountbatten decided that, desirable though it might be in principle, a unified India (in which Congress would form the government) was not really possible. Partition would have to be accepted, in spite of all its inconvenience and difficulty. Although this was what the League had been demanding, and what Congress had been for long resisting with all its might, partition was no longer impossible politically. The two nationalist parties had now been at each other's throats—the progress of negotiations had been held up—for so long that, in the end, Congress resigned itself to the necessity of a split as the only way of getting independence for India and power of government over most of India for itself. The chief practical difficulty lay in drawing the line of partition, in deciding on the boundaries of the two new countries that were to be created. There were some provinces in the North-West that had a large Muslim majority, and should clearly go to Pakistan. But the provinces of the Punjab (in the North-West) and Bengal (in the North-East) had very large Hindu minorities in them, and if they became part of Pakistan there would obviously be all manner of trouble in these places.

The solution was for each province to choose whether or not it wished to accept the constitution worked out by the Congress-dominated Constituent Assembly that was already working on it. Naturally enough, the Muslim provinces would choose not to, and they would be able to unite into a new state of Pakistan. But in Bengal and the Punjab, there was to be separate voting by Muslim-dominated districts and Hindu-dominated districts on their future, and a boundary commission was later to draw a frontier to divide these districts that chose Pakistan from those that chose India.

June 1948 had been set by the British government as the latest date for independence, but Mountbatten decided that independence would have to come long before that time. The government in India, knowing that it was living through its last months, was losing its authority. Mountbatten determined that there should be a quick job made of partition, and after discussions in June with the nationalists, it was agreed that independence should come that very August. In July, the Indian Independence Bill went through Parliament in London without disagreement. In the course of time, everybody, or almost everybody had become accustomed to the idea of independence and realized how little Britain could afford not to grant it.

The difficulties, then, were not difficulties in deciding whether to give it or not. They were difficulties in securing nationalist agreement on the terms under which independence should be given. Once the Viceroy had obtained this agreement (after at least one near-disaster when he misjudged what would be acceptable to Congress), the British Parliament could only agree to his plan.

At midnight on 14 August, British rule came to an end. The name of India remained as the name of the Hindu part of the country, which contained much the greater part of the population. This new, smaller, India, was at first a dominion of the British Commonwealth, and Mountbatten became the Governor-General. As such, he represented the monarch and was a sort of figurehead. He was no longer responsible for the government, as he had been when he was Viceroy. Nehru became Prime Minister of a self-governing and independent India. Later, India ceased to be a dominion and became a republic, but still in the Commonwealth.

The north-western provinces, with a great part of the Punjab, became West Pakistan, and east Bengal became East Pakistan. Though separate geographically, they were one country under one government, with Mr. Jinnah as Governor-General and Liaquat Ali Khan as Prime Minister.

It all came in a remarkable rush. The committees arranging the break-up of the old India had to work overtime to get their job done.

It is ironic that, after so many years in which the nationalists had been banging at the door, it opened so suddenly that everybody was taken by surprise. The people of India had their own free government almost before they realized it. The change was such a big thing that it was difficult to grasp it. But, when they realized it, they found that independence solved only one of their problems, and raised several more.

CHAPTER SIXTEEN

The New India

History does not stop short at some point in time; it continues right up to the present, and the present itself is always moving. We cannot say that the history of India ends at the moment of independence, for example, and that everything that has happened since belongs to some other branch of study. It is a continuous story, still being told.

There are some difficulties that affect particularly the last part of it, the account of India and Pakistan since independence. One difficulty is that there have to be many loose ends in it: we can see what people have been doing, without knowing what will be the results of their actions; we can see what people have been hoping, but the fulfilment or failure of their hopes still belongs to the future.

It is also difficult to make fair judgments about events of the recent past, events that have been hotly debated, have often provoked fierce partisanship, and cannot be seen in their context of past and future. Whether policies were right, whether particular groups or individuals were to blame for things that went wrong—such questions are clouded by doubt and argument.

Again, it is difficult to give the recent past its proper perspective. It bulks so large in our vision because of its immediacy, but these few years since Indian and Pakistani independence are really no more than a tiny morsel in the history of the subcontinent which goes back thousands of years.

But something must be said about the two new countries, some attempt be made to describe their experiences. In the present chapter a survey will be made of the situation with which Indians have been confronted since 1947—the effects of partition, the relationship with the princely states, and the constitutional, economic and social problems that have arisen. In the next chapter we shall see how Indians have dealt with this situation—the story of the political parties, the activities of the government, and the place which India has gained in the world. In the final chapter we shall have a look at Pakistan.

INDIAN POLITICIANS

Mahatma Gandhi, 1869-1948, legendary nationalist leader

Jawaharlal Nehru, 1889-1964, independent India's first Prime Minister

Mrs Indira Gandhi, third Prime Minister

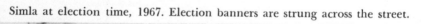

Simla at election time, 1967. Election banners are strung across the street.

(a) The Aftermath of Partition

The gaining of freedom from foreign rule ought to be a joyful event. In India, certainly, many were full of joy, and there were celebrations. But there was also a darker side. The British had been willing to give freedom for some time; what mattered was the question whether freedom should come peacefully and war should be avoided. In the event, freedom did not come peacefully, and though India and Pakistan did not declare war on each other, they later came near it, and there was certainly a war going on in some parts of the subcontinent. Independence was thus not an entirely happy experience. This does not mean, of course, that it was undesirable or that it should not have been granted. The real point is that it was inevitable, for many reasons.

Although there were troubles, they could have been worse. Bengal, where many Muslims and Hindus lived in the same area, might have been swept by anarchy, but it escaped very lightly. Fighting might have spread right across the country, but in fact it did not spread appreciably further east than Delhi from the Punjab. There could have been a declared war between India and Pakistan, but in fact, during the first months of horror, the two countries co-operated in moving refugees. Government in the affected areas could have broken down completely and finally, but in fact it broke down only for a few months, and before the end of 1947 things were more or less under control again

The Punjab

The chief scene of anarchy was the Punjab, in the north-west —the province through which ran the new frontier between India and Pakistan. Its population consisted largely of Hindus, Sikhs and Muslims. Before the British took control, the Punjab had been under the domination of Sikhs. As a community, they have always been regarded as tough and warlike, and have provided some of India's best soldiers.

In the Punjab, all three religious communities were mingled geographically, and partition meant that many Hindus and Sikhs found themselves in a Muslim state—Pakistan—and many Muslims found themselves in a Hindu state—India. With the departure of the British, it was an excuse for long pent up grievances to be worked off. Even before independence, government began to break down. As soon as a date was announced for independence, rioting started. The outgoing British administration had lost most of its authority. After 15 August, the Punjab became a slaughter-house.

The atrocities that were committed were many and various.

Women and children were not spared. A military border force, specially set up to help the police keep order in the Punjab frontier area, could not be relied upon. Abductions and killings, thieving and looting, crippling and torturing were everyday occurrences, and the situation grew out of control. There are many stories of what went on, and there is no need to give details of these. Yet it is necessary to realize how great the turmoil was, since it left enduring scars on the two countries and it lies at the root of much of the enmity that has divided them ever since. For the Punjab, actual casualty figures are extremely difficult to estimate. Altogether, in both countries, perhaps two million people lost their lives in the various disturbances, then and later.

The trouble seems to have started with the activities of organized Sikh groups, who went marauding in Muslim villages putting people to the sword. But, if one group had not started it, another would: the whole of the Punjab was so tense that the first reports of communal outrages sent arson, looting and massacre sweeping across the province like a forest fire.

Refugees

By late in November, eight million refugees had crossed the frontier—Muslims going westwards into Pakistan, Hindus and Sikhs going eastwards into India. These were not members of a mobile population used to moving from place to place: most of them had lived all their lives in one place, and had expected to die there. It took all the fear and insecurity and danger of the partition anarchy to shift them. But once they had started shifting, they moved in enormous numbers. They stretched along the roads in foot processions, scores of thousands strong, carrying with them what they could. And even if they got away from their homes before their enemies found them out, they were not safe, for the foot columns were constantly attacked by armed bands for whom they were ripe for looting.

The governments did what they could. The Indian government set up 160 camps which accommodated a million and a half refugees. Armed escorts were provided for the processions of refugees going by road (but there were occasions when the escorts fired on those they were sent to protect). Trains which transported two and a half million people, were sent shuttling to and fro across the frontier— but often the trains were derailed or stopped, sometimes with the help of the drivers, and the passengers butchered.

(b) THE PRINCELY STATES

The rioting spread into India itself, into Delhi where there was savagery up and down the stately avenues between government buildings, but mercifully it did not spread further into India. By the end of the year, the government was able to concern itself with other problems. One of the chief of these, which led to a continuation of the slaughter in the following months, was the question of the princely states.

These states, 562 of them, occupied not far short of half the area of India and contained about a quarter of the population. Under Britain, they had been semi-independent, with British help in their administration and supervision of their external affairs. When Britain relinquished this position, Lord Mountbatten advised their rulers strongly to take into account the feelings of their subjects and merge with either India or Pakistan. But this was only advice. Theoretically they could stay independent if they wished to, though most of them were too small to last long on their own. Understandably the Indian government was anxious to have them all follow Mountbatten's advice. Three of them, however (one of these not actually within India), gave serious trouble, and of these three, one became the scene of more massacres and, years later, a war.

Junagadh

The first, Junagadh, was a small state on the north-west coast, south of West Pakistan. It had less than a million inhabitants, most of whom were Hindus, under a Muslim ruler. In spite of the fact that it did not have a frontier with Pakistan, the ruler chose to join Pakistan, and Mr. Jinnah accepted. It was legally quite proper for the ruler to do this, but it was inconvenient geographically—it would mean adding another separate piece of territory to Pakistan—and it was not the wish of his subjects, most of whom were Hindu and naturally wished to stay with India. Further, it ran contrary in this to the advice given by Mountbatten. India would not accept the ruler's decision, took over Junagadh by force, and held a referendum there to determine the wishes of the inhabitants. They voted to join India.

Hyderabad

Hyderabad was a large state in the southern part of India. It was also an example of a state with a Muslim ruler and Hindu inhabitants. It occupied a very considerable area, it had a population of about sixteen million, and it was quite prosperous. The ruler, the Nizam, chose eventually to stay independent: though surrounded by India, and wanting to have co-operation with India, he did not want to be submerged. In Indian eyes, however, this was unacceptable. All the facts of geography seemed to point to merger with India; for the convenience of communications and trade it was desirable that Hyderabad should be part of India.

Troubles broke out in and around Hyderabad, partly stirred up from outside. The authority of the government of the Nizam was weakened. Taking advantage of the situation, the Indian government moved in and took over the state.

Kashmir

Both these affairs were naturally very disagreeable to Pakistan, but they were nothing beside the unhappy story of Kashmir, a large but comparatively thinly populated state in the far North, lying between India and Pakistan. It had a population of about four million, mostly Muslim. However, the ruler, Sir Hari Singh, was a Hindu. In this aspect it was the reverse situation from that of Junagadh and Hyderabad. In both of the latter states the facts of geography and religion meant that union with India seemed more natural. In the case of Kashmir, the facts of geography (since roads, rivers and trade went largely from the state into Pakistan), and the fact of there being a Muslim population, meant that union with Pakistan seemed more natural. But the ruler was Hindu. To the confusion of the subcontinent's history, and with dire consequences, the ruler chose to join India.

The decision was made late in 1947, amid increasing disturbances in the state. A rising of some of the people in Kashmir, the Sudhans, led to large-scale bloodshed. In another part—Jammu—a rising was harshly put down and the Hindus of that region massacred Muslims. Hundreds of thousands lost their lives. With the help of the Pakistan authorities, tribesmen in the north-west of Pakistan assembled a fleet of lorries and invaded Kashmir in support of their fellow-Muslims. The Indian government responded by flying in plane-loads of Indian troops to help the ruler quell the disturbances. They were just in time to forestall the invading tribesmen. Fighting raged back and forth. Although regular Pakistani troops did take part in the fighting, they were there as volunteers, or for the purpose of defence only. They were not officially taking part in a war declared by their government.

In 1948, both India and Pakistan appealed to the United Nations Security Council to seek an end to the fighting. Each side thought it was in the right. The Indian government pointed out that the ruler had quite legally chosen to join India, that Kashmir thereupon became Indian soil, and that Indian troops were fighting in their own country to put down a rising supported from outside. However, these states, Kashmir and the others, belong to Pakistan's history as well as India's, and in a later chapter we will look again at Pakistan's point of view.

A commission sent by the United Nations early in 1948 failed to get a ceasefire at first, but in the following January (1949) a ceasefire line was established between the contending armies, and it was agreed that there should be a plebiscite to determine whether the people of Kashmir should join India or Pakistan. Although both India and Pakistan agreed to the holding of a plebiscite at the time, it was obvious that it would result in largely Muslim Kashmir joining Pakistan, and India in the end was not willing to allow the plebiscite to be held. The ceasefire line, intended simply to divide the opposing armies, therefore became in effect an international frontier, dividing the Indian-held part of Kashmir, the most important part, from the Pakistan-held part. So it was to remain indefinitely, a running sore in the relations between the two countries, with Pakistan demanding that a plebiscite should be held, and India refusing. There was so much tension that a renewal of fighting was always possible, and the best part of India's army was stationed on the Pakistani frontier rather than on the Chinese (though eventually it was from China that the most serious attack came).

In September 1965 the undeclared war again broke out when raids into Indian Kashmir from the Pakistani side induced the Indian government to send its troops across the frontier, attacking Lahore. Neither side was strong enough to support a full-scale modern war and the conflict ended quickly and indecisively, leaving the stalemate situation unchanged. It has been estimated that the cost of the war was about £150,000,000 to each side.

(c) Constitutional Problems

The British did not draw up a constitution for India before independence. This was left for the Indians to do for themselves. In 1947 an Interim Government was formed under Mr. Nehru, and there was also established a Constituent Assembly which was to make laws and work out the terms of a new constitution.

The 1948 constitution

Unlike Pakistan, India quickly worked out a new system of political power, a set of rules for government, and the constitution created in 1948 became law in 1950. The chief problems facing the constitution-makers were to ensure justice for all Indians in a society where inequality and discrimination between castes and other groups were the order of the day, to prevent the different parts of India, with their

own languages and traditions, from feeling that the central government was submerging them, and to absorb the princely states into
India as quickly as possible.

The constitution had written into it certain principles and certain
fundamental rights. There was to be no discrimination on grounds of
caste or religion, and the rights of free speech, assembly, and religion
were guaranteed. This meant, for example, that nobody was to be
refused admission to jobs or to public places or places of entertain-
ment because he was of the wrong caste, that political meetings were
allowed and all expressions of opinion tolerated.

A balance had to be struck between the central government and
the provinces. The central government had to be strong enough to
control the development of the country, and the provinces had to
have their own institutions to look after some of their own affairs.
At the centre provision was made for a federal government with
considerable powers, able to legislate on all subjects in emergencies,
and possessing final authority over the states. The provinces were
abolished and a new set of regions, to be called states instead of
provinces, was created with, in some cases, different names and
boundaries. There were at first twenty-eight of them, though some
of these were subsequently divided to make new states and thus to
cater to local demands for separate institutions of self-government.

There were to be two houses of Parliament—the Lower House,
the Lok Sabha, corresponding to the British House of Commons.
Its members were to be elected for five years, from constituencies
each with a maximum of half a million voters. All adult Indians were
entitled to vote. The Lok Sabha was to have 500 members, and the
Upper House 250. Members of this Upper House were to be elected—
not directly by all the people of India, but by the legislatures of the
various states—and they were to be elected for six years. Every two
years, one third of the Upper House was to retire.

The Head of State was to be the President, in whose name the
central government would act—as it has from time to time acted—
to take over the government of particular states where there seemed
to be a threat to law and order, or to change the boundaries of states.
But the President can act only on the advice of the Cabinet, which,
with the Prime Minister at its head, is the effective repository of
governmental power.

As for the 562 princely states with their own rulers, their independence was effectively ended, though it needed a great deal of
persuasion in some cases. Some of them were to be directly
administered by the federal government at the centre; some of them
were merged with the surrounding provinces (or states), and some
were joined together with each other to make larger, more self-

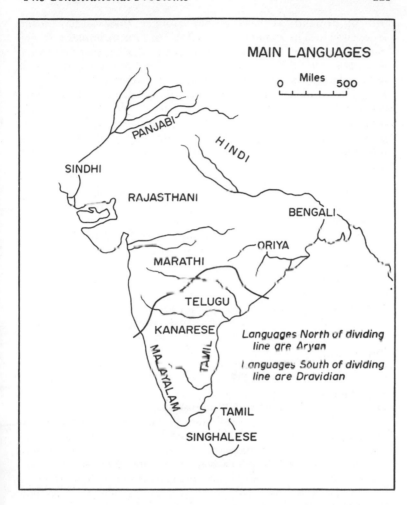

MAIN LANGUAGES

supporting units. What happened to Hyderabad was that some parts were split off to join neighbouring states and part remained as the new state of Hyderabad.

The problem of 'linguism'

One of the factors leading to the sub-division of some of India's original 28 states was the problem faced by the variety of language groups in India and the demands of some of these language groups for separate statehood. 'Linguism' is the term normally used for this sort of demand. It has become stronger since India became independent. The state of Andhra Pradesh, for example, was later created by stages, from different sources, to bring together people who spoke the Telugu language. In the recently divided Punjab, most people speak Punjabi; while the part that has now become Haryana contains mostly Hindi-speaking people. The central government, while reluctant to accede to these demands, has usually had to give way, for the sake of its own support, when the pressure has been strong. It depends after all on the votes from the inhabitants of all states, and must take some notice of minority claims.

(d) Economic and Social Problems

Advantages

Despite her enormous poverty and all the difficulties entailed by partition, India started life with a number of advantages that gave her a sporting chance of making good progress. The effect of British rule was that the subcontinent was now more unified politically than ever it had been in pre-British days. Pakistan was lost, but British India was a single unit of government, and the India of the princes— the semi-independent states—were weak enough in relation to India be be brought into the fold before long. India then was a country of over a million and a quarter square miles with a population of perhaps 337 million people—large enough, at any rate, to support large-scale programmes of development.

Though agriculture was lagging seriously, the war had actually had beneficial effects on India's industry, as we have seen: war needs had meant the sprouting of ordnance factories and the development of every industry that could be sited in the country and could indirectly serve the purpose of the war effort. Further, Britain undertook to pay for India's war effort, and therefore became a debtor of India at the end of the war. India's sterling balances were held in London, and were to be paid in instalments. The funds could be used by India to finance imports of machinery and other materials necessary for economic progress.

Agriculture

We do not usually think of India as a well-equipped modern country, however. We think of her rather as still a land of poverty. The reason is that despite her development in other directions her agriculture was—and has remained—backward. About half of the population made its living directly from agriculture, and far the greater part of the population lived in the countryside, and was engaged in occupations related to agriculture. Yet, despite being an overwhelmingly agricultural country, India failed, and still fails, to produce substantial recurring surpluses of food.

There are various reasons why agriculture is so backward, and most of them have already been noticed. There is not enough land to go round. When a farmer dies, his land is divided between his sons, each of whom may get less than he needs. Plots of land are too small to farm efficiently (to use a tractor, for example, it is necessary to have fair-sized fields), and a man's holdings are often scattered about in different places. Methods of farming are primitive, and the farmer is in no position to introduce improvements. The manure from his cattle is needed as fuel in the household, because no other form of fuel is available; but it would be much better used in the fields as fertilizer.

Because of the farmer's poverty, he falls into debt to the money-lender, and once he is in debt he may not be able to escape from it because of high interest charges. His customs do not help him. According to custom, he is expected to spend large sums on weddings and other ceremonies, and this increases his indebtedness. This is a social problem as well as an economic one, because in a way it is the society he lives in that is responsible for his poverty. The customs of society require him to spend his money in unprofitable ways.

The rent he has to pay does not help either. Even after government reforms, too many peasants are tenants on other people's land, and many landlords are not concerned to spend money on agricultural improvement. Religious customs also are against him. It is a custom not to slaughter cows, and indeed to respect the life of all living beings. This means that pests multiply and damage crops, and that too many cows are allowed to live—underfed, skinny, and doing no good to themselves or anybody else.

Industry

Though India's industrial base at the time of independence was in some ways surprisingly good, it was of course not to be compared with the resources of an advanced Western country. Some things India had in sufficient or near-sufficient quantities; other things she lacked.

Two general defects in the industrial economy at the time of independence may be noticed. One is that India was entirely dependent on imports for many of the things that keep industry going—machine tools, electric motors and so forth. Few or none of these were made in India, and they had to be imported and paid for with precious foreign currency. Secondly partition had the effect of separating raw materials from processing plants in a number of industries. Pakistan had the hides, the jute, the cotton; India had the tanneries and mills where they were processed. Partition meant that these plants were sundered from their sources of supply.

India had steel, oil, coal, paper, cement, manganese, gold, and a great deal of light engineering: that is, she had many of the minerals and industries that she needed, though not always enough for her needs, especially when demand increased and the needs grew. But the development of electric power, high-grade steels, and heavy industry generally—among other things—was necessary, if the country was not to be over-dependent on imports. The most obvious problem that faced the government was that of finding enough money to finance all its planned developments. Each source was limited. Taxation was one, but not all of the money raised by taxation—indeed, only a small part of it—could be spent on industrial development. Private investment by Indian businessmen was another, which the government could encourage if it chose. Foreign investment was potentially a valuable source of funds for Indian industry. And, finally, it was to be hoped that finance could be found from grants and loans by other governments and international organizations, and by tapping some of the hoarded wealth of the country.

Attracting foreign investment raised problems. There were some who saw foreign investment as draining away the profits from what should be native Indian industries. Generally, however, the government was anxious to encourage such investment, on condition that it was spent on industries that the country really needed, and provided that arrangements were made to ensure a share of the profits for Indians.

Industrialization in a poor Asian country is not, of course, like the expansion of industry in a Western country. There are social problems raised by the different customs of the workers. Mobility of labour is important for example. If a factory is to operate smoothly, it should be possible to find the right sorts of workers and appoint them to the jobs that they are most fit to do. But if you try to make a sweeper into a machine operator because he seems to be the right man for the job, you may find that you are making him break caste rules and causing unrest among his fellow-workmen. Caste can thus pose personnel difficulties in the day-to-day running of industry.

Caste

But it is not only in industry that the customs of caste in India are significant; they meant, and mean, all manner of discrimination and injustice in every sphere of life. People would choose their fellow-caste-men in making appointments to jobs. Untouchables, now called the Scheduled Classes, were condemned to lives of degradation with little hope of advancement. Government officers, in distributing funds for village development schemes, were liable to favour the high-caste villages in the apportionment. And it was not possible to change people's behaviour simply by a constitution or an Act of Parliament. The process had to be a gradual one of propaganda and education as well as law.

Overpopulation

Perhaps the biggest problem of all, but one that is very simply stated, was the problem of overpopulation.

At the outset, neither the government nor many other people recognized it as the biggest problem. Since the time when India became independent, the world has become much more aware of the overpopulation problem, and certainly the Indian government has been taking active steps concerning it. But it is a question whether these steps are sufficient. The problem is so enormous that it is difficult to face up to it squarely and accept all its implications. It is a problem for the world, not just for India. The world's population shows signs of being able to double within forty years, whereas the world's food production does not. Therefore there will not be enough to go round. Population is growing fast in a country like India because public health has improved. Fewer people are dying in infancy. This means that more are growing up and marrying and having children. Further, better health means longer life for more people. The increase in population then means for India more children and more aged. These are the very people who do not work for their living but depend on others.

During the Indian government's first five-year development plan, the average expectation of life went up from twenty-six to thirty-two years. Since independence, food production has been increasing, but it has scarcely kept pace with the increase in population. This means that, unless people have fewer children in India, or food production increases very much faster, India's development will not advance; and it will scarcely stand still.

CHAPTER SEVENTEEN

India in the Modern World

(a) POLITICAL PARTIES

Parliament

The first general elections for parliament in India under the new constitution were held in 1951–52. The holding of elections posed enormous problems and the elections themselves displayed a number of very distinctive characteristics.

One problem lay in the sheer size of the country, with a population several times the size of Britain's, nearly forty times the size of Australia's. The mere organization of the election was a major task. People living in remote country areas had to be catered to, and the whole election was spread out over a period late in 1951 and early in 1952. There were 107,000,000 people voting. The problem of illiteracy posed another serious difficulty. The fact that most of the voters could not read or write meant that special systems of voting had to be devised. Party candidates were identified, not by printed names, but by symbols of their parties. If you travel round India when elections are approaching, you will see party symbols stencilled on walls everywhere, so that the streets are like picture galleries. The Congress party, for example, has as its symbol a pair of oxen drawing a plough.

Another important peculiarity lay in the sort of result that the Indian elections had, and still have. There was, right from the start, one big party, Congress, the organization that had led the nationalist movement and brought the country to independence. In the first elections, Congress won about two-thirds of the seats throughout the country. There were, in addition, a few small parties which shared the other seats, none getting very many. The Communists were the second strongest party, and were to remain so in future elections.

It must be remembered that there were two tiers of government: the states, which ran many of their own affairs, and the centre, with its federal government, with overriding powers throughout the country. In each separate state, there was a legislative assembly, for which people voted. In addition there was a parliament at the centre, called the Lok Sabha ('Assembly of the People'), with a Cabinet and Prime Minister, who had to be elected members and who formed the government. There was also a President who was Head of State but who held supreme responsibility in theory and possessed extremely wide emergency powers; there was nothing in law to stop him from trying to run the government himself. In practice he was a figurehead, representing the country on ceremonial occasions. This much we saw in the last chapter.

Congress and the other parties

In this system, there was nothing to stop one party from winning the elections to the Lok Sabha and forming the federal government, and other parties from winning the elections in some of the states. It would be necessary then for the federal government and the subordinate state governments to find ways of getting on with each other. Congress was so powerful that this particular problem arose only rarely, for Congress not only dominated the federal scene but controlled most of the state governments also. The two chief exceptions to this need to be noticed.

The first case is that of Kerala, which for various social reasons became a centre of Communism. In the Kerala elections of 1957, the Communist party won and formed the government. The result was trouble. Conflicts broke out between Communist trade unions and others, the police felt they were being used for Communist party objectives, and the upshot was that the central government took over the running of the state in the name of the President.

The other case occurred after the general elections in 1967. By this time the reputation of Congress had begun to tarnish. There were widespread complaints of corruption at all levels of government and much popular disillusionment with the fruits of independence. In the elections Congress did manage to retain power at the centre, but several states returned non-Congress governments. This posed a problem that the federation hadn't faced before, since it was now necessary for the federal government to do business with a number of state governments that were hostile to it.

Congress

At the time, and in the light of comparisons with the India of the 1950s, many observers feared that this would be the end of strong central government for the country. But if we compare the India of 1968 with any other Asian country with a democratically elected government, we find that Congress is still in a strong position with a convincing majority in the Lok Sabha and in control of the governments of more than half of the states. For Congress, even after twenty years, was still the party of Gandhi, the national hero, and of Nehru, the first Prime Minister: it was the party that had brought India to freedom from foreign rule. It was more than a party; it was a national institution. This, however, carried with it certain dangers.

One danger was that it might lose its sense of purpose. People were likely to join it for the wrong reasons—not because it represented a particular point of view but because it was the party that one had to join in order to achieve success in politics. Those who criticized Congress thought that this process had gone too far already. Allied to this was the danger of corruption. Congress was a sort of bandwaggon for all who wanted power. As it seemed bound to be the party of power and success, it didn't matter so much what people did once they were in it: they could use their positions in government—state or central—for their own benefit. It was this aspect that turned so many people away from the party in 1967.

So long as the party had strong and well-respected leaders, great names who had fought for independence in the war and before, Congress held together and had a sense of purpose. Gandhi, Nehru—these were the best known—and, around them, people like Jayaprakash Narayan, Chakravarti Rajagopalacharia, Lal Bahadur Shastri, Vallabbhai Patel belonged to the respected generation of Congress leaders. But Gandhi was assassinated soon after independence; some others later left Congress to form parties of their own; and Lal Bahadur Shastri succeeded Nehru as Prime Minister only to die soon after.

The other parties

Apart from Congress, no other party had a really strong organization throughout India. Some of them might be strong enough in one or two particular areas to win state elections—as happened in 1967—but none could make a good showing in the country as a whole.

If an exception to this existed, it was the Communist party. But it has been said that the Indian Communists were their own worst enemies. Although India is a poor country, and the sort in which Communism might well make a strong appeal, the party in India has never looked like a serious challenger to Congress. After independence, the Communists spoiled their chances by using violent tactics—being responsible for much of the trouble in Hyderabad, for example. They had successes when they adopted constitutional methods, particularly in areas where frustration and discontent with the existing state of affairs were strongest. This sort of frustration and discontent was to be found especially where there were large numbers of educated people without employment commensurate with their ability—where university graduates for example might have to become bus drivers. Kerala, with its long traditions of good schooling, was such an area, and this is where the Communists scored their big success in 1957. But in the 1960s the party lost its strength and its appeal because it split into two factions, one supporting China and the other supporting Russia. In the minds of many Indians, the Communist party was associated especially with China, which it had supported in the 1950s, and China now had become India's bitter enemy.

On the left wing of politics, the Praja Socialist party is also worthy of notice. It was formed as the result of the merging of two separate socialist parties founded some time after independence by Jayaprakash Narayan and Acharya Kripalani respectively. Congress took some of the socialists' thunder in the 1950s by itself proclaiming its adherence to socialist policies, as it did in the Avadi Declaration of 1955, in which the Congress party set itself the task of making India a socialistic state.

To the right of Congress in political views were several conserva-tive parties whose doctrines were strongly tinged with Hinduism. Hindu political organizations, chief among them the Mahasabha, wanted to see Hindu customs made law and were fiercely hostile to Muslims. One such party, associated with the Mahasabha, was the Jan Sangh, which became increasingly strong in the 1960s. One of the chief demands of the Jan Sangh was that the slaughter of cows should be made illegal, a demand that dogmatic Hindus had been making for a long time.

Currents of political change revealed themselves clearly in the 1967 elections. Support for Congress was ebbing away, and new forces were at work—some favouring the Communists, some favouring Hindu parties, some favouring regionalist anti-Hindi parties and representing 'linguism', the self-government of language areas. What the future held was difficult to see. What was very much to be hoped was that things would not stand still in the sphere of economic development either, though many feared that this was the case.

(b) PLANS AND PERFORMANCES

Planning

There was a time when it was taken for granted that economic progress was something that came about spontaneously, and within limits could be left to look after itself. These *laissez faire* views no longer find many adherents. Some people may favour rather more private enterprise than others, but most accept the fact that govern-ments should take at least some part in controlling a nation's economy and managing its development so that communications can be improved, factories built, investments chosen, and workers paid in an efficient and just way. Thus, the benefits of progress can be made available to all. In India, both before and after independence, there was a very strong belief in the necessity of government planning.

There are several ways in which a government can improve economic controls. It can itself take over all the enterprises in the country—factories, railways, buses, mines, shops, everything—leaving no scope at all for private enterprise. This would be a full-scale socialist solution, and the Indian government did not wish to commit itself to any such absolute course of action. Alternatively a government can impose more limited forms of control. It can take over certain important industries (such as steel), run them itself, set the prices, and take whatever profits there may be. At the same time it can leave other industries in private hands, reserving to itself in some fields the right to set up new enterprises. It can set up a state trading corporation to handle some or all of the country's foreign trade. It can direct investment and decide which lines of development are desirable and which are not. It can decide how particular industries are to be run. It can insist on having government representatives on the boards of directors of private companies.

The government can also make rules about the way in which profits are to be shared. By this method private enterprise is left to provide capital and run the industry, but the government supervises it for public purposes. The disadvantage of this system of control is that if there are too many rules, businessmen (foreign or otherwise) are wary of venturing their capital in new enterprises, and even if this does not happen, the operation of bureaucratic regulations may be so complicated that concerns cannot operate efficiently. This is the problem that has given rise to most complaints in India.

The Five-Year Plans

The governments of independent India have shown an interest in all these methods of control over the economy, especially the last. From the beginning, there was an interest in planning which led to the formulation of targets for the country's development. In 1948 plans were made for automobile assembly, oil refining, steel mills, and many other avenues of development. When it became obvious that these plans had not succeeded in dramatically improving the country's economy, a more comprehensive approach was adopted. A series of carefully worked out plans for Indian development over five-year periods was based on a sober assessment of how much money would be available for the government to finance them.

The first five-year plan was launched in 1951. Targets were set for agriculture, industry and all kinds of public works. Nearly half of the money that the government was to spend was to be put into agriculture and irrigation: impressive schemes were put into effect for dams and the provision of hydro-electric power. There were enormous possibilities in the rivers as a source of power: only 6% of their flow was actually harnessed at the time, and it was clear that India stood to gain much both in irrigation and in electricity by exploiting them. During the period of the first five-year plan, the country's industrial production increased by about 50%.

The second plan was launched in 1956. The mid-fifties saw a trend towards socialism in the Congress party; many of the new members of parliament, elected in 1952, wanted to see more dramatic social changes than the old generation of leaders had seemed to contemplate, and consequently there was a greater interest among the party's members in state control of the economy. Accordingly, a list of seventeen major industries was drawn up which were to be the concern of the state, not private enterprise. And twice as much money was to be spent as under the first plan.

Under the third and fourth plans the country experienced difficulty in keeping to its programme. This was partly the result of over-optimism, a tendency among the planners to exaggerate the funds they could expect to find available for their schemes, whether from private investment, foreign loans or taxation. Another cause lay in the simple fact that, after thousands of years of history, India's economy still depended immediately on favourable weather conditions. If rains failed, harvests were bad, there was a danger of famine, and large quantities of grain had to be imported. This meant that there was less to invest in the execution of the five-year plan. In the mid–sixties, famine conditions developed in many parts of the country. In the North-East, many died. The outlook for the economy as a whole was bad, and the value of the rupee, India's unit of currency, had to be lowered.

Agriculture

The problem in developing industry is largely the problem of finding money for it. Once the funds are available it is possible to go ahead and employ competent engineers and construction firms to set up the industry, and to know more or less what one is getting.

It is different with agriculture. The problems only begin when the money is found for agricultural improvement. Problems arise because the money and resources for improvement have to be distributed through a large organization of officials on whose honesty and intelligence the state must rely. They also arise because technical improvements such as pumps, tractors and fertilizers are useless unless the millions of people in the fields both want them and know how to use them. The whole process depends on many people, each doing the job properly, and this is not easy for a government to control. Since the process involves the education of farmers in new methods, it is likely to be a slow one.

In fact, there has been no dramatic improvement in Indian agriculture—no question of increasing production by fifty per cent in five years. In the early years of independence, there were bad harvests, production slumped, and India had to buy abroad more than she could sell. The mid fifties were much better for agriculture, and in the years 1951–61 the average increase in food production has been estimated at 2.6%. This was a good steady increase, but it was still not enough to do more than feed the extra mouths created by the simultaneous rise in population.

Land reform

Two general methods of tackling the farming problem are worth noticing. One of these is land reform. This was intended to cut down tenancy and give to peasants their own land. Too many of them had to pay large rents to landlords, or they had fallen deeply in debt to moneylenders who claimed the land in payment of the debt. They could scarcely subsist, let alone improve their land and learn modern methods. The government therefore aimed at redistributing the land. Each family was to be given a minimum of five and a maximum of thirty acres.

The famous Bhoodan movement was not part of government activity, but it was in line with the government's aims. This was a movement aimed at persuading people to give land, which could then be passed on to the poor. The movement was founded by Vinoba Bhave, who went about like a preacher, talking to villagers and asking them to give him land so that his movement could let the landless benefit. In this way, millions of acres were redistributed, but much of it was inferior land, and not all of Vinoba Bhave's helpers, responsible for the redistribution, were reliable and efficient.

However no amount of redistribution can solve the land problem if there is not enough land in the country to be redistributed. At the root of the problem lies the overpopulation of India.

Village self-help

The other general method of tackling the farming problem used by the government was the idea of community self-help. This meant getting villagers to do a thing for themselves, instead of devoting some of the scarce government funds to the task of doing it for them.

The scheme worked by employing government officers to visit villages and encourage people to undertake enterprises such as building wells, starting schools, preparing roads (on which crops could be taken to a market town or rail-head, to the benefit of agriculture). The villagers supplied most of the resources in the form of labour, materials, and sometimes cash; the government helped by providing teachers when schools were built, surfaces for roads when the foundations were made, farming machinery when people had learned what they were for and wanted them, and so on. This community development scheme was launched in 1952; villages were divided into groups of about a hundred, called blocks, under Block Development Officers (B.D.O.s), and the blocks were grouped together with staffs for each group containing experts in agriculture and engineering.

This was another project that seemed very good in theory but did not work perfectly in practice. Suppose that a B.D.O were assigned a sum of money for building wells in his block—there is little to stop the money from disappearing from view. Too few wells may be built, or they may be built quite cheaply so that they are unsatisfactory for their purpose. The area of a block is too vast for supervisors and inspectors to examine everything on the spot, and they have to rely on reports drawn up for them by officials who may wish to deceive them. Again, a model village may be set up where modern farming methods are demonstrated on somebody's land and a tractor is provided for everybody to use. But the villagers, even if they see the modern methods and are impressed by them, may not have enough money to buy the pumps and so forth that are required to put the methods into practice. And their fields are too small for a tractor to be useful, so it rusts away. Perhaps the government pays a veterinary surgeon to stay in the area and give free service; but he may refuse to answer any calls unless he is paid, and most people will not be able to benefit from him.

For all that, a great many valuable improvements have been set in motion in the villages by schemes of this sort. In the course of time, there may be great changes in the outlook and methods of farmers.

Welfare and justice

Inequality and discrimination were social evils that the government set itself to eradicate, and here, too, good intentions could not easily be turned into realities. The constitution of the country provided, as we have seen, that nobody was to be refused access to public places or to employment simply because he was of a particular caste or outcaste. In the states, the governments took steps to ensure that some positions in government service would be reserved specially for outcastes or untouchables, now called the Depressed Classes. Lists were made of poor castes that had suffered injustice from the rest of the population and were in need of special treatment —development funds, special free schools, reserved jobs, and so on. Naturally, all the castes that were not obviously wealthy and powerful clamoured to be counted as poor and put on the lists, so that they would enjoy these benefits.

In the particular matters of health and education, there were solid achievements that could be recognized. The proportion of literate people steadily increased. Hospitals and schools appeared in all parts. Universities sprang up like mushrooms. The expectation of life increased, with successes in anti-malaria schemes and public health generally. But the deficiencies from the standards taken for granted in Western countries were so great that all these achievements were a drop in the ocean. And the quality of many social services was not high. People could get free treatment in government clinics, but in many cases the treatment was notoriously poor. Hospitals were very congested. Teachers were paid wretched salaries—as little as Rs80 or £4 a month in many village schools— and the teaching profession did not attract the best people. By the mid sixties, universities were being created at the rate of about five a year, but most of them were thoroughly inferior, with poor staff and too little equipment. This is not to say that high standards were not maintained in some, but a mood of frustration set in and student riots became commonplace.

It is difficult to know whether to be optimistic or pessimistic about India's chances of worthwhile development. A visitor to India in 1967—the year when elections ousted Congress from power in several states, famine swept the North-East, and rioting broke out in many northern cities—could only get a gloomy picture from all that he was told. Everybody would complain of corruption in government, inefficiency and waste of money, general disintegration and openings for Communism. But if we stand back and look at India in the framework of the rest of Asia, there is no denying that the country's performance could have been much worse, and there is much that is encouraging.

(c) INDIA IN THE WORLD

Nehru was the chief architect of India's foreign policy and the chief feature of the stand he took in world affairs was the doctrine of non-alignment.

The relationships with friends and enemies would probably have been the same whoever was running India's foreign policy. But India's reputation in the world, and the development of non-alignment as a doctrine, were largely the work of Nehru himself. Other Indian leaders left foreign affairs very much to him. Non-alignment did not mean that India did not align herself with either side in any quarrel. India had quarrels of her own, and there were many conflicts in the world on which Nehru was prepared to take a stand. Rather non-alignment meant not taking sides in the cold war, the tension between the West and the Communist powers. It meant trying to have good relations with as many countries as possible on both sides, and indeed getting help from both sides.

India between East and West

Although India stayed in the British Commonwealth, this did not mean taking sides with the West against Communism. In 1949 a way was found of ceasing to be a dominion of Britain, and becoming a republic, without actually leaving the Commonwealth. But the Commonwealth could not be thought of as a group of countries dominated by Britain; it was a group of countries that had certain things in common and consulted together, but were completely free to form their own relationships with Russia and other nations. Other countries in Africa and Asia became independent after India, and most of these also adopted a position of neutrality or non-alignment in world affairs. Among these, India was one of the first to gain independence, and the biggest. This gave her a position of leadership among them.

Though all these countries had their own differences with their neighbours, they were all ready to form friendships with both Western and Communist countries. As neutrals, they had a valuable part to play in settling international disputes. India especially took a part in international affairs, being active in the United Nations, helping to settle the Korean war, and playing a part in the Geneva settlement which brought for a time an uneasy truce in Vietnam.

In 1955 a conference of African and Asian powers was held at Bandung, in Indonesia, and again India played an important part. At that time, there was a great sense of confidence among the non-aligned countries, which felt that they were following peaceful policies, benefiting from all, harming none, and with the future on their side. In later years there came to be so much trouble within and between them that the mood evaporated. While it lasted, however, the mood was well expressed in Nehru's set of five principles of foreign policy, which he said India was following. These were respect for the land of other countries, non-aggression, not interfering in other countries' affairs, equality, and peaceful co-existence. They were called the *Pancha Shila*.

Friends and enemies

It would be silly to pretend that Indians were, or are, more peaceful by nature than other people. There is no reason why they should be. And it would have been silly for an Indian government to ignore what was going on in the world and seek no allies. India was confronted by the genuine problem of two hostile neighbours to the north: Pakistan and China. Relations between Muslims and Hindus had become so bad, and the disorders at partition so appalling, that there was bound to be no love lost with Pakistan. We have already seen that Kashmir was a running sore in their relations, that a ceasefire was not agreed to until 1949, and that a referendum for the Kashmiris to decide their own future was agreed to but never took place.

India hoped for friendship with China, especially during the socialist phase of Congress when China, as a Communist power, could be seen as a model of planned development by an independent Asian power. In 1954 Nehru visited China and was impressed by what he saw. India and China agreed on following the *Pancha Shila*. China's takeover of Tibet in 1950 had been accepted by India.

But Chinese maps showed parts of India as being in China, and the disputed territory was a source of friction which eventually brought outright war. Relations worsened. In 1962 Chinese troops refused to move from a part of Indian Kashmir, claimed by China, or from the North-East frontier of India, where also there were disputed claims to territory. A short war followed, and there were genuine fears of full-scale invasion. But the Chinese forces stopped short in the area that they claimed was Chinese.

Part of India's northern frontier is with Pakistan (both East and West), and part is with China (the North-East Frontier Agency, Himachal Pradesh, and Indian Kashmir), but there are certain smaller states also in between India and China. These are Nepal, the biggest, Bhutan and Sikkim.

Nepal is independent, and has its own monarch. The Indian government was anxious to have the friendship of Nepal and to bring the country under its influence. In Khatmandu, the capital of Nepal, many Indians worked in missions to help with Nepal's development —engineers, agriculturalists and others. But Nepal was equally anxious to preserve her independence and she cultivated friendly relations with China also. As for Sikkim and Bhutan, these are small and weak states which came very much under Indian influence, receiving military as well as economic assistance. But with both major neighbours hostile, allies were urgently needed. The British connection was not abandoned; close links were always maintained. Nonetheless, the Indian government felt disappointed that the West as a whole showed less readiness to help India than was wanted. The West did not take India's side over Kashmir, but stayed aloof. America was particularly distrusted because of the alliance between the U.S.A. and Pakistan. Arms and tanks were supplied by America to Pakistan, actually for defence against any Communist attack, but they could be—and in fact were—used against India in the Kashmir fighting of 1965.

We should not be surprised that India turned to Russia for help and support. In 1955 the Russian leaders, Bulganin and Khrushchev, toured India and scored a major propaganda success. They declared that India was in the right over Kashmir. Eventually agreement was reached for Russia to build advanced fighter aircraft in India; and in the mid–sixties hostility between Russia and China made an understanding between Russia and India only natural. This does not mean that Russia was willing to support India in any adventures. Like the Western powers, Russia did not want to stir up possibly very expensive trouble in Asia. In 1966 the Russian leader, Mr. Kosygin, persuaded India and Pakistan to bring the Kashmir war to an end.

Some small bits of coastal territory in India were actually possessed by other European colonial powers even after independence. They were ports that had been taken over as colonies long before. Understandably the Indian government wanted to have them as part of India. In 1954 by agreement the French gave up Pondicherry. But the Portuguese were unwilling to give up Goa, South of Bombay. In 1955 there were border clashes, perhaps provoked in part by Indians so that there would be an excuse to invade. The government wanted to settle the question peacefully. However, no amount of persuasion would budge the Portuguese, and in 1961 the army was sent in, to take forcible possession of Goa.

This sort of action damaged India's reputation in the West, largely because in the 1950s people got into the habit of regarding Indians as especially peaceful, and judging their actions by specially high standards. Judged by the standards we commonly apply to other countries, India's conduct of her foreign affairs was neither worse nor better than anybody else's.

CHAPTER EIGHTEEN

Pakistan

(a) PAKISTAN AFTER PARTITION

If you get to know a number of people who live in Pakistan or the North of India, you may be surprised to find how many of them suffered injury, or bereavement, or at least terrifying experiences, during the months that came before and after partition. They do not boast about it, but from casual references in conversation you may learn how the father of one was killed, how the whole family of another spent nights of fear huddling on a rooftop waiting for rioting crowds to come and kill them, how the mother of another was attacked by a rioter and has been an invalid ever since.

Refugees

Pakistan was born amid rioting, slaughter, and organized massacre. The trouble was especially bad in the Punjab, where Muslims and Hindus lived side by side, and could not trust each other. The frontier itself was not finally decided and clearly marked out until some time after independence. Therefore there was chaos both before and after independence, with refugees pouring in both directions—Muslims crossing to Pakistan, where they would be safe among their fellow-Muslims, and Hindus going to India, where they would be safe among their fellow-Hindus. There was less trouble in Bengal, the other province of the old India that had to be split. Calcutta, the capital city of the province, went to India, and the frontier was drawn through the Ganges delta east of Calcutta.

These facts were noticed in an earlier chapter, because they are facts of Indian history as well as Pakistani. But what were the consequences for Pakistan?

The most obvious was the refugee problem. In 1947 and the following year, by fits and starts, no fewer than eight million refugees entered the country. These were nearly all Muslims who did not want to live in India. An enormous number came at the time of partition itself, having chosen beforehand to live in Pakistan. Others were slaughtered on the way, or before they could leave their Indian homes. A wave of refugees came later while there was war in Kashmir—from the part of the state that was overrun by India. Others came in later years, especially in 1950 when anti-Muslim riots in Indian Bengal drove many to make their way to East Bengal, which is the eastern wing of Pakistan. There have been other occasions since. And a trickle of refugees has been coming in all the time. Not all of them are driven out of India at a time of rioting—many have various private reasons for wanting to make the move.

Lack of facilities

Another consequence was the necessity to start a government and build up all the apparatus of state from scratch. A civil service had to be created with its ministries, its army administration, its documents and records. All the main centres of government in the old India went into the new India. Not only Delhi, the capital of India as a whole, but large provincial capitals possessing major government buildings also went to India. Pakistan in consequence lacked a suitable home for its government. Karachi was made (temporarily) the capital, but Karachi lacked the buildings, equipment and facilities that were needed for a capital, and for some time after independence the staffs of the ministries were working in hastily erected huts at tables bought from nearby bazaars. It was an improvised, orange-box government.

Relations with India

Other consequences of partition belong to the history of India and Pakistan jointly—the various things that contributed to continuing hostility between the two countries. The case of Junagadh has already been mentioned. The rulers of the native states had to make up their minds whether to join India or Pakistan. The semi-independent tribes of the north-west frontier, the rulers of Bahawalpur and Khairpur, and the Baluchistan states joined Pakistan. So did the ruler of Junagadh, but Junagadh does not have a border with Pakistan and would therefore have been a third separate section of the country, almost surrounded by India (not entirely, because Junagadh is on the coast). Mr. Jinnah was willing to accept Junagadh as part of Pakistan, but the Indian government was not willing to let this happen, and took over Junagadh by force. This was one thing that poisoned relations between Pakistan and India, but it was a very small thing beside the problem of Kashmir.

The Pakistan point of view on Kashmir can be briefly stated. While it was true that rulers of princely states were legally free to make up their own minds whether to join India or Pakistan, or stay independent, it was not reasonable or just in the circumstances for the ruler of Kashmir to opt for India, and when he did so it seemed that this was the result of much plotting by Congress that had been going on for a long time. There were comings and goings of Congress men, including Gandhi himself, between Delhi and Kashmir, which suggested that some mischief was afoot. It seemed that the Indian government was bringing pressure to bear on Sir Hari Singh, and probably promising the help of the Indian army to make Kashmir a part of India. These suspicions seemed to be confirmed when India actually did fly in troops to put down the rising against the Kashmir government after the decision to join India.

Though Kashmir had borders with both India and Pakistan, it seemed to belong naturally to Pakistan rather than India. The most obvious reason for this was that three-quarters of the population were Muslim. But even apart from this, geography suggested it. Rivers flowed into Pakistan, and roads were into Pakistan rather than India. The rivers that fed Pakistan with water rose in Kashmir. By religion and geography it seemed Kashmir should be part of Pakistan. By law, the ruler had a right to take it into India. India insisted on this legal right when she went to war for the state. But when it came to another princely state that was obstinate, Hyderabad, the Indian government seemed to forget the legal argument and use a geographical one. Hyderabad had the legal right to stay independent. But it was surrounded by India, and would be better off in the modern world as part of India. Therefore it seemed to the Pakistanis that the Indian government was just using whatever argument suited it to gain its own ends in trying to take over both Kashmir and Hyderabad. The Indian refusal to let the future of Kashmir be decided by a referendum, even though this was agreed to with the United Nations, seemed to confirm the opinion. And, ever since 1947, Kashmir has been the chief obstacle to normal relations with India, the chief cause of friction and even undeclared war.

Other problems in relations between the two countries have been solved, though not without acrimony. The rest of the frontier (apart from Kashmir) has been settled. Agreement has been reached over the division between the two countries of the waters of the Indus river, flowing through both.

(b) PAKISTAN SINCE INDEPENDENCE

The new country

A survey of facts about the effects of partition, then, looks like a list of disadvantages for Pakistan. It is a disadvantage for any country to be in two separate sections. It is even more so when these two sections are separated from each other by nearly a thousand miles of another country which is hostile. Travel between the two wings of Pakistan is usually by air or the long way round by sea—right round India.

West Pakistan consisted of various princely states which joined, the frontier tribes, the Western Punjab, Sind, and the part of Kashmir that the army was able to take over. These have an area of about 300,000 square miles, and at independence the population was about seventy million. The provinces of West Pakistan have since been amalgamated to form one unit. This means that it is on a more even footing with East Pakistan, which has always had only one province —East Bengal—but has a rather greater population than the whole of West Pakistan.

Mr. Jinnah became Governor-General. Unlike the Governor-General of India (Mountbatten did not run the government) Mr. Jinnah was the effective leader of the Pakistan government until he died a year later. Nazimuddin, from East Bengal, then became Governor-General. Liaquat Ali Khan was the first Prime Minister. There was at first no constitution. Instead, a Constituent Assembly was elected to draw up a constitution and to carry on as a sort of parliament for the time being.

The leaders of the new country therefore had a difficult task ahead of them. They threw themselves into it with gusto, and most of the purely administrative problems were eventually solved. But other problems—chiefly lack of ability or purpose in many of Pakistan's politicians—held up seriously the development of Pakistan as a modern state.

Pakistan in the 1950s

Government did not work well, despite the dedication of Mr. Jinnah and other early leaders. The Prime Minister, Liaquat Ali Khan, was assassinated, and the second Governor-General, Nazimuddin, took his place. Politicians were reputed to be corrupt. Ministers were said to hinder the efficient working of their departments by using their position to make doubtful deals, and to protect people who were carrying on illegal activities. That government was not working efficiently is quite clear. Education and public health were not being catered to as they should; refugees were being neglected. Plotting and intrigue were regular features of the political scene. In 1951 a plot to overthrow the government was uncovered. In 1952 proposals were made which were intended to form the basis of a constitution for the country, and these started off a long-drawn-out controversy.

The controversy was between moderate Muslims and extremists.

Since Pakistan had been created for the sake of the Muslims, it was only to be expected that the constitution of the country (when it was drawn up) would declare Pakistan to be a Muslim state. But it was a question to be debated how strictly Muslim the country should be, how far the laws of Islam were to be adopted as the laws of the country. Many people, particularly in the government, thought that the laws of Islam were out of date and unsuited to the needs of a modern state. But strictly orthodox Muslims, particularly the mullahs or teachers, wanted a full-scale introduction of Islamic law.

In 1953 there was rioting in Karachi, started by students and continued by mullahs. There was friction, not only between extremist and moderate Muslims, but also between the two wings of the country. The East Bengalis felt that their province was too much dominated by Westerners. Urdu was supposed to be the official language of the country, but Urdu belonged chiefly to West Pakistan and not many Bengalis knew it. Bengalis therefore wanted to be more free of West Pakistan, to have more self-government. At elections in 1954, a Bengali regionalist government came into being, violently against the West. This led to general rioting and confusion; martial law was imposed—the army had to take over to keep law and order.

In 1955 there was a return to government by the elected provincial and central bodies, and a new Prime Minister took office, who treated East Bengal with consideration. It was then that the various provinces of West Pakistan were joined to make one unit.

In 1956 a constitution finally came into being. This declared Pakistan to be an Islamic republic. The system of government combined two features. One was a strong parliament with political parties and a Cabinet of elected members (familiar in British Commonwealth countries). The other was a fairly strong president—who could take much of the responsibility for government if the parliament could not function properly. He possessed, for example, a veto on the laws passed by the parliament. And he was to be commander-in-chief of the forces. Nevertheless, his powers were limited. The advice of the Prime Minister and Cabinet was to be binding on him.

The constitution did not put an end to Pakistan's unhappy political life. Dissatisfaction grew, and in 1958 a group of army officers, impatient with the whole system, took action.

The army takeover

The complaint was that the politicians were corrupt and were interested in their own power rather than in efficient government.

The object of the army coup leaders was to reform the government and put Pakistan back on its feet. The method adopted was to arrest the politicians and take over all the powers of government while the necessary reforms were being carried out.

At first the previous President was kept on to give legality to the new military regime. But he was himself, in their view, too much tainted with the corruption of Pakistan politics, and was dropped. An army officer, Ayub Khan, later a field-marshal, took control; and he became responsible for most of the steps that were taken in the following years to change the political face of the country.

Political reforms

The changes brought about by the new military regime can be considered under two headings: political and social. The political changes were intended to hand back power to elected politicians—preferably not the same ones—with a more effective system of government. The social reforms, which were carried on by Ayub Khan when he became President eventually under a new constitution, were intended to do for Pakistan's agriculture, industry, health, education and so forth the sort of things that should have been done before, but had not been undertaken.

In 1960 a commission was appointed to give advice on the form of a possible new constitution. In 1962 a new constitution was actually put into effect. By it, there was to be a strong president at the head of the government elected directly by the people, and a National Assembly to exercise law-making powers. The president could veto the decisions of the Assembly, and if necessary he could dissolve it. If he dissolved it, a new one would have to be elected, and he would have to stand for election again himself. If the Assembly for its part wished to remove the president, it could do so by a three-quarters majority vote.

But any system, to work well, is dependent upon the quality of the people operating it. Ayub Khan wanted to keep the old-style politicians out. The Basic Democracies that formed part of the new system were intended partly to achieve this. The idea behind the Basic Democracies was that the ordinary folk, the villagers, didn't know enough about political affairs to be able to vote for their politicians in the Assembly. They did not know these politicians personally, and did not understand the things they talked about. On the other hand, they could vote perfectly well for somebody they knew, who would represent them in *local* affairs, which they understood. So Pakistan was to be divided into a large number of small units. These were the Basic Democracies.

People in the Basic Democracies would vote for representatives who would be concerned with government activities at the village level, who would be personally known to those who elected them, and who would be doing a job that the voters could more easily share in and understand. The people elected in this way would be themselves educated enough to be able to vote wisely for members of larger regional assemblies, and the members of each regional assembly would vote for a higher body. Thus the government was to be like a pyramid by the time the whole process was complete, with the National Assembly at the top and the Basic Democracies at the bottom. Each level in the pyramid would vote for the one above.

When the first elections were held, about 80,000 people were elected from the Basic Democracies. Most of these were literate, although only a minority of the whole population of the country was literate. Some of them were university graduates. An un-expected feature of the way the system worked was that many of the old-style politicians managed to get back into the elected bodies, in spite of the intention that the system should keep them out.

Social reforms

Land reform was possibly the most important item to be dealt with by Ayub Khan's government. Too much land was in the hands of too few people, according to the government's view. There were zamindars, who bought or inherited land on which the workers were their tenants, and there were jagirdars, whose families had in the distant past been given their estates tax free in return for services to the government. It was now proposed to take estates away from the big landlords, to break them up and parcel out the land to the peasants. Accordingly it was laid down that nobody could inherit more than a certain amount of land, and anything in excess of this was forfeit to the government, which would give compensation to the dispossessed owners. The result of this scheme was that about 2,300,000 acres were redistributed to the peasants, who were given grants by the government to help them improve their agriculture.

In 1959–60, only 36% of children of primary school age were actually attending schools, and only 12% of the age group in secondary schools. This meant that much had to be done for educa-tion, and plans were made by which there should be eight years' schooling for all by 1975. Scholarships were to be given for overseas study, and television was to be used for education.

In the villages, efforts were made to promote self-help schemes. When the Basic Democracies were established they were made responsible for co-ordinating government activity in the villages, encouraging a spirit of constructiveness among the people, running schools and dispensaries, promoting agricultural improvements, and other things which would improve conditions at the grass roots level.

Conclusion

On March 25, 1969, Ayub Khan announced his resignation as President of Pakistan and called on the Army to take full control of the affairs of the country. Martial law was proclaimed the same day, with General Agha Mohammad Yahya Khan, Commander-in-Chief of the Pakistan Army, as Chief Martial Law Administrator. By a proclamation issued on April 1, General Yahya assumed the office of President, with retroactive effect from March 25.

(c) Social and Political Problems

Pakistan is a country of problems. The whole idea of Pakistan seemed ridiculous when it was first put forward—it scarcely looked practicable to create a country out of nothing by disentangling a Muslim population from a land of Hindus and by giving them bits of territory that were separated by a large tract of Indian soil and lacked the requirements of a modern state. It seemed ridiculous—but it came to pass; and, with all its tribulations, Pakistan has survived and shows signs of life and purpose even. We should not wonder that the country has problems. We should wonder rather that it has managed in spite of them.

Pakistan and the world

In a way, the biggest problem was India. There was every reason for India and Pakistan to be hostile to each other, and Pakistan, being smaller, had more to fear from a state of hostility. In Pakistani eyes, the Indian takeover of Junagadh was villainy, and the invasion of Kashmir by India was far worse.

During the years of independence, the friction between India and Pakistan was likely to turn into violence at any moment. Just a little more heat, and the pot would boil over. Already in 1965, over Kashmir, there were open hostilities. Apart from Kashmir, there remained, even after all the slaughter at partition, substantial numbers of Muslims in India (about forty million) and substantial numbers of Hindus in Pakistan. These minorities were like hostages for their co-religionists across the border. If for any reason there was a surge of Indian enmity towards Pakistan (such as over Pakistan's later invasion of Kashmir), the Muslims in India would be made to suffer; and Pakistanis in turn could, if need arose, take out their anti-Indian feelings on the hapless Hindus in their midst.

Relations with India are at the heart of Pakistan's foreign policy.

A weak country with many internal problems, Pakistan has not wished to take a very active part in world affairs; but Pakistan has wanted friends. This has meant two things. Firstly, instead of being neutral, Pakistan has turned to those who were willing to give practical help. Secondly, Pakistan has tended to regard India's enemies as her friends, and India's friends as her enemies.

The first of these facts is shown by the way in which Pakistan became increasingly involved with the U.S.A. The American government was prepared to give practical help in the form of loans and arms sales. In 1954 a defence agreement was signed with America, by which Pakistan obtained large quantities of war materials. And, being committed to the West in world politics, Pakistan joined the anti-Communist alliances of the Middle East and Asia—SEATO and CENTO.

The second of these facts is shown by the way in which—in spite of being an ally of America—Pakistan developed friendly relations with mainland China, India's bitter enemy. There was an agreement with China to settle the line of the frontier between them. Air services were opened between the two countries. This flirtation with China was naturally not popular with the United States, but it was a natural consequence of the pattern of friendships and enmities in Asia.

Afghanistan and the Pathans

The search for practical friendship led to America and the West, though Pakistanis were disappointed when—despite her neutrality—India had great quantities of military assistance lavished on her by the West after the Chinese attack. The Pakistanis were also disappointed in their fellow-Muslim states. From North Africa to south-east Asia, there are many Muslim countries, and Pakistan hoped to have fruitful relations with them. This was not to be. Other Muslim governments would not forsake friendship with India in order to please Pakistan. And of all the Muslim countries, her neighbour Afghanistan was perhaps the most worrying to Pakistan.

Afghanistan was a fairly small, weak, backward country, with a population several times smaller than Pakistan's. The worry came, partly through fear of the Russians on the other side of Afghanistan, and of their possible activities in it, and partly through the links between Afghanistan and tribes within Pakistan.

These links were formed by the Pathans. The Pathans are a people with their own language, living on both sides of the border between Pakistan and Afghanistan. Though they are only a small part of the population (about five million in Pakistan), it used to be feared that they could cause trouble, for they are a militant, close-knit people. The fear was that there would be, as there had been at times in the past, a demand by the Pathans to be united. This would mean, either that the Pathan area of Pakistan would join Afghanistan, or that a new Pathan state would be set up.

Afghanistan, instead of cultivating friendly relations with Pakistan, made repeated demands for the Pathan area. Clearly there was a possibility of disorder and disaffection on the northern frontier, a part that was important for Pakistan's defence. In fact, serious trouble was avoided. Pakistan proved to have much less trouble from her tribal areas and language regions than did India. The North-West Frontier tribes, and the states of Baluchistan, Khairpur and Bahawalpur, were absorbed without much difficulty.

Language problems

All was not plain sailing in the matter of language, however. Many of the problems in running India since independence have been caused by the demands of language areas—the people who speak a particular language wanting to form their own state or province, separate from others and running as much of their own affairs as possible. There was a similar problem in Pakistan.

In the west wing of the country, the chief language actually used for everyday speech is Punjabi. The language of the east wing is, naturally enough, Bengali (East Pakistan consists of East Bengal). The language of Islam is Urdu.

At first, Urdu was adopted as the official language of Pakistan. This was because of its associations with the Islamic religion, and because it is a sort of lingua franca among educated Muslims (and indeed many Hindus) in the north of the subcontinent. But in East Bengal, very few people can speak or understand Urdu, and the Bengalis objected to having it forced on them. This was one of the reasons for the 1954 attempt by Bengali politicians to throw off the control of West Pakistanis.

The military regime of Ayub Khan's government solved the problem by giving Bengali and Punjabi equal status as official languages. Urdu was no longer to be forced on everybody. And English, the language still normally used in the courts of law and by the government, was recognized for the time being as the language of administration.

Education and health

When Pakistan was born, one of its disadvantages was that Muslims were generally more backward than Hindus. This meant that the country did not get its share of highly trained people, or colleges, or schools.

This problem has already been noticed in dealing with the reforms attempted by Ayub Khan. Eighty per cent of the country's population was unable to read or write, and a gigantic task lay ahead. Similarly the hospitals, family planning clinics, rural health centres and anti-malaria programmes started by the new regime were faced with a chronic situation. Much was said during the 1950s about government plans and local organizations to run health and education, but it appears that little was actually done.

Poverty

None of the social problems of the new Pakistan can be separated from poverty. It is not just that, if individual people are poor, they cannot afford to buy medical treatment, schooling for their children and improvements for their farms. If the entire country is poor, and if there are too few trained teachers and doctors, then the government cannot afford to provide these services and they are not there to be bought.

One aspect of the problem of poverty is the congestion of the agricultural population. Famines or food shortages, such as those in 1952–53, caused untold suffering. There is not enough land under cultivation to satisfy everybody's needs adequately. East Pakistan especially has a very high density of population. Most farming families do not own the land that they work but are, effectively, the tenants of landlords who live somewhere else and have no particular interest in improving the agriculture so long as they get their rent. Taking land away from many of the zamindars and jagirdars and giving it to the peasants is a start to the tackling of the problem, but by itself it is not enough to make crops grow more abundantly. A lot of money has to be spent on training farmers in ways of cultivating their land efficiently, and providing them with the means to do it.

Another aspect of the problem of poverty, one that was glaringly obvious to visitors to Pakistan from outside, is the presence in the country of many refugees. Most had no jobs to go to, and were regarded with suspicion by the other inhabitants, as rivals for the jobs that were available. We noticed before how Ayub Khan's regime made a start on the task of settling them.

A third aspect is the growth in population. In twenty years, the population of Pakistan increased by over thirty-four per cent. This was not simply because refugees were coming in—many refugees were leaving as well. The population has been growing because, as in India, fewer people are dying in infancy, or before maturity, and adults are living longer. And, as in India, it may well be that in the long run, this will turn out to be the most important and toughest problem of all.

Industry

Pakistan is under-industrialized. Industries mean more jobs that pay steadily, and more things to sell abroad for much-needed foreign money (which can then be used to buy things overseas that Pakistan cannot produce). Pakistan produced a number of commodities for export, such as jute, cotton, and wool, but did not have the industries to process them. Governments have increasingly abandoned their original idea of having the state run all new industries, in favour of the idea of encouraging private enterprise and helping foreign firms to set up factories in the country.

Religion

There are about twenty million non-Muslims in Pakistan. The Muslims are about seventy six per cent of the population of West Pakistan and seventy-one per cent of the population of East Pakistan. The non-Muslims are Hindus and Sikhs in the West, Hindus in the East. There are a few Christians and others as well. Since the Hindus and Sikhs are minorities surrounded by Muslims, they are not a problem in the way that religious conflicts were a problem in the old India. But in East Pakistan, at any rate, there are so many Hindus (about a fifth of the population of the province) that there is a constant danger of rioting; and in 1950 and in 1964 there were serious anti-Hindu riots.

Conclusion

Not only did Pakistan have enormous obstacles to surmount: she got off to a slow start in overcoming them. It is difficult to turn an underdeveloped country into a modern one; it is like trying to lift yourself up by your bootstraps. Efforts have been made to tackle some of the worst problems, with varying degrees of success; and only the future can tell how far the seemingly impractical idea of Pakistan can be made into a strong modern state.

The Writing of Indian History

There is no one single version of Indian (or any other) history that is right, all others being wrong. You might read one historian's books and think that, for example, India in the nineteenth century enjoyed peace, justice, reform of social ills, constant improvements in all the amenities of life and unprecedented prosperity under British rule. Then you might read another historian's books and think that in the same period there were exploitation, persecution, oppression, a whole catalogue of tyrannies endured by the Indians at the hands of their foreign masters. And you might suppose that one of these historians, and perhaps both, must be giving the wrong version.

But it is not as simple as that. The truth does not have to correspond with one of these opposite opinions, and it does not have to come somewhere in between either; it could very well be a mixture of both. Oppression and reform, exploitation and improvement could all be there. Therefore when historians differ in their interpretations this does not mean exactly that some of them are making a mistake; it means that some of them are choosing their evidence too selectively, or that they are over-influenced by their bias in assessing the evidence.

It would be nonsense to say that they should have no bias at all, for then there could be no history. Everybody has bias; but what an historian should do is to recognize it in himself, to allow for it as far as possible, and to judge the evidence as objectively as possible in spite of it.

Bias does not mean simply wanting to believe that a particular thing (such as British rule) is good or bad. That sort of prejudice, a prejudice in making value judgments, is only one sort of bias. There are others. For example, looking at one sort of evidence only, such as government records, and neglecting others, such as village traditions, is another form of bias. Never mind whether the government is good or bad, we might get a different and more useful picture of life in the country by using other sorts of evidence besides government records. Again, treating only one aspect of history as important and neglecting others is a form of bias. To write only about the accession of kings and the wars they had, as if only these were important, would be to write a very incomplete sort of history.

Every generation of historians has had, inevitably, its own forms of bias, but this does not mean that the literature of Indian history is worthless. On the contrary, a century and a half of devoted research has produced an abundant, rich and valuable treasury of historical writing.

The writers

It would be possible to say a good deal about the writing of Indian history before Westerners—chiefly British—took it up. But, although the literature of Indian languages before the eighteenth century included historical writing, it belonged to a tradition very different from history as we know it. The mediaeval chronicle of Kashmir, for example, is valuable and interesting for the historian, but does not distinguish between history as we understand it and legend.

The tradition of history-writing that we inherit grew from the labours of the eighteenth-century scholars who were keenly interested in Indian culture and did important pioneering work in studying Indian languages and translating Indian literature. Sir William Jones, first president of the Asiatic Society, was most notable among these. Thus the beginnings of Indian history-writing were orientated to linguistic studies.

The nineteenth century saw the growth of a class of scholar-administrators, men in the government service who were keenly interested in Indian languages, literature, religion, archaeology and art, and who devoted much of their time to the assembling and evaluation of evidence touching on India's past. Though some of their work is unsophisticated by modern standards, their achievement was enormous: they did not have the basis of literary knowledge and the framework of previously gathered historical evidence that we have—they were building these things up from scratch by translating manuscripts and deciphering inscriptions. A modern researcher today still refers often to the work of people like E. V. Cunningham in the decaying volumes of old journals.

As British rule was consolidated, and Victorian England—with its optimism, and its belief in progress and in the superiority of British achievement to whatever else the world had to show—came, for many men, to seem like an institution ordained by providence for the betterment of the human race, the writing of Indian history came to dwell increasingly on the effects, and the assumed benefits, of British rule. Drawing on a tradition of political philosophy that was fostered early in the century by utilitarians such as James Mill, historians concerned themselves with the activities of the British and their effects on the Indians. Particularly notable is Vincent Smith, whose praise of British achievement is often held up as an example of 'imperialist' complacency. However, in our concern with his value judgments we should not overlook the sheer scholarship of his writing, which made his work standard until well into the present century. Among more recent historians, the work of Sir Percival Spear, with less emphasis on the contribution made to India by British institutions, is among the most notable.

So far mention has been made only of British historians, but they are not the only ones. Other European countries—notably France, with its own colonial interests in Asia, and Germany, with a strong tradition of oriental studies amply endowed at numerous universities —have also made substantial contributions to the history of India. And in the last few decades of course it is the Indians themselves who dominate the scene.

In the circumstances of the early part of the twentieth century, it was natural that Indians engaged in scholarly activities should be intensely interested in the political developments around them, the growth of nationalism and the demand for independence. Many were active nationalists. And in the study of Indian history the attention of many turned to the achievements of Indian culture and government in the past, which might serve as an inspiration to nationalists in the present and as proof that India had a civilization as good as the West's. There is little dispute now that some, like K. P. Jayaswal, exaggerated these achievements unwarrantably and read into ancient India modern ideas and institutions which had no meaning then. But this does not mean that their Indian bias was more disabling than their predecessors' British bias, or that their work was less scholarly.

As for the study of Indian history today, in the middle part of the twentieth century, it is difficult to characterize this simply. There is a proliferation of different sorts of research at numerous Indian universities, seeking new bits of evidence to make our picture of history constantly more complete, trying to tap new sources of evidence, such as village genealogies which can tell us about population and migrations for centuries back. There is a closer scrutiny than before, a focusing on particular areas rather than the whole subcontinent or a whole region.

Above all, in tune with the modern trend in historical writing, there is an interest in society and economy, in the village rather than the court, the market-place rather than the audience hall. Historians such as D. D. Kosambi typify this trend. An interest in Communism often goes with this, and indeed in India today the term 'Marxist' is very loosely used to refer to an outlook orientated to society as a whole.

Though only a few names have been mentioned here, the number of those who have made important contributions to our understanding of India's past is very great. But however great it may be, there can never be any point at which everything has been discovered, everything written; for each new generation will have a new point of view, a new perspective on history, and the work of all its predecessors will seem incomplete.

Bibliography

The following list contains a mixture of primary and secondary sources which may be used. For the whole history of India, there are few general works in existence which are well-balanced, readable and scholarly. That by Moreland and Chatterjee, though dry, is valuable for coverage and simplicity. Edwardes' *History of India* contains numerous documentary extracts with linking narrative and a wide variety of illustrations. Tinker's *South Asia* conveniently summarizes trends and broad aspects of the history of India and neighbouring parts.

Some books listed touch on traditional Indian culture. For religions especially, and for early history as a whole, Basham's substantial *The Wonder that Was India* is a clear and readable outline. For early history as such, Thapar's paperback reflects modern research and has a wealth of detail on social history. *Traditional India* is a useful collection of readings. *Prehistoric India* describes the archaeology of the Indus Valley civilization.

For the Muslim period, Gibb will offer a useful introduction to the religion. Other books listed here include primary sources.

Colonial and modern history are represented by British and Indian writers. Something of the pace and excitement of the ending of British rule is caught in books such as those by Edwardes and Moon. Nehru's *Autobiography* is naturally valuable as a historical document in its own right; *Asia and Western Dominance* is an important work on colonialism in Asia.

General

Basham, Arthur. *The Wonder That Was India: A Survey of the History and Culture of the Indian Sub-continent Before the Coming of the Muslims,* 3d rev. ed. New York: Taplinger, 1968.

Conze, Edward. *Buddhism, Its Essence and Development.* Magnolia, Mass.: Peter Smith, 1959.

DeBary, William T., Jr., and Embree, A. T. (eds.). *Approaches to Asian Civilizations.* New York: Columbia University Press, 1963.

DeBary, William T., Jr., et al. (eds.). *Sources of Indian Tradition,* 2 vols. New York: Columbia University Press, 1964.

Edwardes, Michael. *A History of India.* New York: Farrar, Straus, 1961.

Fabri, C. L.   *An Introduction to Indian Architecture.* New York: Taplinger (Asia Publications), 1964.

Filliozat, Jean.   *India: The Country and Its Traditions.* Englewood Cliffs, N.J.: Prentice-Hall, 1962.

Hutton, J. H.   *Caste in India,* 4th ed. New York: Oxford University Press, 1963.

Khantipalo, Bhikku.   *What is Buddhism?* London: Probsthain, n.d.

Kosambi, D. D.   *An Introduction to the Study of Indian History.* London: Probsthain, 1957.

Moreland, W. H. and Chatterjee, A. C.   *A Short History of India,* 4th ed. New York: McKay, 1957.

Nilakantha Sastri, K. A.   *A History of South India from Prehistoric Times to the Fall of Vijayanagar,* 3d ed. New York: Oxford University Press, 1966.

Panikkar, Kavalam Madhu.   *A Survey of Indian History,* 4th ed. New York: Taplinger (Asia Publications), 1963.

Rawlinson, Hugh George.   *India: A Short Cultural History,* 2d rev. ed. New York: Praeger, 1952.

Smith, Vincent.   *The Oxford History of India,* 3 parts, 3d ed., edited by Percival Spear. New York: Oxford University Press, 1958.

Tinker, Hugh.   *South Asia: A Short History,* 2 vols. New York: Praeger, 1966.

Wallbank, Thomas Walter.   *Short History of India and Pakistan,* rev. and abridged ed. New York: New American Library, 1965.

Wolpert, Stanley A.   *India.* Englewood Cliffs, N.J.: Prentice-Hall, 1965.

Zinkin, Taya.   *India,* 2 vols. New York: Walker & Co. (Nations and Peoples Library), 1966.

Early History

Auboyer, J.   *Daily Life in Ancient India.* New York: Macmillan, 1965.

Beal, Samuel (trans.).   *The Travels of Fah-Hian and Sung-Yun.* Santiago de Compostela: 1964.

Chavarria-Aquilar, Oscar L. (ed.).   *Traditional India.* Englewood Cliffs, N.J.: Prentice-Hall, 1964.

Majumdar, R. C.   *Hindu Colonies in the Far East.* London: Probsthain, 1963.

Piggott, Stuart.   *Prehistoric India.* New York: Barnes & Noble, 1962.

Puri, Baij N.   *Cities of Ancient India.* Mystic, Conn.: Verry, 1966.

Thapar, Romila.   *A History of India,* I. New York: Penguin, n.d.

Muslim Period

Gibb, Hamilton A.   *Mohammedanism: An Historical Survey,* 2d ed. New York: Oxford University Press, 1963.

Husain, Yusuf. *Glimpses of Medieval Indian Culture.* London: Asia Publishing House, 1962.

Karim, Abdul. *Social History of the Muslims in Bengal to 1538.* London: Luzac, 1959.

Sharma, S. R. *Mughal Empire in India,* rev. ed. Mystic, Conn.: Verry, 1966.

Modern India

Boxer, C. R., *in* Livermore, Harold V. (ed.). *Portugal and Brazil,* 2 vols. New York: Oxford University Press, 1953.

Collier, R. *The Great Indian Mutiny,* 2 vols. New York: Dutton, 1963.

Edwardes, Michael. *The Last Years of British India.* New York: World, 1964.

Griffiths, Sir Percival Joseph. *Modern India,* 4th ed. New York: Praeger, 1965.

Karunakaran, K. P. *Religions and Political Awakening in India.* Mystic, Conn.: Verry, 1965.

Lach, D. F. *India in the Eyes of Europe: The Sixteenth Century.* Chicago: University of Chicago Press, 1965.

Lamb, Beatrice Pitney. *India—A World in Transition,* 3d rev. ed. New York. Praeger, 1968.

Moon, Penderel. *Divide and Quit.* Berkeley and Los Angeles: University of California Press, 1961.

Nehru, Jawaharlal. *An Autobiography.* New York: Paragon Reprint, 1965.

Panikkar, Kavalam Madhu. *Asia and Western Dominance: A Survey of the Vasco da Gama Epoch of Asian History, 1498–1945,* 2 vols. New York: Hillary, 1959.

Roberts, Paul E. *A History of British India,* 2 vols., 3d ed. New York: Oxford University Press, 1952.

Spear, Percival. *India: A Modern History.* Ann Arbor: University of Michigan Press, 1961.

Stephens, Ian. *Pakistan,* 3d rev. ed. New York: Praeger, 1967.

Tinker, Hugh. *India and Pakistan: A Political Analysis.* New York: Praeger, 1966.

Varma, V. P. *Modern Indian Political Thought,* 3d ed. Mystic, Conn.: Verry, 1966.

Weber, Max. *The Religion of India: The Sociology of Hinduism and Buddhism.* Glencoe, Ill.: The Free Press, 1958.

Woodruff, Philip. *The Men Who Ruled India,* 2 vols. (Vol. I: *The Founders;* Vol. II: *The Guardians*). Mystic, Conn.: Verry, 1963.

Index

Attitude to British, 190
Becomes President of Congress, 185
Becomes Prime Minister, 212
Foreign policy of, 234
Nationalism of, 187
Nehru, Motilal, 185
Nepal, Relations with India, 236
Nerbudda, R. (also NARMADA), *map*, 3
Nizam of Hyderabad
At time of Warren Hastings, 140
Chose independence in 1947, 217f.
Non-alignment, 234f.
Northern Sarkars (also CIRCARS)
map, 138
Franco-British rivalry, 129
Northwest Frontier, 151
Nur Jahan (Wife of Jahangir), 112f.

Ormuz
map, 24
Taken by Albuquerque, 122
Oudh
In Mutiny, 155, 157
map, 138
Relations of Warren Hastings with, 136-9
Taken by Wellesley, 148
Oudh, Begams of, 143
Outcasts. See Harijans
Overpopulation, 225, 232, 249

Pahlavas (Persian dynasties), 61
Pakistan
And Kashmir, 218f., 239f.
And partition, 211, 215f., 238f.
As Muslim state, 242
Military coup in, 242f.
Relations with India, 236, 239f., 245f.
Relations with China, 246
Relations with Afghanistan, 246f.
Pala dynasty (Bengal)
Kingdom, 70
map, 63
Pali (Sacred language of Buddhism), 29
Pali Canon (Buddhist Scriptures)
Source material for history, 52
Contents, 52f.
Pallavas (Southern kingdom)
Empire, 72
In early trade, 25
map, 63
Pancha Shila (Five principles), 235f.
Panchayat (Village Council), 28
Pandyas (Southern dynasty)
Kingdom, 73
map, 63
Panipat
map, 106
Site of Maratha defeat, 1761, 119

Parliament
In independent India, 219f., 226f.
Partition
Aftermath in India, 215f.
And Constituent Assembly, 212
And industry, 223f.
Problems of, 202, 211
Pataliputra (capital of Magadha)
Gupta capital, 62
Centre of power and culture, 51
map, 50
Patel, Vallabbhai, 228
Pathans, 247
Patna
map, 138
Near site of Pataliputra, 31
Scene of war, 131
Patna War, 131
Pegu (Province of Burma), 150
Persians, Invade Mogul empire, 118
Peshwas (Marathi rulers)
And British, 141, 148f.
Origin, 118
Pigot, Sir George, 140
Pitt's India Act, 1784, 145
Plantations, Develop in late 19th century, 169
Plassey
Battle, 130f.
map, 138
Plebiscite, Proposed for Kashmir, 219
Police
Brutality, 197
Strike (1946), 209
Polygars
As independent Hindu rulers, 117
map, 106
Pondicherry
Ceded to India, 237
map, 123
Scene of war with British, 129
Site of French settlement, 125
Portuguese, 98, 110
Piracy, 125
Seafaring, 121
Settlement on Hooghly, 115
Trade, 120-3
Post Office, Establishment, 170
Poverty
In Pakistan, 248f.
Reflects subsistence agriculture, 5
Praja Socialist Party, 229
Prakrit (Ancient language), 18
Presidency of Bengal, 133, 145
Presidency of Bombay
Administration, 145
In Mutiny, 159
Relations with Marathas, 140f.
Presidency of Madras
Administration, 145